# Hon
# Not Alone

916033

4.95

# Home but Not Alone
## The Work-at-Home Parents' Handbook

© 1998 by Katherine Murray

Published by **Park Avenue Productions**
*An imprint of JIST Works, Inc.*
720 N. Park Avenue
Indianapolis, IN 46202-3490
**Phone:** 317-264-3720   **Fax:** 317-264-3709
**E-mail:** jistworks@aol.com
**World Wide Web Address: http://www.jist.com**

See the back of this book for additional JIST or Park Avenue titles and ordering information. Quantity discounts are available.

Other Books by Katherine Murray

*The Working Parents' Handbook: How to Succeed at Work, Raise Your Kids, Maintain a Home, and Still Have Time for You*

*Printed in the United States of America*

1 2 3 4 5 6 7 8 9      02 01 00 99 98 97

**JAN 0 3 1998**

Library of Congress Cataloging-in-Publication Data
Murray, Katherine, 1961-
        Home but not alone : the work-at-home parents' handbook /
    Katherine Murray.
            p.   cm.
        ISBN 1-57112-080-7
        1. Home-based businesses—Management. 2. Home labor. 3. Self
    -employed. 4. Telecommuting. 5. Work and family. I. Title.
    HD62.38.M87  1997
    658'.041—dc21                          97-20392
                                              CIP

**3 9082 07106322 9**

We have been careful to provide accurate information throughout this book, but it is possible that errors and omissions have been introduced. Please consider this in making any career plans or other important decisions. Trust your own judgment above all else and in all things.

ISBN 1-57112-080-7

*To Connie,*
*Friends forever.*

iii

# Acknowledgments

Thanks to all the talented people at JIST Works, Inc., for welcoming, publishing, and promoting Home but Not Alone: The Work-at-Home Parents' Handbook. Every step of the way, from concept to printed book, I had help and support in putting this book together. Special thanks to Jim Irizarry, Sara Hall, Sherri Emmons, Wendy Prescott, and Kathleen Martin. And thanks—in advance—to the Bobs, Hamilton and Grilliot.

At the heart of this book are stories and inspired advice from the people who've been there: other work-at-home parents and their kids. I have gratefully included stories and suggestions from the following people:

| | |
|---|---|
| Joe Hawthorne | Connie Horner |
| Julie Pophal | Sandra Leshaw |
| Jenny Watson | Susan McCullough |
| Julie Chappell | Kevin Friedly |
| Roxanne Garber | |

Mrs. Garber's third grade class at Southside Elementary School

I also need to say thank you to the many, many people who have shared their experiences with me online, in person, and on the phone. Their names may not appear here, but their ideas and values are represented in the pages of this book.

Finally, the second biggest thank you (the first goes to God) is for my children, Kelly, Christopher, and Cameron, who continue to give me things to write about, and who continue to make writing worth while.

# Preface

About an hour ago, I was standing in a pumpkin field with 43 3- and 4-year-olds—the entire Monday-Wednesday-Friday enrollment of my son Cameron's preschool. It was his first field trip. He held hands with his classmates as we (teachers and parents) led the group out into a field dotted every few feet with huge orange pumpkins. We listened to the farmer tell us how pumpkins were planted, how they grew, what they looked like as babies, and what you did with them when they grew up. The kids wiggled, kicked, fidgeted, and poked one another. We went back to our cars windblown and frosted, ready for cider and gingerbread cookies.

That's why I'm a work-at-home parent.

This was not a life-changing event. It may not have been a significant moment for anyone except me, Cameron's mother. But as I stood freezing in that field, I was amazed that he is growing so fast, and thankful that I am here to see it.

Working at home is an incredible blessing—if that's what you want to do. If it's not something you want to do—but is, instead, something that's been forced on you by company policy or because of downsizing or layoffs—it is a challenge now, with the potential of feeling like a blessing later.

As I researched and wrote *The Working Parents' Handbook* (the first book I wrote for Park Avenue Productions), I was struck by the number of parents I interviewed who said they wanted the opportunity to do something at home, to be closer to their kids, to have more say in the priorities they set for their lives. This book is the result of those discussions—a how-to guide for getting started working at home. I want those moms and dads to be able to follow their hearts, as I have been able to follow mine.

I think the key to raising happy families—and to being happy ourselves—is being true to our hearts. Not everyone is happy being a work-at-home parent. Not everyone is happy being a work-at-the-office parent. The trick is figuring out what is right for you, and then taking the steps you feel comfortable with toward that goal.

Working at home might be something you've always wanted to do or something you've never thought much about. In either case, it's an option to consider as you evaluate your choices and dream about how you can help your family grow stronger each day.

As for me, I know the pumpkins will be back every fall. But Cameron will be three only once.

Hey, no contest.

# Table of Contents

# Part II: Getting to Work

# Part III: On the Home Front

# Introduction

How many times have you closed the door to your office with a heavy sigh and headed for the company parking lot counting your "somedays"?

 *Someday* I'll be out of here!

 *Someday* I'll be able to be home with the kids.

 *Someday* I won't have to worry about whether they're closing this plant.

 *Someday* I'll get that business started.

Why someday? Why not now?

An ever-increasing number of parents are taking a bold step into a new frontier. Yesterday's image of the slick entrepreneur is giving way to a new one: a Mom or Dad juggling home, kids, and an exploding career, often from the spare bedroom, a corner of the dining room, or the wired minibarn in the backyard. And still more parents, while remaining employed by someone else, are taking their offices home, where they can be productive, challenged, and available for their kids with Band-Aids and Kleenexes as the needs arise.

*Home but Not Aone* will help you investigate and then get started working at home. Maybe

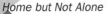

you're just thinking about it right now. Great—think away! And while you're thinking, use the checklists and write-in pages to help organize your thoughts. Perhaps you're already working at home and you're looking to make your life a little less complicated. The tips and advice scattered throughout the book will tell you what other moms and dads have done is similar circumstances.

Working at home isn't for everyone, but it's a great option if (1) it's something you want to do and (2) it's something you want to do. You'll also find it extremely helpful if it's something you *really* want to do.

The desire to work at home is a great starting point, but many people don't have that luxury. With a changing economy, corporate cutbacks, downsizing, and layoffs, more and more people find themselves becoming entrepreneurs in self-defense. They need to support their families, and the businesses they had relied on for stability suddenly have become unreliable or dried up altogether.

The day you shut that office door for good doesn't have to be "someday." It probably won't be tomorrow, either. But with some thoughtful planning, careful setup, and tenacity, it could be soon. And whether you are moving from the office to the family room by choice or out of necessity, there are a number of ways you can make the transition a smooth and successful one.

## Who Is This Book For?

If you are working at home, or you are considering it, and you are a parent, this book is for you. The number of hours you work doesn't matter. The type of work you do—or you think you may do in the future—doesn't matter. You'll find information here that applies to your

situation whether you're working at home for yourself or for someone else.

Whether you are leaving the corporate world because you've always wanted to run your own business or because you've just received a pink slip and you need to do something to support your family, you will benefit from the practical business information, the common-sense organizational tips, and the "been there, done that" advice from other work-at-home parents as you start your new work-at-home experience.

# What's in This Book?

Chapter 1, "Dream a Little Dream for Me," will help you focus on what you want to accomplish by working at home. More time with the kids? Shorter commutes? More control over your life? We'll start off with a look at the home business boom happening in America. Then you'll do a little daydreaming and picture yourself in your own home business. What do you want most for yourself and your children? Are your family's goals set up to reach those dreams? This chapter will help you make sure you're spending your energy working toward what you want.

Chapter 2, "Exploring the Possibilities," will help you begin thinking about the kind of work you can do at home. Starting with a quiz to rate yourself on how well suited you are for working at home, this chapter also has exercises designed to spotlight your better qualities and the things you like to do. There may be a career in there somewhere.

Chapter 3, "Starting Out at Home," addresses home-office basics—all the practical issues involved in getting set up to work at home, from computers to paper clips. You'll need a workspace, of course; and, depending on what you do, you'll need a few or a mountain of material goods. With worksheets to record what you'll need (and how much your

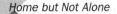

needs will cost!), this chapter will help you get a firm grip on what's involved in setting up a home workspace.

Have you prepared your clan for the changes that are coming? Chapter 3 also includes tips on how to communicate the excitement and challenge of your new undertaking so that the whole family gets involved.

In Chapter 4, "What About Child Care?" we'll look at one of the most important topics you'll consider as you start your home business. You may be staying home, at least in part, to be closer to the kids, but you'll soon find that you're swimming in a sea of details while your kids are playing video games on the shore. You need time to get things done. They need supervision. How are you going to handle it? This chapter will help you evaluate your child-care options and provides suggestions for finding a solution to the daycare dilemma.

If you work for yourself, you have a unique set of stresses to deal with. No one is regularly sending you a paycheck; you earn it, write it, and deposit it yourself. The work you do depends on one person: you. As a parent, you may feel the pinch even harder, knowing that your children—in addition to relying on you for parenting—depend on your business for their financial well-being, too.

Chapter 5, "The Self-Employed Parent," deals with issues specifically related to the entrepreneurial parent, with checklists and guides for creating a budget and a business plan, strategies for reducing stress, finding the help you need, and more.

The situation may be different for you if you work at home for someone else. In today's world of connectivity, many employers are becoming more flexible in their work-attendance rules. Some permit employees to work a schedule split between home and office—you might work at home three days each week and be in the office two. Or perhaps you're temporarily working at home full-time, maybe for eight weeks after the birth of your child. Some parents are moving their offices home for good—with their employer's blessings—and employers are finding the home workers happier, with less absenteeism, higher productivity, and better results. What kind of work-at-home work is best for you? What kinds of jobs lend themselves to this arrangement? How do you approach your employer and open a discussion in favor of working at home?

Chapter 6, "The Home-Working Parent," deals with setting up office at home, with advice on how to handle benefits, sick days, vacation time, and overtime. Tips and checklists will help you anticipate and side-step trouble spots along the way.

Chapter 7, "The Parents' Guide to Business Management," will give you some basic information on how to get organized and stay that way, a day at a time. You will learn the value of Post-It notes and Day-Timers, set up a phone schedule, and plan out that billing system long before you need it. You'll also get good advice on marketing your business, scheduling your work, invoicing customers, organizing and storing your files, and maintaining customer contact.

In Chapter 8, "Adjustments, Adjustments," we'll focus on the changes that are happening in your family. No matter how stressful your job was before you left it, working at home is no picnic by comparison, especially in the beginning. Your entire family will feel the change. This chapter will help you plan for change, deal with it successfully, and help your family cope with it, too. Tips and checklists will help you pinpoint trouble spots and take steps toward resolving family issues.

Chapter 9, "Housework? What Housework?" takes a no-holds-barred approach to household management. Now that you're home all the time, your house should be spotless, right? Ha! After you've been home for a few weeks, you'll find that things you had a system for in your work-at-the-office days seem impossible now. You never get dinner on the table at a reasonable time. The laundry is never done. There are always dishes in the sink. You need to get on top of the housework before it gets on top of you. This chapter will give you ideas for organizing, breaking up, and delegating household chores.

Chapter 10, "Kids at Work," will give you another perspective on what your work-at-home endeavor can mean to your children. You'll hear the voices of kids explaining what their moms and dads do for a living. You'll see the lessons these children are learning by watching businesses unfold and grow, right in their own living rooms. And you'll find out how to hire your children and turn your business into a family affair!

Chapter 11, "Time for You," is a must-read, even if you don't have the time. When you work at home, you can't go home and relax after a harrowing day. There's always one more phone call to make, one more report to read, one more letter to write. Use the quizzes here to check out how well you're taking care of yourself. Need to find more quiet time? Do something you enjoy? Improve your diet? Get out more? Use the tips and techniques in this chapter and spend some of your precious time on your most precious resource: *you*.

In Chapter 12, "Living and Working Happily Ever After," we'll take a leisurely look at the balanced work-at-home life. What kinds of benefits will you and your family enjoy? This chapter ends with three inspirational stories of work-at-home parents who have navigated the difficult startup stages and moved on to enjoy the fruits of their labors.

This book concludes with three appendices. The first lists the top opportunities for work-at-home parents in the United States. The second lists online addresses and Web sites you might want to check out. And the third includes important addresses for work-at-home parents.

## Special Features

What do work-at-home parents like best about their lifestyle? What's the worst thing about working at home? How do we know? We asked them! Scattered throughout the book, you'll find tips, stories, and suggestions from other work-at-home parents who have been right where you are today. The special elements are these:

### Best & Worst

Other work-at-home parents tell you their favorite aspects and their biggest challenges of working at home.

### Professional Parent Panic!

When you're doing it all from home, there will be times when your career and your kids clash. Learn how other parents have navigated that crash course successfully and lived to tell the story.

### Been There, Done That

What can you learn from others who have gone before you? Here parents talk about what they've learned in answer to specific situations and help you avoid the same trouble spots they encountered.

### Profiles

These are brief sketches of parents who successfully run businesses from home, including their biggest challenges and how they meet them.

In addition, you'll find tips, notes, sidebars, illustrations, charts, and checklists to keep you awake, interested, and moving forward.

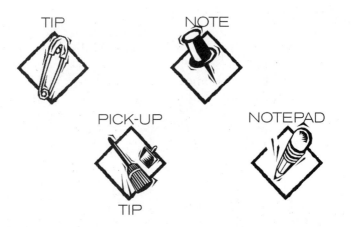

TIP          NOTE

PICK-UP          NOTEPAD

TIP

Now, if you're ready, get yourself a cup of coffee, a pen, and a notebook (or use the checklists and write-in spaces in this book—that's what they're for), and let's start at the beginning, dreaming the dream.

# The Work-at-Home Potential

*We've all thought about it: working at home. Who wouldn't want to get up late, stumble into the office in sweats, make a few calls, go out to lunch with friends, take a nap in the afternoon, and—best of all—get paid for doing it? Unfortunately, working at home isn't that kind of a picnic for most of us. The first part of this book introduces you to both the great potential and the hard-nosed realities of working at home and helps you get started putting your work-at-home plan in place.*

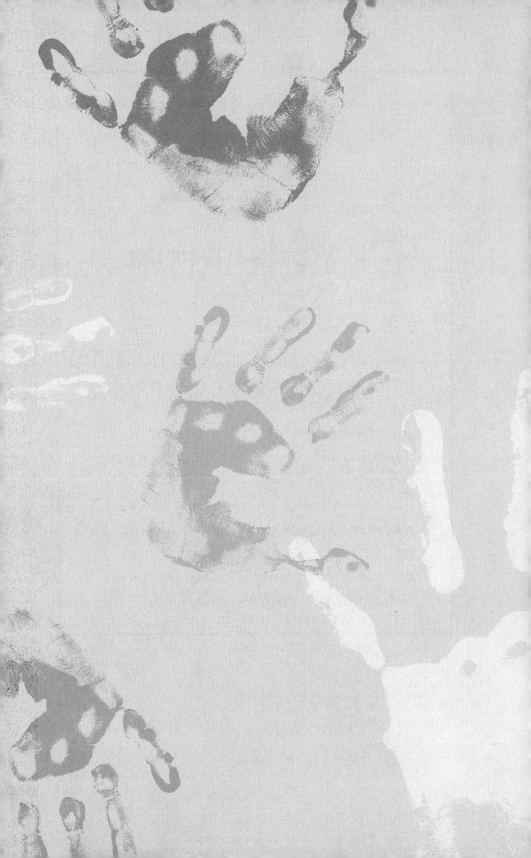

# Dream a Little Dream for Me

*"Some people look at the world and say, 'why?' I look at the world and say, 'why not?'"*
—George Bernard Shaw

Do you wish you could be there every day when your son gets home from school? Do you miss volunteering in your daughter's class? Are you tired of worrying about your latch-key kids for that last anxious hour of your workday?

Working at home is the answer.

When I first considered leaving the corporate world and working at home, I thought I was doing it for my soon-to-be-born second child. Little did I know I was also doing it for my third-grader and for myself, too. It was a decision I made because it seemed like the right thing to do at the time—and it was. But back then I had no idea how far the benefits of working at home would go in my life.

# The Benefits:
# I <u>Knew</u> This Was a Good Idea!

Depending on *why* you want to work at home, you'll pick up on the benefits right away. Maybe you're tired of paying for child care. Maybe your children are unhappy at the sitter's all day. Maybe *you're* unhappy at work and want to lessen your stress load, which will help you be a better parent.

- Working at home gives you flexibility— something you need plenty of if you're raising kids. (No doubt you've already noticed that!)

- Working at home gives you freedom. You can set your own priorities for yourself and your family and stick to them.

- Working at home gives you accessibility. Now your kids can get to you whenever they need you. In emergencies, in thunder storms, when flu strikes—Mom or Dad is right there.

Working at home offers special benefits for parents. You can arrange your schedule the way that works best for you. You don't have to rely on others for full-time child care. You can be with your children when they need you. And they know you are nearby, which is comforting even if they don't need you right now.

**BEST** &
WORST

*Best:*
"Knowing
that I'm
here for
my children."

Working at home also benefits you personally. You have to get organized. You learn to take risks. You learn to work hard and smart. You get better at making your own decisions. If you're working for an employer out of your home, you learn to get really good at communicating with others on your team. If you work for yourself, you learn to weather storms. After a few squalls, you even learn to forecast them and navigate around them. You discover that you are motivated, intelligent, capable, and successful. Pretty good perks, aren't they?

And all those benefits carry back to your children, who see you doing what you want, earning a living, and being there for them. And when it's time for them to make their own decisions about going out into the workforce or working at home and raising their kids themselves, they will have your successful experience to draw on.

Now *that's* a far-reaching benefit.

# The Challenges:
# I <u>Can</u> Do This ... Can't I?

Let's not get too carried away here, I don't want to deceive you. There are challenges unique to working at home. Notice that I use the word *challenges*, because they are only temporary situations that can be overcome with some constructive thinking and creative problem solving.

## "Are You Crazy?"

Just a few years ago, jumping off the corporate ladder was not considered a smart thing to do. People would roll their eyes. Inevitably, the rumor would surface that you couldn't handle the pressure.

Today, people look on with curiosity. They are not so quick to judge. They might be thinking about working at home themselves, and they want to see whether you make it. Even if you get that "Are you crazy?" look from coworkers, don't let it shake your aplomb. Sooner or later, we all learn that most people agree with us only if we mirror the decisions they have made in their lives. If we make a different decision, they shake their heads and say there must be something wrong with us. That's okay. We'll let those people work for other people; we'll be the entrepreneurs.

## Facing the Green-Eyed Monster

When you first start working at home for an employer, the reactions of your coworkers may be mixed. Some people will cheer you on and begin thinking about how they could do the same thing. Others will grumble that you will be hard to reach and that working at home will affect your job performance. They may have a "sour grapes" problem and begrudge you this added flexibility. Again, keep your eyes on what you want and give the situation your best effort. The most important line of communication in this arrangement is the one you have with your employer. If she's happy and you're happy, you can ignore the water-cooler comments. The success of your work-at-home position will make itself clear over time.

Make sure you are working at home for yourself and your family. If you do it for the accolades and respect of other people, you may be seriously disappointed.

## All I'm Asking ... Is for a Little Respect

Today, work-at-home businesses are so prevalent that people aren't shocked when they discover you are working from your basement. A few years ago,

### Case in Point

When I first decided to work at home, in 1987, I was in the employ of a large book publishing company. I had a personal computer at home, which I often used in the evenings and on weekends to work on various writing projects, so the move wasn't going to require any expense for my employer. And my house was only a few minutes from the office, so I could easily make it in for meetings.

I was surprised and hurt when stories began circulating about me and my reason for leaving. And I was affronted when I heard that a few people had decided I was pursuing some kind of illicit relationship with my employer, which must have been the reason for his sudden flexibility. Soon, management circulated a memo stating the company's policy on work-at-home employees: "Every full-time employee must work within the walls of this organization." Enough said. I resigned my position and began my freelance career.

a customer might have been turned off at hearing your 3-year-old playing video games in the background. Most work-at-home parents don't try to hide the fact that they are work-at-home parents. One work-at-home dad, who runs an Internet publishing business from his home office, puts it this way:

*"When clients call, I don't feel like I need to explain anything. If Jason interrupts, which he doesn't do very often, I just say, 'Excuse me, my son wants to talk to me for a second.'"*

Of course, you do need to draw guidelines for what's an acceptable interruption and what's not. If the curtains are on fire, you need to check it out. If your daughter wants you to untie the bow in

Barbie's hair, she probably can wait a few minutes until you're off the phone.

*For more on setting guidelines for acceptable interruptions, see Chapter 3.*

The best way to solve the respect issue is to respect what you're doing. If you feel comfortable—not apologetic—about working at home, others will too. There are several things you can do to present yourself as professionally as possible; we'll talk about that in Chapters 3 and 4.

# Daddy's Home, but He's Working

Working at home will be new for your entire family. Your *kids* will be affected. Your *spouse* will feel the change. And *you* will be scrambling to make your idea work as quickly as possible, trying to balance all the changes in your family, and trying *not* to let that "What-have-I-*done?*" monster get the best of you.

The office-to-home change itself may happen quickly: One day you're working in an office; the next day you're working at home. But adjusting to the change may take some learning. Your kids need to learn when you're working and when you're not. They need to find out when you can play a game with them, when you need quiet time, and when interruptions are okay. They need to learn not to make airplanes out of your business stationery. They need to learn how (or whether) to answer the phone when you're not by your desk.

How can you help your kids learn the boundaries? Define them yourself. Know how much time you need and when you need it; then plan for their activities during that time. Communicate your needs as clearly as you can, and be willing to reevaluate on a regular basis. When you are clear about what you want, your kids have a guideline by which to judge their own actions, which makes the transition a smoother one for everyone.

## I'm Starved for Adult Conversation!

This is one of the unique challenges of the work-at-home *parent* as opposed to a work-at-home person who is not a parent. Without your kids, you might feel isolated and alone working at home all day every day. With kids, you don't feel isolated, but you may feel numbed by Barney songs, "Sesame Street" characters, and questions like, "Can you take me to the potty now?" I've had days when I simply cannot get the Donkey Kong theme music out of my head. Such is the nature of work-at-home parenting.

There are several things you can do about this. First, have realistic expectations. If you're moving home from an office environment, you *are* going to be spending quite a bit more time with your kids. And there *will* be days you'll feel the loss of those office relationships—even if you keep up on the phone or at occasional lunches.

> If you ever feel tempted to hold the kids accountable for your choice—"See what I gave up for you?"—jump on the feeling right away and revisit the issues that made you decide to work at home. Making your kids feel responsible for your choice isn't going to help anybody adjust any faster.

Second, admit that you're missing the company of other adults; then do something about it. It doesn't make you a failure as a work-at-home parent; it simply means you need to talk to other adults. Go to the gym or to the park—let the kids play while you talk to other parents. Schedule a lunch out with other work-at-home parents or with clients. Organize a group of other at-home parents in your neighborhood. Network with other business owners. Get on the Internet and chat in a work-from-home forum.

## Facing the "What Have I Dones?"

One morning, sometime soon, you'll probably wake up screaming, "What have I *done*?" In fact, it may not be just one morning. It may be several. It may be *every* morning until you conquer that monster once and for all.

Doubts are not unique to entrepreneurs. Everyone worries. Everyone second-guesses the decision to work at home. If you are moving your office home but will continue to work for an employer, you may worry that the boss will tire of your "special privileges" and look for a reason to let you go. If you work for yourself, you may wake up with night sweats about finances, career moves, and the changes in your family.

The best thing for a bad case of the doubts is resolve. There's a question that needs to be answered: "Is working at home a good idea?" If necessary, revisit the issues that caused you to make the decision in the first place. Reevaluate your decision and ask yourself whether you would make the same choice again. If the answer is "No," ask yourself why not. If the answer is "Yes," ask yourself why.

The most important thing to remember about the "What-have-I-done?" monster is that it dogs everybody's footsteps at some point along the path. Accept it as a normal part of the process, but seek to get rid of it once and for all. Remind yourself, when the monster gets close, it could be because there's something in your life that needs to be addressed: Maybe you're working too many hours; maybe you're trying to do too much; maybe you're not handling your finances as creatively as you might. Go ahead and look at your situation, but not with the intention of giving up. Look at it with a constructive eye and discover where it's making you panic. Then you can shore up your business at its weak point and move on, better for the experience.

## Staring Down the Monster

In my own business, I didn't eradicate the "What-have-I-done?" monster for almost eight years. It didn't hound my steps every day, of course—only when I was too tired, too stressed, or too tapped financially. Then I would begin to question my decision to work for myself and fantasize about what a "secure" life working for a large company would be like.

One day, after a particularly bad bout with the monster, I called a publisher and discussed the possibility of full-time employment. When I hung up the phone, I sat down and had a long talk with myself. I thought about what this would mean to my kids, to the dogs, to the house. I reminded myself of all the wonderful things about being at home, and how it fits the free, creative lifestyle I want to live. It lets me be a room mom, go to preschool picnics, and visit my daughter's driver's education teacher.

Finally, after quite a bit of recounting, I sat back and thought, "What am I, crazy?" I resolved to put everything I had into this business—100 percent invested. No little doubt phantom was going to make me give up after eight successful years. I'm in it for the long haul. And you know what? The monster hasn't been back.

# With Friends Like These, Who Needs a Paycheck?

Like your kids, your friends may need retraining.

Your fishing buddy is home on vacation this week and wants to reroof his house. He knows he can count on you for help, since you're home too.

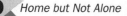

Your neighbor sees the light on in your family room and thinks, "Oh, great! Marge is home. I can show her my new wallpaper samples." So instead of contacting clients this morning, you sit politely staring at 120 bathroom wallpaper samples.

Not a real productive day.

Again, communication is the answer. Make sure everyone who knows and loves you understands that you are home *working*, not sitting on the couch watching soaps and eating bonbons. Let them know specific hours when it *is* okay to contact you—and tell them the kinds of things it's okay to contact you about.

*Before you tell people about your hours and your boundaries, you've got to define them for yourself. For more about that, see Chapter 3.*

## Surprise! You're the Neighborhood Catch-All Parent!

One mother I interviewed had this horror story to tell:

"I finally was able to move my work home, after talking with my employer about it for several months. Within weeks, however, I found that all the other parents in the neighborhood, working friends of mine I'd known for years, were calling me and asking me to do things for them, since I was 'at home' now. One wanted me to wait on her doorstep for the refrigerator repairman. Another asked me to watch her two older kids after school every day. Another asked me to mail a few things for her. The last straw was when a neighbor asked me to make cookies for her son's class party. They all thought that since I was home, I had time to do the stuff they didn't have time for."

What you're fighting here is a misconception that says, "Home can't be a workplace because it's home." What any career mom—that is, a mom who makes raising her family her career—will tell you is that home is, indeed, a workplace. The fact that love, joy, laughter, clutter, and stuffed animals abound there doesn't negate the fact that there's work to be done. Setting clear boundaries, having realistic expectations, and saying so when things aren't working are three major steps in working at home happily and successfully.

"One time I was negotiating with a printer to try to get my project done faster than he was offering. It was pretty tense. I was trying to be as professional as possible. All of a sudden my 2-year-old wandered in and said, 'Mommy—gimme lunch now!' I was so taken aback, I just laughed. The printer laughed too, and said, 'Yeah, I've got one of those at home. Pretty demanding little fellas aren't they?' And then we talked more reasonably about dates and came up with something we could both live with. I guess my demanding little guy broke the ice for us."
          —work-at-home mother of one

So now you've got an idea of some of the monsters that may lurk along your path to home employment. But they're nothing some planning and communication can't banish. The trick is to watch the signals: Catch any of these issues early, if you can. Some good, open conversation about what you're doing and why you're doing it will help other important people in your life—friends, neighbors, family, coworkers—see the choices you've made in a better light.

## Who's Working at Home?

The first answer that comes to mind is the obvious one: People running home-based businesses. But there are others, too. The accountant down the hall who wanted to extend her maternity leave has worked it out so she can be home three days a week with the new baby. That's a work-at-home option. The salesman in the downsizing company takes his office home because he's been asked to. That's working at home, too. And the manager who has a full-time job in the office but also runs a small business on the side is working at home.

**BEST &
WORST**

*Worst:
Working
late nights*

It's not the number of hours you work or the amount of money you make while you're doing it. People from all walks of life are spending at least part of their working week at home. According to the American Home Business Association, 39 million people in the United States worked at home in some capacity in 1996. Over 20 million of those workers have started their own home-based businesses—in consulting, sales, marketing, publishing, and more.

We've all heard the story: Starting your own business is tough, right? That's why so few people attempt it, and why even fewer succeed. The failure rate is enormous. The cash outlay makes us quake in our boots. The risk is tremendous.

But home-based businesses (also called cottage industries) are proving themselves different. They are changing the face and statistics of small business. Home-based businesses are incredibly successful as a whole, easy to start, easy to maintain, with a low initial investment and a quick road to often massive sums of money.

Sound good? Combine the low-risk, low-investment opportunity with the draw of being home to raise your kids the way you want to, and you've got a great idea for today's parent.

Here are some current statistics on home-based businesses:

 There are currently more than *23 million* home-based businesses in operation in the United States.

More than 8,000 new home-based businesses are started every day.

 Home-based business have a success rate of over 90 percent, meaning they are still around after three years. (Traditional small businesses, by comparison, have only a 20 percent success rate.)

Home-based businesses appeal to both sexes: 60 percent of home business owners are women; 40 percent are men.[1]

What do you need to start a home-based business? The desire, a product or service people need or want, the time to get your idea off the ground, and a space to call "office." Chapter 2 will help you explore some ideas and opportunities for home-based businesses.

# Work and Family: Priorities, Priorities

It's no surprise that families are a hot topic in the '90s. It's about time. Our generation has done the corporate-ladder thing and the two-career-family thing. Now, most of us want more: not more things, more status, or more power, but more time, more peace, more fulfillment, more love.

We've all seen changes in our society, in our families, and in ourselves. We've got the data to support the claim that crime is a problem, drugs are a problem, gangs are a problem. We've got politicians and ministers telling us that the fabric of family life is coming unraveled. We have waited for our companies, our churches, and our government to *do* something about it.

But ultimately it comes back to us. We're the ones paying the price. We may achieve high positions, good salaries, impressive perks, but if we sacrifice our families or the quiet happiness we experience with those we love, what's the point? We may try— and be able, for a while—to do it all, keeping everybody happy, healthy, and well-adjusted while running our corporate careers, but we may ultimately pay a huge price health-wise.

That's why working at home is so great. *You* set *your* priorities the way *you* need to for *your* family. You aren't living someone else's dream.

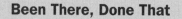

### Been There, Done That

*"I started out my business working part-time at home. That way I could see whether I liked it and whether it would support me. After about 18 months, I left my day job to work full-time at home."*

—source?

## Setting Your Priorities

If you've never had this discussion with yourself before, now is the time. What's most important in your life? Your spouse? Your kids? The car? That time-share condo in Fiji? Your priorities might be emotional, physical, or spiritual. Here are a few ideas:

 The safety and well-being of my children

 The financial and physical upkeep of our home

 My own professional and personal fulfillment

Or, if you're not as wordy as I am, you might list priorities like this:

 Family

 Work

 House

That's pretty simple, isn't it? You can easily see what goes where in your heart of hearts.

> *If getting out of a financial tight spot—or gaining some kind of financial security— ranks high on your list of priorities, you are not alone. Many families today are in a crisis financial situation, and the fact that many employers are downsizing or closing shop altogether makes the financial world a scary place for the typical two-income family. If the safety and well-being of your children is one of your top priorities, you quickly realize that it's hard to be safe or well when you can't afford the necessities of life. For many of us, finances rank high on our lists of priorities, not because we want that vacation condo but because we are trying to reach a point at which our families are financially protected.*

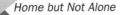

So now it's your turn. What are the priorities in your life? Go ahead, write down whatever comes to mind.

It's important to remember that your priorities won't necessarily be the same as anyone else's. Your spouse may have a different idea of what's most important. (We'll get to that in a minute.) Your kids are pretty likely to have different priorities than you do. But brainstorming the list—in whatever order it comes to you—is the important first step.

Which one of those items is *most* important? We can assume that your children rank right up there on the list, but you may have other items too, including good health, financial stability, and your faith (not necessarily in that order). Number the priorities you included on your list, from most important (that's 1) to least important.

My personal priorities are these:

_____

_____

_____

_____

_____

_____

_____

_____

## What "Everybody Else" Thinks *Is* Important

Sometimes it's hard being a parent: You're the one with the uncool ideas. You think it's important to do things like get out of debt, raise your own kids, pay off your mortgage (or buy that first house). Your teenagers think you're boring. Your third-grader thinks you're no fun. Here's a list of how *they* would list your priorities, if you turned the job over to them:

🧦 **Most important:** A cool car

🧦 **Next most important:** Great shoes

🧦 **Next, next most important:** A great Spring-break vacation

🧦 *Way down there* **on the list:** Feeding the family well-balanced meals

Or:

🧦 **Most important:** The latest video game

🧦 **Next most important:** Not having a little brother

🧦 **Next, next most important:** No homework!

🧦 *Way down there* **on the list:** Paying the bills on time. (Bills? *What bills?*)

## Setting Couple Priorities

Now get your spouse to do the same thing, and then compare notes. Is there a priority on your spouse's list different from the ones you wrote? Use your personal lists to create a couple priority list, like this one:

*Our priorities as a couple are:*

*Raising healthy, happy children.*
*Being financially secure in*
*retirement.*
*Having time together as a couple.*

Now, write your own couple priorities below.

Our priorities as a couple are these:

_____

_____

_____

_____

_____

_____

_____

_____

_____

If you have different ideas about what your priorities as a couple should be, talk it through until you reach a consensus. Remember, you are seeking to answer the question, "What are the most important things to us as a couple?"

*If you're a single parent, like me, you won't have this step to do. You should, however, consider if having a relationship is a priority in your life. If it is, include it on your list.*

## Setting Family Priorities

Once you have thought about and written down the priorities in your life individually and with your spouse, it's time to have a family discussion. You will ask everyone who lives under your roof what your family priorities should be.

---

### Tips for Your First Family Meeting

Family meetings should be fun. They usually aren't, the first time. To increase your chances of having a successful first family meeting, follow these tips:

- Tell everyone about the meeting several days in advance. Tell them you want them to be thinking about what's important to the family for the next few days.

- Post a note on the fridge to remind them of the meeting. Include the time and place (7:00 in the dining room with the hammer). Make sure you have the meeting on a night when everyone can attend.

- Promise something fun afterward (a movie, a pizza, a game).

- Go to the meeting with an agenda and realistic expectations. Write down specific questions you want to ask. Ask the questions, and *write down* whatever answers you get.

- Be grateful. You wouldn't gather a bunch of account executives together, and then yell at them for not cleaning their rooms first. Treat the meeting attendees with respect, do what you need to do, then disperse.

- Relax and laugh. Don't expect the meeting to be perfect; relax and listen while Janie tells you about the hamster getting loose at school today.

- Give everyone a chance to talk. Although you are leading the discussion, it's important that everyone has a voice. If your kids don't volunteer, ask them, "What do you think the priorities in our family should be?"

So what did your family come up with? Remember that most families will not have identical priorities, although we can expect to see some similarities: love, safety, communication, health, and financial stability are important to all of us, no matter what the age.

Once you've got a handle on what's most important for your family, you're in a better position to make a decision about your work

Our family priorities are these:

_____

_____

_____

_____

_____

future. Does working at home fall in line with your family priorities? Is it important in your household for one parent to be home with the children? Do you need to make an income, either to supplement or to support your family?

If you answered "Yes" to those questions, you've got the basis of a work-at-home decision. Now you need to think about which kind of work-at-home situation will fit your family's priorities and enable you to use your gifts and talents to earn a living and be there for your kids at the same time.

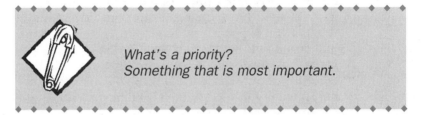

*What's a priority?*
*Something that is most important.*

## Dreaming the Dream

How does this sound? You wake up at 7:00. Your spouse (who is all ready for work and feeding the kids breakfast in the kitchen) has made coffee, and it's waiting for you—nice and hot—as you shuffle into the kitchen in your robe and slippers. You sit down at the table with your family while they finish their breakfasts and gather their things for the day. Your spouse takes Peter to preschool; the older two kids grab their book bags and head off toward the bus stop. At 7:45, the house is quiet, and you shut the door and start up the stairs to take your shower—a nice, leisurely, hot shower— before you start your work for the day.

Let's look in on you at 10:00. You've made a number of phone calls and started writing that report that's due on Friday—three days from now. You're wearing your favorite jeans (the ones with the hole in the right knee) and your San Francisco 49ers jersey. Oh, and don't forget the slippers.

Does that keep you from sounding professional on the phone? Of course not! You only sound more ... comfortable.

At noon, you pick Peter up from preschool. You talk with the other parents for a few minutes, visit with his teacher, pick up lunch on the way home. At 2:45, while Peter is still napping, the older kids get home. Life is louder, but still workable. The slippers are back on.

Your dream of working at home may be much different from this. You might see a faster pace, more people, more excitement, more money. For me, heaven is peace—which is pretty much what I just described. Before you start making arrangements for your work-at-home life, think carefully about what kind of life you want that to be. How do you see yourself? What would be "great!" to you?

Ask yourself this question: "What would *my* perfect work situation be?" What's the answer? You can use this space to describe the situation you're dreaming of:

My perfect work situation:

_____

_____

_____

_____

Now play out the scenario.

Where is your workspace? What does it look like? Is there a desk? Is there a large, open work area? Are there file cabinets? Is there a computer on the desk? Is there a fax machine? A photocopier? Are there tools in the work area specific to the kind of work you want to do?

_____

_____

_____

How many hours do you work? What hours
are they? Perhaps you're a morning person—
up before dawn, with half a day's work accomplished
before the kids get out of bed. Or maybe you're a
night owl, doing your best thinking when the rest of
the world is asleep.

_____

_____

_____

Who works with you? Are you in a single office, home
with your kids all day? Or will you hire an assistant, a
programmer, an editor, a friend? Will clients be
coming to your house for meetings or will you go out
to meet them? Will you conduct your business in
cyberspace, so no one ever actually meets at all?

_____

_____

_____

What kind of work are you doing? Are you on the
phone, talking to customers, or do they come to your
office? Are you painting or writing? Are you a
musician? Are you a bookkeeper? An editor? An
electrician? A child-care provider? A counselor?

_____

_____

_____

Now use this space to distill your dream into a bite-size idea you can focus on:

Where I work: _____

What I do: _____

How many hours I work: _____

When I work those hours: _____

Who does it with me: _____

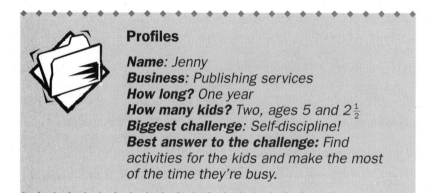

**Profiles**

*Name*: Jenny
*Business*: Publishing services
*How long?* One year
*How many kids?* Two, ages 5 and $2\frac{1}{2}$
*Biggest challenge*: Self-discipline!
*Best answer to the challenge*: Find activities for the kids and make the most of the time they're busy.

# Believing the Dream

Walt Disney once said, "If you can dream it, you can do it." That's true not just in Disneyland; almost anything you envision, you can make happen in your life.

What you see in the world has a lot to do with what you bring to it. Have your experiences made you cynical or hopeful? Resigned or determined? Defeated or victorious? Your general outlook will either help you or hinder you as you begin brainstorming ideas of what you want and thinking about ways to achieve that.

> *What's the flavor of your life? Sweet, bitter, sour, or pleasant—we tend to choose the flavor we find most in our daily experience. Rest assured that your kids are watching the way you experience life—and if you find it sour, they'll expect it to be sour too. Life is really a palette of all tastes, but if you've got to choose one to have most often, make it sweet!*

Working for yourself and being a great parent have something very important in common: Success will come more easily if you believe in yourself. Know what makes you happy, what challenges you, what makes you look forward to tomorrow. Don't blind yourself to your limitations, but do spend time concentrating on your good points.

Think, plan, and dream about working at home. If you don't have an idea about what kind of work to do yet, don't worry—you'll find one soon. The next chapter will help you explore your work-at-home possibilities by investigating different business opportunities and matching them with your talents and priorities.

## Notes

1. *Home Business News*, published by PT Corp., in 1996.

# Exploring the Possibilities

*"Life is like a ten-speed bike. Most of us have gears we never use."*
—Charles Schulz

You've thought about working at home. Maybe you've seen those "infomercials" that run on the cable channels late at night, the ones telling you how to get into real estate fast.

(They usually alternate with 30-minute spots for exercise equipment and food dehydration machines.) Have you wondered whether those things—*any* of those things—really work?

**BEST** & WORST

*Best:* "Being able to work in my jeans."

Wondering is good, as long as you don't stop there. The next step is considering your possibilities. And that takes a little research and a little education. This chapter does the research part for you, so read on and consider how, where, and what you might do to earn your living at home.

# How Do You Work at Home?

Choosing to work at home is as individual a decision as deciding what color shoestrings to wear in your tennis shoes. What you will do at home, when you will do it, and how you will begin depend on your current situation, your talents, your desires, your family situation, and so much more.

The first step is to look at your life. Not your neighbor's or your mother's. Your situation is unique. You've got your own bills, your own goals, your own family to think about. You've got individual likes and dislikes you must consider in the situation you create for yourself. You've got specific talents that no one else has, and experiences that (seen in the proper light and put to proper use) could earn you a living at home. You can put those talents to work at home for an employer or for your own business, or in some combination of the two.

## For Someone Else

Some people work at home while remaining under the umbrella of an employer. They have the security of a regular paycheck, with taxes taken out (which means they have less figuring to do in April), and a sense of job stability. In exchange for this security, they agree to stay tied to the schedule of the employer, answerable for all the responsibilities of an in-office employee, and (ordinarily) accessible during normal work hours.

## Security Isn't Secure Anymore

Relying on a company for job security isn't as safe as it used to be. Today, downsizing, layoffs, and closings are a very real part of everyday life in America. In my small Midwestern community, a manufacturing plant recently closed three days before Thanksgiving, leaving 120 workers without jobs for the holidays.

Brian Tracy, a motivational speaker on self-improvement and business issues, suggests we should each think of ourselves as the CEOs of our own personal services corporations. In this mindset, you aren't somebody's employee; you are a business offering an employer your services. This keeps you from relying too heavily on the employer's promises—either real or implied.

If you are a victim of downsizing or a layoff, you may be reading this book in somewhat of a panic. You might want to get started doing something—*anything*—fast, in order to bring in an income. Even though the pressure's on, take some time to think about the ideas in this chapter. Then begin educating yourself about things you might *like* to do at home.

Transitions are scary—especially sudden ones over which you have no control. But with some clear thinking, good information, and a little opportunity, you may be able to turn a scary situation into the best break you ever had.

## For Yourself

Others leave the corporate system and start their own businesses at home. They have the ultimate freedom in a work environment, but they also have the ultimate responsibility: Everything depends on them. As one work-at-home dad put it,

◆ ◆ ◆ ◆ ◆ ◆ ◆ ◆ ◆ ◆ ◆ ◆ ◆ ◆ ◆ ◆ ◆ ◆ ◆ ◆ ◆ ◆ ◆ ◆ ◆

*"I'm the most understanding employer I've ever had, but I'm also the toughest. When one of my kids is sick, I love it that I can be right there for them. But when there's a job I've got to get done, I'll stay up till 3:00 or 4:00 A.M.—sometimes several nights in a row—to get it finished on time."*

◆ ◆ ◆ ◆ ◆ ◆ ◆ ◆ ◆ ◆ ◆ ◆ ◆ ◆ ◆ ◆ ◆ ◆ ◆ ◆ ◆ ◆ ◆ ◆ ◆

Your first step in exploring the work-at-home option is evaluating what you've got now and determining what you want to keep and what you want to change. The next few sections will walk you through that process.

# How's Your Life?

### Case in Point

Tyler threw a fit on the way to daycare this morning. It was the third time this week.

Brittany let the dog out just as you were walking out the door this morning, and you spent ten minutes running around the yard in your high heels trying to catch him. You were late for work, and a coworker gleefully pointed out a muddy paw print on the back of your leg.

Work is piling up: The to-do list on your desk has spilled over onto the second page. You're supposed to take a client to lunch and meet with designers this afternoon. Your boss just called and scheduled a "15-minute" meeting this morning in the conference room, which means you'll be in there for at least an hour. You know you'll have to come in on Saturday morning—again—to catch up on all the work you haven't had a chance to finish.

Sound familiar? Many people have trouble getting work done at work. Office communications—face-to-face meetings, telephone conferences, and e-mail messaging—take quite a bit of time in an office setting. According to a recent survey done by *Entrepreneur* magazine, 80 percent of home-based workers say they are more productive at home than they were in the office.[1]

## Listing the Positives

What do you like about your current work situation? Perhaps you're happy with the money you're making. Maybe you like the people or the work itself. Perhaps you'd like to keep building window frames, but you want to do it at home. Maybe you like your schedule, but you don't like driving an hour each way to get to work.

Use the space below to write down what's good about your current work situation:

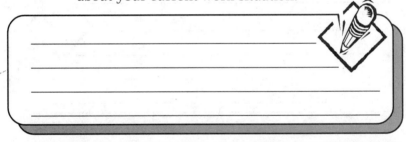

### Positives That *Shouldn't* Play a Part in Your Decision

- You like to see the boss sweat.

- You enjoy fanning the flames of office gossip.

- Getting home late means they have to start dinner without you.

- You won't have as many opportunities to use your expense account.

- The candy machine.

- Free—if unethical—Xeroxing.

- Company Christmas parties.

## Now, the Negatives

Now think about what you don't like about your current work situation. If you're working in an office, you may not like your boss, your schedule, the pressure, the pay. If you're in a warehouse, you may not like the physical labor, the hours, your coworkers, the pay. Maybe there's a lot of insecurity at your workplace—rumors of layoffs or downsizing. If you're not working, you're probably tired of worrying about your finances and anxious to build a better future for yourself and your family.

In the space below, write down whatever bugs you about your current work situation:

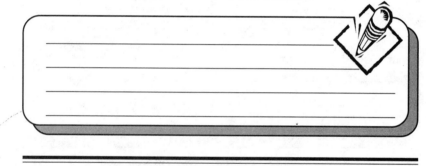

### Negatives You'll Take Home with You

There's a philosophy some of us adopt early in life that goes something like this: "When things start looking bad, move on." The problem with that philosophy is this: You wind up digging all these holes in your life that, sooner or later, you'll just fall into. Case in point: grades. You can't change schools just because you flunked English—what good would it do? Oh, sure, you can fool the new English teacher for a paper or two— but then what? You've taken your bad study habits with you.

Making the switch to working at home isn't much different, in some respects, from changing schools. If you were disorganized at work, you are likely to be disorganized at home. If you didn't use your time wisely in the office, time will fly by even more quickly at home, where there's even more to steal your attention. If you had a tendency to look at the downside of all your work-related tasks in the office ("I *hate* filing these claims! I wish I had something else to do today!"), you will no doubt take those attitudes with you when you change environments.

If you see any negatives in your current situation that are likely to come home with you, make a decision to leave them behind. Starting your own business will have its own challenges—you don't need to bring any bad habits with you that will make your mountains more difficult to climb.

## What's Missing?

There's another category that doesn't fall under positive or negative. These are the things that are missing in your life right now, things that would help you feel more settled, fulfilled, challenged, capable, whatever. It might be that you have no time to think, no time to do fun things with your family, no laughter, no challenge, no responsibility, or no room for advancement. When you ask yourself, "What's missing in my current work situation?" what answers do you come up with?

It may be that these things aren't completely absent, but they are seriously low on your current list. What do you need more of? Here are a few ideas:

- Time for yourself
- Time with your family
- Peace of mind
- Freedom
- Flexibility
- Control of your circumstances
- Money
- Security

When I was a work-in-the-office parent, I scurried through my day, from one thing to another, a blur of perpetual energy, like a hamster in a hamster wheel. At the end of the day, I came home, fixed dinner, talked to my daughter, helped her with homework, and then it was bath time, story time, and bedtime. More often than not, I was asleep before she was—and a few short hours later, the whole scenario started again.

When I first began to consider working at home, I had no idea what was missing in my life—my days just ran together, from work to home and home to work. My daughter was my first priority. My job was another one. Everything else—housework included—just fit in around the edges.

After a few months at home, however, I started noticing things I hadn't noticed before. I took time to listen to the radio while I worked. I went to a lunch-time concert; I met a friend for lunch at the art museum. I held my baby son on my lap while I worked, and I started falling in love with *Sesame Street*. I began actually enjoying the time I spent helping my daughter with her math homework— we took our time to do it instead of struggling through the pages in *Hurry-Up!* mode. I started singing to my kids again.

In my own life, I had overlooked the largest thing of all, and I hadn't even known it: Life. I was forgetting to live—to do the small things, to take pleasure in the moment, to be creative and open to new experiences. I was so locked into running my hamster wheel, with nothing new except the challenge of being better, faster, and more on time than ever, that I never looked outside my own little track— until the day I jumped off.

Now, what have you been missing? Write your missing items in the following list (and if you can't think of any now, don't worry—they'll come!):

_____

_____

_____

_____

## Putting It All Together

What all this identifying does is help you see what you have, so you can see what you *don't* have. You know what you like and don't like about your current situation, and you know what important items are missing in your work life right now. When you start investigating different work-at-home options—whether you work for yourself or work for someone else from your home—you'll be more educated about which choices fit you and which ones don't.

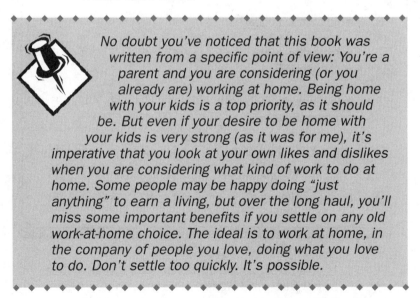

*No doubt you've noticed that this book was written from a specific point of view: You're a parent and you are considering (or you already are) working at home. Being home with your kids is a top priority, as it should be. But even if your desire to be home with your kids is very strong (as it was for me), it's imperative that you look at your own likes and dislikes when you are considering what kind of work to do at home. Some people may be happy doing "just anything" to earn a living, but over the long haul, you'll miss some important benefits if you settle on any old work-at-home choice. The ideal is to work at home, in the company of people you love, doing what you love to do. Don't settle too quickly. It's possible.*

Now that you know what works and what doesn't in your current work situation, you can begin playing with the possibilities of working at home.

Have you wondered whether you would make a good at-home worker? Use the following quiz to rate yourself on various work-at-home qualities.

## Is Working at Home for You?

|  |  | Not True |  |  | Very True |  |
|---|---|---|---|---|---|---|
| 1. | I believe I would be more productive at home. | 1 | 2 | 3 | 4 | 5 |
| 2. | I'm a good time manager. | 1 | 2 | 3 | 4 | 5 |
| 3. | I don't like office gossip. | 1 | 2 | 3 | 4 | 5 |
| 4. | I use my resources well. | 1 | 2 | 3 | 4 | 5 |
| 5. | I can solve problems creatively. | 1 | 2 | 3 | 4 | 5 |
| 6. | I enjoy what I do. | 1 | 2 | 3 | 4 | 5 |
| 7. | I want to be more available for my family. | 1 | 2 | 3 | 4 | 5 |
| 8. | I know how to reduce my stress level. | 1 | 2 | 3 | 4 | 5 |
| 9. | I really want to work at home. | 1 | 2 | 3 | 4 | 5 |
| 10. | I enjoy challenges. | 11 | 2 | 3 | 4 | 5 |

If you rated all 5s in the list, you already are a Super-at-Home-Worker, and you should be writing this book. Most people starting out in home-based businesses or in work-at-home positions fall in the low-to-mid range. Much of it you learn as you go.

### 0 to 10

You really don't have much interest in this work-at-home thing. You're probably reading this book because your wife made you. You may be happy with the way things are, or you may be cynical about working at home. In any case, it's probably not your bag right now, but keep considering. Sometimes life surprises us.

### 11 to 20

You have some interest in working at home, but you're doubtful about your own abilities, especially when it comes to managerial tasks like scheduling, project managing, and stress control. If the doubts are really insecurities, they can be overcome. Keep reading.

### 21 to 30

This is a healthy response for someone considering working at home. You think all these things are possible, but you're not convinced. You need more information—about work possibilities and about your own strengths and weaknesses—before you'll know what to think.

### 31 to 40

A great start—you already have most of the basic skills you need for working at home successfully. You probably know how to manage projects, solve problems, and handle people (that's family) situations. If you had a high-scoring answer for the "want to" question (#9), you're all set.

### 41 to 50

Not only should you be working at home if you're not already, but you'll probably have an easy time making the transition. Not that there won't be challenges, but, hey, you said you enjoy them—right?

The most important question in the quiz is #9, "I really want to work at home." If you answered 3 or higher on that question, even if your overall score was 10, you should consider yourself a candidate. Keep learning about working at home. Don't give up the idea. If the desire is there, the rest will fall into place sooner or later. (I think everyone who wants to should work at home. Can you tell?)

## The Dangers of Working at Home

I would be guilty of infomercial tactics if I told you about all the benefits of working at home without mentioning the negatives. Personally, I can't list any negatives because it's all been a blessing to me and my family. But, in the "bigger picture," sociologists and theologians have a different idea about this at-home-ism that is taking root in the '90s.

These people tell us of the dangers of cocooning, of pulling ourselves and our families inside the warm walls of home, keeping everyone safe and cared for, at the risk of excluding the rest of the world. It becomes "us" and "them," the experts warn. The Internet joins people across the world, but those people are faceless, pseudonymed phantoms; and, even when pen-pal relationships develop, they are no replacement for the flesh-and-blood contact we must have with the outside world.

Contact is important. Real people are important. Working at home should not be an isolating experience. Depending on the nature of the work you do, you may have to make a concentrated effort to get out and talk to adults. I know I could go several days talking only to my kids and the dogs. Lucky for me I've got a truck with a battery that dies if I don't drive it every two days. I've got to get out and do something—take the kids to the park, go shopping, visit a friend, schedule interviews—so I can keep my truck running and my sense of humor recharged.

# In-Company Possibilities

Up to this point, I've given equal time to the ideas of working at home for yourself and working at home for someone else. They are two very different situations, however. This section will help you investigate the possibility of working at home if you want to keep your current job (or one similar to it), working for your current employer.

You might be surprised to find out about the different tasks employers are lettings workers do at home these days. Depending on the flexibility of your employer, these kinds of tasks (and more) could be handled out of the office:

- Appointment scheduling

- Bookkeeping

- Computer programming

- Correspondence

- Data entry

- Data tracking

- Desktop publishing

- Editing

- Envelope stuffing

- Graphics design

- Market analysis

- Order taking

- Project design and management

- Research

Reviewing

 Simple assembly work

 Tax preparation

 Telephone solicitation

 Transcription

 Various writing projects

 Video composition

**Professional Parent Panic!**

*"I stopped using my sitter when I moved my office home. But one day we had an emergency meeting at the office and I had to take my son, who was just starting to walk. During the meeting, he pulled down the blinds on the board room windows. He was fine, but I was embarrassed! That afternoon I went home and called people until I found a sitter who would be willing to watch Will on an as-needed basis."*

—*work-at-home mother of one*

## Could You Do at Home What You Do?

Suppose you're sitting there at your desk. It's 3:00 P.M. What are you doing? Would it be possible to do this at home? What would you need in order to do it?

Just a few years ago, working at home was next to impossible. The personal computer has changed all that. Now, if you have a computer and a modem, you can work in the next town as easily as you could work down the hall. You can still trade files with your editor; you can send artwork to the printer; you can enter a report, input debits and credits, and more.

Electronic mail (or e-mail) enables you to send messages to coworkers, bosses, or clients faster than you could make a phone call. The Internet makes massive research projects doable from any source with Internet access. Overnight couriers, although expensive if you use them often, enable you to move projects and products as quickly as possible in our fast-paced world.

If you assemble gadgets, build PR kits, create baskets, or work on other products that require light assembly, you might be able to do that at home.

If you are in a service industry that relies on your going to the client—such as a maid service, a window-washing service, or a pet-sitting service—you might be able to run your own schedule and set appointments from home.

If you are in sales, you might be able to use your home as your home base, making sales calls, setting client appointments, and doing your paperwork from the office in your house.

## Why Would an Employer Want You to Work at Home?

If you're a good employee, the boss wants you around, right? Not necessarily. More businesses than ever are looking at whether they need all their staff on-site, and if they can offer at-home advantages to those who seek them. Why? Well, for several reasons, among them these:

- Employees who work from home at least part of the work week are happier, more productive, and more loyal.

- Employees who work from home take fewer sick days.

- Employees who work from home spread good will to other employees and people in the community.

- Allowing employees to work from home reduces the overhead costs of the employer.

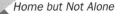

## Starting the Discussion

How do you open a discussion with your employer about working at home? First, know what you're asking for. Don't wander into the boss's office right after lunch and do this:

*"Uh, Bruce? Can I talk to you a minute?"*

He stretches. He's had a large lunch.

*"Sure," he says.*

You step tentatively into his office.

*"I've been wondering about something ... "*

*"Okay."*

*"And I'm, well, not sure it's possible, but ... "*

*"Yes?"*

*"If I promised to make sure nothing slips— nothing at all—do you think I could try working at home?"*

*"Working at home?" he asks with a blank look on his face.*

*"I miss my kids."*

*"Oh," he says, not seeing what good this will be to him at all. "I'll think about it and get back to you."*

He won't, of course. All he knows is that one day recently after lunch you were missing your kids. He doesn't see what that has to do with your job.

You have to help him see that. After a couple of practice sessions with the mirror, you go into your boss's office a few mornings later at 10:00 A.M. (Long enough after breakfast for him to be getting hungry again, so he's awake.)

*"Bruce, I have something I want to discuss with you. It will take about 10 minutes. Can we talk now, or should we set a time for later?"*

Bruce waves you in. You enter the office in a businesslike manner and sit down opposite him.

*"You know I've been working on the Peterson account for the last several weeks."*

*"Yes,"* he says.

He's listening. That account is an important one to the company.

*"There are a number of challenges I'm facing on that account. First, I'm having trouble getting Internet access, which is seriously hindering my ability to do the research on this project. For the last three days, our computers have been down a total of 12 hours—that's really hanging me up."*

*"That is being addressed,"* Bruce says. *"But I know it's a problem."*

*"I'm also having trouble getting a solid block of time to compile the results of all the testing we've been doing. The report is due a week from Friday, and all the interruptions I deal with make it impossible to write more than one paragraph at a time."*

Bruce nods.

*"And you know, if I can't get the research done, the report is not going to be up to snuff, which isn't going to impress any shareholders, which means we don't get the account for next year."*

*Bingo.* Bruce has made the connection.

*"Maybe you should work at home for the next couple of weeks. Come in on Monday mornings for the staff meetings, and e-mail me every day and let me know how you're progressing,"* he says.

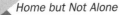

You smile and stand up.

*"I thought you'd know what to do," you say.*

Bruce stretches.

*"That's why they pay me the big bucks," he says. "Now I'm wondering, what's for lunch?"*

Now, granted, this is an idealistic scenario. (Isn't fiction *supposed* to be?) But it sets the stage for you to show your employer what you could do if you were working at home. The three things to remember are these:

1. Don't apologize for what you're proposing, because it will benefit the employer as well as benefiting you.

2. Don't start the discussion unprepared.

3. Don't get upset if you get a "let's-give-it-a-week-or-two-and-see" attitude. That may be the best answer you can get. If you get a chance to show your employer you can work success-fully at home, take it. You can prove yourself with your performance.

### Before You Talk to the Boss

**Know what you want.** How many hours do you want to work at home? Afternoons? Two days a week? Full time? Make sure you know the answer *before* you ask the question.

**Know what you will do at home.** If there are some parts of your job you *can* do at home and others you can't, make sure you can identify for your boss the specific tasks you will accomplish at home.

**Know how you will do the work at home.**
Explain what equipment and materials you
have at home that will enable you to do the
work there.

**Know how much you will get done at home.**
Be prepared to tell the boss you can increase
your productivity by working at home. Give her
specifics about how much better you will do.

**Know how long you plan to work at home.** Is
this a temporary move, until your kids go back
to school in the fall, or permanent? Is it
something you want to start right away, or
something you want to consider now for after
the baby is born?

**Know how to answer questions.** Practice a
question-and-answer session with your
spouse, a friend, or a trusted coworker so
you'll know how to respond to questions and
challenges your employer might offer.

Remember, the key is to show your employer how
it will benefit the company for you to work at
home. The trick, then, is to deliver on those
promises. Be truthful, precise, and as realistic as
possible, so you'll be able to achieve the goals you
promise and work in the environment you want.

*Some employers really like to see things
in writing. If yours is one of those—or if
writing is your strong point—write out a
proposal showing your boss exactly how
your working at home will enhance your
job performance.*

## Points to Remember

Okay, supposing Bruce gave you the thumbs-up and now you get two weeks to prove yourself at home. There are a few things to keep in mind that will help you be successful (and keep Bruce happy, which *is* part of the deal as long as he's the employer):

 **Communication is crucial.** The biggest complaint employers have about employees working off-site is that they don't know what's going on. Some people think there's a huge potential for abuse in a work-at-home situation: After all, you could be lounging on the couch watching talk shows instead of doing the research you promised, couldn't you? It's important to keep communication channels open so that your employer is reassured and people at the office can reach you if they need you.

The whole idea is to make working at home as much like you being in the office as possible for your coworkers so they have nothing to complain about. If the proofreader can't reach you by phone during the day or your boss can't get hold of you when he's got a question from a client, there's going to be trouble down the road. Make sure you are accessible, that you answer all phone messages promptly, and that you keep your employer or supervisor apprised of your progress each day.

**Be punctual.** Now that you've made the case for working better at home, *you have to meet your deadlines.* Deliver the report when you promised. When you're called in for meetings, be there on time—not a minute late. Present yourself in the best possible light and show your employer that you really want to make this work for her—and for yourself.

**Keep your promises.** Whatever you promised as part of your work-at-home reasoning—"Shorter commutes, so I can work more" or "I do my best work after midnight, so I'll be able to finish all three chapters by Monday!"—you'd better deliver on it. Otherwise, your credibility may fly out the window, along with your chance of turning a temporary work-at-home gig into a permanent one.

Be real, be honest, and be fair. Don't promise something you can't deliver. Have the best interest of the company at heart, and be clear about your intentions. Working at home can benefit everyone, though not every company will go for it. Still, you'll never know until you ask.

## Starting Your Own Show

Up to this point, we've been talking about the possibility of working at home when you're employed by someone else. There's another body of workers out there, a group that's growing by some 8,000 people a day: entrepreneurs.

What is an entrepreneur? According to *Webster's Ninth New Collegiate Dictionary*, the definition used to be "a person who organizes, manages, or otherwise runs a business or enterprise." Today, the lady on the corner running a home daycare center is an entrepreneur. The pet-sitter who advertises in the *Yellow Pages* is an entrepreneur. The guy who designs business cards in his den is an entrepreneur. The woman down the block who sells air time for local television stations is an entrepreneur.

In short, if you're running your own show, and doing it for money, you're an entrepreneur. For those of you into etymology (which is the study of words, *not* the study of bugs), the word itself is taken from a French phrase meaning "first thought." Luckily, it's not only the originator of an idea who is considered an entrepreneur. Every person, everywhere, who is doing his or her own thing his or her own way and making money at it is an entrepreneur.

## What Could You Do at Home?

By now, I know two things about you.

1.   You're interested in starting your own business.

2.   You've got kids.

At first glance, those might seem like mutually exclusive interests. Owning your own business is more than a full-time proposition. And every parent knows that having kids requires much more than full-time hours. (And you don't get overtime, either.)

You can come up with ideas for your home-based business by answering just three questions.

## 1.  What would you like to do?

This might be harder than you think. If you're having trouble, a little brainstorming is in order. See "Brainstorming 101" for a specific exercise in recalling the various goals you've had for your career. In general, give some time to each of these items as you consider what you want to do at home:

### Think about your talents.

For a long time, I sneezed at my talents. ("Talents are nothing to sneeze at," my mother used to say.) I played piano; I had perfect pitch; I could write; I could draw; I had a talent for making my brother blow milk all over the dining room table in the middle of a gulp; and I could antagonize my cat to the point of attack.

Okay, some good talents, some not so good.

Today, I use all those talents in the work I do. Although my business revolves around writing, I also write music, perform in a band, and design and publish the materials related to both the band and my business. But it hasn't always been that way. I've been writing professionally for over a decade, but the other talents—music, art, and the milk-blowing thing—I didn't start using again until recently.

You, too, have talents you may or may not use. Are you a gardener? Mechanically minded? A great cook? Tremendously organized? Think of the areas in your life where things seem to come more easily to you than they do to other people. You'll find clues there. Take a look at things you love— animals, kids, photographs, boats, anything—and ask whether there's a potential business in there somewhere.

These are my talents:

These are the topics that interest me:

_____

_____

_____

_____

_____

_____

_____

_____

**Think about things you've done in the past that you really enjoyed.**

This is similar—but not identical—to thinking about your talents. What experiences have you tried that you really liked? Perhaps you planned a great birthday party for your son. You could turn that into a kids' party service. Maybe you know a lot about aquariums, and you set a great one up for your brother's law office. The office next door might want one too. And perhaps they need another one for the conference room? There's a business opportunity!

## 2. What's realistic?

Suppose you come up with a few ideas on the kinds of things you like to do. Under talents, you listed talking with people, athletics, and *Jeopardy*. Under good experiences, you listed sky diving, scuba diving, and water polo.

It's a fair guess you're into sports.

The next step is matching your idea with some reality. What type of business opportunities are there that match your talents and experiences and gel with your real-life responsibilities? And what are your real-life responsibilities? Your family needs certain things. Your house needs certain things. You need certain things. It's your job to meet the basic needs of your family, so you need to know what those needs are. Start by answering these questions:

How much money do you need to make?

How many hours do you need to be home to be accessible to the kids?

How many hours do you have to be available for outside interviews and meetings?

How many hours do you need for yourself and your spouse?

Get a clear picture of what kind of opportunity will fit your lifestyle. If you are planning on being a work-at-home parent, it's fair to say that being home is an important part of the equation. That means your business probably won't take you scuba diving in the Bahamas or sky diving in the Waimea Canyon on Kauai.

But you could do something sports-related closer to home. How about a specialty sports vacation travel agency, where you set up scuba diving or sky diving vacations for clients? You could sell specialty sports equipment by phone or catalog. You could design and manufacture your own line of sports gear. You could design and market a sports game that challenges players to test their knowledge of sports trivia.

## 3. Where do you see yourself in five years?

Finally, when the ideas start popping, don't get carried away thinking about today. Consider tomorrow, too. Where do you want to be in five years? Consider how your family will change by then. Where do you want your business to be?

In five years, I plan to be

_____

_____

_____

_____

_____

Don't worry if this seems open-ended. It is. You might have answers ranging from "alive" to "independently wealthy" to "living in Fiji." The point is to avoid getting stuck in the excitement of now and ask yourself where you hope to be, what you hope to be doing, and how you hope to be doing it in five years.

## Brainstorming 101

Now comes the fun part. Get yourself a cup of coffee and sit down with the book and a pen. Do you remember all those "When I grow up, I'm gonna' be" statements you made when you were little? Search back through those memories, everything you ever thought you wanted to be, were interested in, thought might be fun, or found exciting. Write them down—the silly ones, too—in the spaces below:

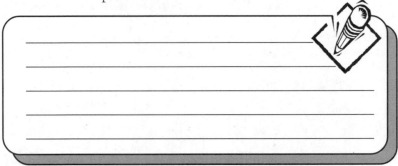

*What, exactly, is brainstorming? It's capturing every idea that goes flying through your brain—good or bad—after you ask it a question. Fight the temptation to throw out the "crazy" ideas while you're brainstorming; those might the ones with enough spark to set your idea on fire.*

Brainstorming is fun, once you get the hang of it. You'll be amazed at the wild answers you come up with—the more creative, the better. And brainstorming with a friend or your spouse can give you additional perspectives. Instead of asking yourself what you always wanted to do when you grew up, ask your spouse, "What do you see me doing? What do you think I'd be good at?" Remember, however, that when you ask for someone else's opinion, you're likely to get it—and it may not mesh with the way you see yourself. Accept the ideas in the spirit of fun and use them to enlarge your perspective as you weigh the possibilities of what you might be able to do at home.

My daughter had considered more careers by the age of 8 than most of us have in a lifetime, although she seemed to adopt a kind of cyclical approach:

- A garbageman (now we call them "trash collectors")

- A doctor

- An artist

- A teacher

- A writer

- A geneticist

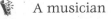 A musician

 An artist

 An art teacher

My list is shorter but surprisingly similar:

 An artist

 A concert pianist

 A writer

What you might find in your list of wanna-be's is a pattern that will give you a clue about your lifelong interests. Maybe certain things have always caught your eye and certain topics have always captured your attention. This brainstorming may help you see a pattern or topic that holds a future career for you.

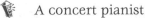

## A Second Opinion

You might want to ask your kids what they think. I tried that at my house.

"If I wasn't a writer, what do you think I'd be good at?" I asked them.

My youngest son, who was playing video games at the time, said, "I think you'd be good at games!"

My older son thought a moment and said, "I think you would make a good archeologist."

When I asked him why, he said, "Did they find the Ten Commandments yet? That would be a good job for you. You could get pretty famous for doing something like that. Maybe even get paid!"

Hmmm. I thought he was going to say that anyone who could find a matching sock in *his* sock drawer had to have some kind of archeological gift!

> *Similar but not the same are those things you've always wanted to try but haven't. Perhaps you've always wanted to go skiing in the Rockies, but you've never done it. That's a "want-to," not a "wanna-be," and you should put it on your list of ways to reward yourself someday. It doesn't mean you should start a home-based business as a ski instructor.*

## Educating Yourself

Once you've got an idea of the kinds of things you're interested in, you can start finding out more about the businesses that might relate to those topics. There are a number of ways you can go about it. Here are just a few ideas:

 **Let your fingers do the walking.** People underestimate the *Yellow Pages*, that treasure trove of ideas and resources. Look up the topic you're thinking about. How many mobile pet-grooming salons are there in your town? What about auto-detailing companies? Who offers gift baskets? How many computer consultants are there? The *Yellow Pages* will tell you (1) what businesses are making it in your community and (2) what needs are *not* being met. If you have an idea and you don't find it represented, great! It may be that you're on to something your town really needs.

**Search the Internet.** Because the Internet is a world-wide network of smaller networks, you can literally search the globe to find information on the topic that interests you. You might, in fact, receive a truckload of information, depending on how popular your topic is. Much of it won't be relevant to your individual city or town, unless you specify that in your search. (For example, entering

"Dog-grooming-Seattle" will produce documents that have references to those three words in them.) The information you gather from the Internet, however, can show you what people are doing in the world related to your topic: What's going on with in-home child care? Are there any new resources for dried flowers you could tap into? What about searching for a place to get the lowest price on packing materials? The Internet gives you a world of information, accessible through your phone line—but you need to think and use it creatively to make the most of it.

 **Talk to your local Chamber of Commerce.** Let's bring things back to a local level. Your local Chamber of Commerce will have lots of useful information: How many new businesses have started in your area in the last year? How are they doing? Are there any surprising new businesses? How many home-based businesses are represented in their membership? The Chamber of Commerce relies on business memberships to keep going, so they will want you to succeed and, someday soon after you open shop, they'll no doubt contact you and try to get you to join. Fees vary; in my area it costs $125 a year, which entitles me to a monthly newsletter, discounted Internet access, low-cost or no-cost seminars, and an option to join a group health plan. If your business relies on networking, joining the Chamber is a great business move.

**Head for the library.** We all know that libraries are great. Yet it's been said that less than 3 percent of American adults set foot in a library during a year's time. The library is a terrific resource for all kinds of things: ideas on at-home businesses, statistics on business success and failure rates, the *Yellow Pages*, directories, all kinds of things. Tell the librarian you're investigating home-based businesses and let him point you in the right

**Been There, Done That**

*"In my mind, I started about ten businesses a week. I had all these great ideas, but I didn't act on any of them. When I finally did start my craft business, I was afraid I wouldn't stick with it. But I really love what I'm doing, so that hasn't been a problem."*

—work-at-home mother of three

direction. Just remember to speak softly so you don't get shushed.

**Get out more.** It's amazing the number of businesses you start noticing when you're thinking about starting your own. You notice places you never saw before. Your town is currently supporting thousands of businesses. When you're out and about, read store signs and notice advertising. See what seems to be big in your area and what's dying out. And, in the back of your mind, reserve a spot for that special missing something, the service no one seems to offer or the product everybody needs.

**Take a class.** Many community colleges offer classes that explain the basics of starting a home business and offer ideas and resources you can check out on your own. The conversation with other people in the class is probably worth the price alone—you can make some valuable contacts in this startup phase with others who share similar goals for themselves and their families.

Of course, everything we're talking about here falls under the heading of *networking*. Whether you are taking a class, joining the Chamber, making contacts with new businesses, or simply talking to your son's friend's mother at hockey practice, you are creating relationships that can help you learn more about what you're planning to do. These networks will help you in the education phase of building your business now, and they may help you reach customers down the road, too!

We've looked at a number of ways you can find out about the needs of your community. Now let's think globally. The personal computer lets you offer your services to a world-wide community. If you decide to start a sales business, for example, you can offer your product internationally using the Internet. If you work in a service business—such as writing, publishing, or graphics design—you are not tied to local clientele; you can work with people all over the world who need your services. As a writer, I work with publishers on both coasts and a few in-between, but I have yet to do any business at all in my home town. The computer and the Internet make it possible for me to work as easily with a publisher in New York as I could with someone down the block.

## Franchises: Prefab Businesses

One opportunity we haven't talking about is the possibility of buying a prefab business: a franchise. Yes, I know, you aren't interested in running a fast-food operation from home. But you might be surprised to find there are a number of franchises that are run from homes all over the country.

### What's a Franchise?

When you buy a franchised business, you are becoming the owner of one segment of an existing business. You get the ongoing support of the parent company, as well as advice, discounts on materials and services, the company name, and more. Many businesses owners buy into franchises to reach a level of success quickly, relying on proven methods, products, and reputations to sell their services or products to the local market.

## Write It Down!

Now that you've explored what you've wanted to do, and compared that to information you've gathered on what it's *possible* to do, you can fit the two together and determine whether there is a need for that type of product or service in your community. Suppose you wanted to be a firefighter when you were growing up, and through your life you have been interested in fire-safety issues. Maybe your niche is consulting with area businesses to make sure they are within the local fire code. You might design fire-safety suits for firefighters. Perhaps you could do fund-raising for volunteer fire departments. There are any number of ideas that could spring from that initial brainstorming session.

Look back at your brainstorming list and see where your primary interests are. How could those interests fill a need? Write your ideas here:

| | |
|---|---|
| _____ | _____ |
| _____ | _____ |
| _____ | _____ |
| _____ | _____ |

It may not be something you've thought a lot about, but franchising is a concept that's working in a big way in America. According to *The Entrepreneur Magazine Small Business* Advisor, a new franchise is born every 17 minutes.[2] And here's another whopping statistic: Over one-third of all sales in the U.S. in 1996 took place in franchises, coming in above the $250 billion mark.

Granted, you won't find a huge number of retail franchise outlets you can run from home. But you might be surprised to discover that many popular franchises *are* run from homes, or have at least a percentage of home-based franchisees.

A recent issue of *Entrepreneur* magazine listed the top 101 home-based franchises in the country.[3] Here is a sampling of the different companies and the number of home-based franchises they currently run:

## Top Home-Based Franchises

| Franchise | Description | How Many Franchises at Home? |
|---|---|---|
| Snap-On Tools | Professional tools | 2,943 |
| Molly Maid | Home cleaning | 146 |
| Jani-King | Commercial cleaning | 5,424 |
| Jazzercise, Inc. | Dance and exercise classes | 4,415 |
| Travel Network | Travel agency | 52 |
| Lawn Doctor, Inc. | Tree and shrub care | 288 |
| Computertots | Computer program for kids | 147 |
| Safe-T-Child, Inc. | Child identification program | 70 |
| United Coupon Corp. | Direct-mail advertising | 49 |
| HouseMaster | Home inspection services | 105 |
| The Sports Page | Youth photography | 104 |
| Candy Bouquet | Candy gift packages | 9 |
| The Dentist's Choice | Dental equipment repair | 60 |
| Video Data Services | Video production services | 167 |
| General Business Services | Business services | 220 |

## The Upside of Franchises

Buying into an existing idea—that has proved successful for others and offers a specific startup method you can follow—brings a number of advantages. First, you know it's been done before. You're not risking your career, your finances, and next year's vacation on an idea that's never been attempted. Second, there are a number of systems already in place to help you get started successfully—that's part of what your franchise fees go toward. You will get information on setting up and running the operation, from books to payroll.

Another benefit of purchasing a franchise is that you are buying a company name. With the name comes recognition and a prescribed method of doing business that (as the franchiser will tell you) leads to professional and financial success. This means you also enjoy the power of buying collectively, perhaps straight from the franchiser, which saves you money and guarantees some degree of product or service quality. Most franchisers also will help you with the startup phase—from evaluations to advice to financing. They also may help with business planning because, ultimately, your success is their success.

## Down the Downside

All the perks a franchise offers come with a price. First, there's the initial cash investment, which may run anywhere from $5,000 to $150,000—or more. Next, there's a monthly franchise fee, which runs from 2 to 6 percent or your profits, depending on the franchise.

Aside from the financial hits, you also have an emotional issue to deal with: You are not in complete control of your own business. You sign a contract with the franchiser, agreeing to basic business guidelines, how sales will be handled, what costs you'll pay, where you'll get your merchandise, how you'll handle advertising, and so on. With some franchisers, your hands are tied in a big way; with others, you have more freedom in the way you run your business.

## Franchise Q&A

When you begin investigating a specific franchise opportunity—perhaps informally, by talking to someone who owns a franchise in your area, or more formally, by speaking to a company representative—ask questions that give you answers to these important questions:

- How many franchises are in operation?
- How long have they been operating?
- Are they strictly work-at-home franchises?
- What is the success rate?
- What is the average income?
- What is the average expense per franchise?
- What is the startup cost?
- What percentage do franchises pay monthly to the franchiser?
- What is the company's mission statement?
- How marketable is the franchise in your area?

Other questions you'll need to answer include the all-important ones: Does this franchise fit my priorities? Will I be able to have the work-at-home lifestyle I want if I become a franchisee for this company? Don't rely on gut feelings for this one—make sure you have plenty of data to back up your decision. Interviewing other franchisees will tell you how their expectations compared with the reality of running a franchise. Their experience can be invaluable to you as you consider your long-range goals.

*For more information on choosing and owning a franchise business, check out LaVerne Ludden's* The Franchise Opportunity Handbook.[4]

**Profiles**
**Name:** Joe
**Business:** Internet publishing services
**How long?** One year
**How many kids?** Two, ages 7 and $2\frac{1}{2}$
**Biggest challenge:** Keeping work from taking over.
**Best answer to that challenge:** Take more breaks and remember to spend some time away from the office.

## The Idea

I hope by now you've got something cooking in your head (besides a headache, I mean). A potential idea. Something that sounds good to you, would fit your family responsibilities, and would fill a need in your local or world-wide community.

Stop now and answer the following questions on the next page. Don't fret over them: Just think of your answers as rough drafts. You're crystallizing your idea here, and you can expect to revise whatever you start with. It's the starting that's the important part.

## Testing Your Idea

I have to be honest here: this isn't my favorite part. I love ideas, but I don't like testing them. I don't want to be wrong, so I'd rather just believe in the good points than see the bad.

What's your topic?

_____

What hasn't been done (or isn't being done enough) in relation to that topic?

_____          _____

_____          _____

_____          _____

What specific service or product could your business offer to fill that need?

_____          _____

_____          _____

_____          _____

How do I find out more?

_____

_____

_____

_____

*If you're still having trouble coming up with the idea that really fits you, check out Kelly Reno's* 77 No Talent, No Experience, and (Almost) No Cost Businesses You Can Start Today! [5] *This book includes fun, creative, and good ideas you can use to kick-start your own mental processes and find the business that works for you.*

Maybe you're the same way. It's important, however, especially when your money, your time, and your family's security depend on it, that your idea be a sound one. Now that you've got the basic idea for your business, you need to test it rigorously to make sure it holds water. You can use questions like these to test it:

1. Does this idea seem realistic?

2. Does it meet a specific need?

3. Will it require a large investment?

4. Will I be able to earn a living doing this?

5. Does the idea fit my family priorities?

6. How many other people are doing what I am considering?

7. How successful have they been?

8. If this idea depends on a local clientele, is there room for my idea?

9. Do I want to do this?

10. Do I have the equipment I need, or will I need to purchase it?

11. Do I have the finances I need, or will I have to raise funds?

12. Do I believe in this idea?

13. Do I have the space I need to start this business?

14. Do I have the time I need to run this business successfully?

15. How does my family feel about the idea?

16. What are the best things about this idea?

17. What will the challenges be?

Now, before you go any further, talk to at least three people whose opinions you respect about your business idea. What do they think? If possible, choose advisors who have circumstances similar to yours, who are running home-based businesses, or who at least understand the family priorities you hold dear. When you have gathered your information, looked at the idea from every possible angle, discussed it with people you respect, and resolved any issues it poses for you or your family, you're ready to make the decision.

## Partners in Grime

Many home-based businesses today are run by husband-and-wife teams, who are able to combine their talents to make their businesses successful, profitable, and fun for their entire families. When you are considering your home-based business, it's important to take it on as a team project. What does your spouse think? Is it something he or she would be interested in doing, too? Perhaps your spouse will keep a full-time position until you get the business moving enough to support both of you. There are any number of options you can come up with, but you need your spouse's endorsement and support.

## Uh ... Go for It?

I wish I could be more definitive here, but that choice is one you shouldn't be pushed into. The best advice is this: Don't make the move until you feel ready for it. But don't let yourself sit around stuck in indecision forever, either. If you're considering talking to your employer about working at home, you won't know until you ask. If you're thinking about starting your own business, remember that businesses open every day, and if you don't act on your idea, someone else will.

But time spent thinking never goes to waste, so use your time to sift through your hesitations and unanswered questions about what you're pondering.

### Entrepreneurial Options

Many people start their home-based businesses as part-time efforts to test the waters without losing the security of their full-time jobs. That way, they find out whether they like the business, whether it fits their family, whether the market will support it, and whether it has the potential of supporting them. Over 50 percent of the home businesses operating today are part-time businesses, but many of them go full-time within their first year.

◆ ◆ ◆ ◆ ◆ ◆ ◆

BEST &
**WORST**

*Worst:*
"Financial
worries that
hit me in the
middle of the
night."

◆ ◆ ◆ ◆ ◆ ◆ ◆

For different ways to ease into life in a home-based business, see Chapter 5.

# What We've Got So Far

By this point, you've thought about working at home and learned enough about it to have come up with an idea you're mulling over. You're gathering all this information with the idea that sooner or later you'll be ready to make a huge decision—one that will change your life and the dynamic of your family. Intimidating, yes, but also exciting and wonderful. You're on the verge of a major change that will put you back in the driver's seat of your life.

There are three key ingredients that can help make your leap a successful one:

- **Belief.** You must believe in yourself, in your family, in your abilities, and in the idea.

- **Realistic expectations.** Most successes don't happen overnight. Plan for your success and celebrate the small triumphs along the way.

- **Resolve.** Once you've made your decision, be determined to make it work. Don't give up on yourself or your business when you are tested. (And you *will* be tested.)

Whether you are prepared to take the leap and begin working at home now or you plan to sleep on the idea for a few days (weeks? months?), knowing what you need in order to get started is the important next rung on the ladder.

# Notes

1. *The Entrepreneur Magazine Small Business Advisor* (New York: John Wiley, 1995), p. 213.

2. *Small Business* Advisor, p. 213.

3. *Entrepreneur,* "Top 101 Homebased Franchises," compiled by Stephanie Osowski (September 1996), pp. 167-169.

4. LaVerne Ludden, *The Franchise Opportunity Handbook* (Indianapolis: JIST, 1996).

5. Kelly Reno, *77 No Talent, No Experience, and (Almost) No Cost Businesses You Can Start Today!* (Rocklin, Calif.: Prima, 1996).

# Starting Out at Home

*"Luck? I don't know anything about luck. I've never banked on it, and I'm afraid of people who do. Luck to me is something else: hard work—and realizing what is opportunity and what isn't."*
—Lucille Ball[1]

Whether you are preparing to face self-employment for the first time or you are moving your work office to your home office on someone else's payroll, you have some preparing to do. You'll need certain essentials to begin with—and to hold onto—work-at-home sanity. This chapter helps you look at the practical issues involved in working at home. First, we'll cover the basics, from workspace to paper clips, from calendars to computer systems. Then you'll learn where you can find each of these essentials. You'll also need to plant the seeds of cooperation in the family flower bed, so a few weeks down the road, when you're really into the throes of change, you can count on everyone pulling together when things seem to be falling apart.

# What Do You Need to Work at Home?

Your initial answer to this question may be, "Not much." But when you start looking seriously at the various items—material and otherwise—you need to keep on keeping on. Your answer may change. This section gives you an idea of the kinds of things you need to plan for as you start your work-at-home business.

### Shoestring Businesses

It *is* possible to start a business on a shoestring. Especially if you're concerned about money, you'll watch the expenses like a hawk, cutting out everything that's not absolutely essential. You don't need paper clips, right? You can simply fold down the corners of pages you need to keep together. But you'll find that, after a while, the papers get shuffled, the crimped edges annoy you, and you're losing pages. At that point, you might be more than willing to spend 39¢ for 100 paper clips. Most business owners go through shoestring periods from time to time, but nobody exists on a shoestring forever. Once in a while you've got to loosen your belt so you can laugh a little, even if it's only over paper clips.

If you're working at home for an employer, of course, the company might give you all the supplies you need, including a computer, paper, envelopes, disks, labels, whatever. This isn't always the case, however, and some employers simply reimburse their work-at-home employees for expenses rather than have them carrying reams of paper and cases of disks out of the building.

# I Just Need My Space

Everybody needs one's own little corner of the world. When you start working at home, you need a place to call your office. The best situation, of course, is when you've got a spare bedroom, the basement, the attic, the pole barn, or even the garage to create the office you need. In countless homes around the country and the world, however, businesses are being run on desks in living rooms, on tables in bedrooms, and even on kitchen counters.

The amount of space you need, and its access to the outside world, will depend on what kind of work you'll be doing at home, as these examples show.

 If you're a work-at-home insurance agent and you'd like your clients to come to you, you need an enclosed space—like a spare bedroom or den—that is easily accessible from the outside. A room over the garage, a front bedroom, or a library close to the front door would be great.

 If you teach music in your home, you need some space with room for instruments and privacy from the rest of the family. And a path from the music room to the door that doesn't run through your living room would be ideal.

 If you're a freelance speech writer and you send and receive most of your information by fax, you need a space for your files, your typewriter or computer, your fax machine, and other support items. You don't have to worry about clients coming to your office, though, so whatever suits you in terms of size and accessibility would fit the bill.

If you run a home daycare center, of course, you need plenty of room for children. You'll also need open space, room for small tables and chairs, easels, cars, baby buggies, and more. Check with your local Family Services office to find out how many square feet you should allow per child.

If you run a cleaning service business from your home, you need space to store the equipment. If you have employees, you'll want to consider the accessibility of the office: Will employees be coming in to pick up schedules and paychecks? If so, make sure the office is as easy to reach as possible so you can maintain the privacy of your home.

### Professional Parent Panic!

*"My two partners and I started our programming business in the basement of my house. The trouble was that, to get to the basement, you have to go through my bedroom. There were plenty of nights when my wife and I were tired and wanted to go to bed and my partners were still down there working ... we learned the hard way how important privacy is."*
—a work-at-home father of one

Take some time to think about the space you need, where you need it, and what type of access it should have. Use the following checklist to help you identify the space issues that are unique to your work.

Not everyone has the space or the money to start out with the office envisioned. It's important, however, to think about what you would love to have, and then decide what you realistically can achieve now.

**Ideas for Your Workspace**

Does your office need to be accessible to clients? _____

Do you need a separate room for your office? _____

Do you need room for (check the following that apply):

_____ A computer

_____ A printer

_____ A fax machine

_____ A file cabinet

_____ A work table

Other: _____

_____

This is the office I'd like to have:

_____

_____

_____

_____

_____

This is the office that will do at first:

_____

_____

_____

_____

_____

*If you rent your house or apartment, check your lease carefully or speak to your landlord about any legal constraints on running a business from your home. There may be insurance liability issues to deal with if clients come to your residence and it is not your own.*

What can you do if you don't have space? Many people have handled this dilemma successfully, especially in the startup phases of working at home. Listen to what a few work-at-home parents have tried when they were setting up their home offices:

*"I was determined not to spend any money on working at home until I knew it would work. So I took two old file cabinets that I had in the basement and an old door from the garage, and I made a desk in the corner of the dining room. I used my son's computer and printer, and plugged into the phone line in the kitchen. (I just stretched the phone cord to the computer when I needed to use the modem.) I worked with this setup for about six months, until I was sure I was going to keep working at home. Then I splurged and bought a real desk and chair, and my own computer, and set everything up in the spare bedroom."*
—work-at-home mother of two

*"I live in a small house with my three kids and my wife, and there just wasn't any room to set up office space. So I use a laptop computer to do my freelance writing work and keep all the files I need in a filing cabinet tucked away in my bedroom closet. When I need to use the modem, I plug into the phone line. Most of the time, I sit on the couch and work while the kids play right there beside me. Sometimes I miss the privacy of a 'real' office, but my laptop gives me the freedom to go to the park and work too."*
—work-at-home father of three

*"I work at home in a spare bedroom I've set up as an office, but my office area really only takes up about a third of the room. The rest is my kids' domain—Super Nintendo, TV, VCR, books, an activities table, a futon to flop on, a bookcase with more of their books than my own. But I like it this way; I want them to feel 'at home' in my office with me. I think that's one of the biggest benefits of working at home."*
—work-at-home mother of three

*"If you don't have space, go up! I built bookshelves from the top of my desk (which is along the back wall in the family room) all the way to the ceiling. I keep everything up there—books, files, fax machine, a light, supplies—my whole office, in an area about five feet wide, four feet deep, and ten feet high. And one of the best things is that the kids can't reach the things on the top shelves, so I put all my bookkeeping and client files up there."*
—work-at-home father of two

*If you have to set up your office in the corner of a busy room in your house, consider getting a folding partition to put around your workspace. This will help you concentrate and will help your family members know where the boundaries are.*

## Details, Details: Zoning and Permits

If you're starting your own business at home, you have a few more details to gather as you research work-at-home ideas. How is your area zoned? You can find out by visiting your township clerk's office and getting a copy of the city ordinances for home-based businesses. Have your lawyer take a look at the ordinances, so you can be sure you are on the up-and-up with your idea.

Permits also take a little legal digging. What kind of permits do you need to operate your business? Does your county require a standard business license? If you make cookies in your own kitchen and sell them, do you need a permit from the health department? If you work with flammable materials, the fire department will want to know—and you'll probably need a permit. In any case, your attorney can help you solve this issue, too, by reading the ordinances on licensing and helping you understand how they apply to your business.

**BEST** &
WORST

*Best:*
"Being able to stay home and work when the weather's bad."

# Equipment Essentials

The items listed in this section probably won't surprise you. You might think you need one or all of these things, and the prospect of buying them all right off the bat might make your eyes roll. But hang in there—I'll talk about where you can get equipment the cost-cautious way in the next section.

## The Practical PC

If you think you can run a business from home without a computer, think again. Consider these testimonies:

*"It's the first piece of equipment you should buy."*
—an optometrist

*"You cannot run a business without a PC these days."*
—a marketing specialist

*"The days of the typewriter are over."*
—a journalist

*"My editor would shoot me if I couldn't save files to disk!"*
—okay, I admit it—that's me

The personal computer isn't simply a luxury for people who are fairly well off. It's an important tool for most homes these days: Current statistics indicate that close to 50 percent of American homes now boast at least one PC. And it's an *essential* tool for work-at-home parents.

*I use the term* PC *here to refer to the* personal computer, *not the IBM PC, as past generations have done. A PC can be an IBM compatible, a Macintosh, an Amiga, or a computerized toaster. (Well, maybe not the toaster.)*

What will you do with your computer? Perhaps the question more easily answered is what *won't* you do with your computer? You will keep track of clients; work on files; print reports and mailing labels; balance your checkbook; keep your kids busy playing games while you're on the phone with a client; draw a logo for your business cards; write that first financial statement for the bank; send e-mail to your accountant; and much, much more.

So how much computer do you need? That's a whole different question. The kind of computer you need, how powerful, and how expensive depends in large part on the kind of work you do with it. Today's computer systems range in price from $1,000 to $5,000—and up. For many simple office tasks, you can get by with a low- to mid-cost system. Expect to pay $1,400 to $1,800 for a basic PC that does everything you want. Here's a list of must-have items for any PC you get for your office:

 At least a 486 microprocessor

 At least 8 megabytes of memory

 At least 850 megabytes of hard disk storage

 At least one floppy drive

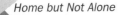
 A monitor

 A printer that gives you the quality printout you need

 A modem, if you plan to communicate by e-mail or the Internet

 A mouse (which should come with the computer at no cost)

 A keyboard

Other add-on items that are nice but not necessary for many business applications include a CD-ROM, a sound board for multimedia programs, extra memory, and more disk storage.

*The good news is that many PCs come with "bundled" software, meaning that several popular programs are already installed when you buy them. You'll probably get programs like Microsoft Works—which includes word processing, spreadsheet, and database programs—along with a few games and other miscellaneous programs you may never use.*

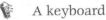

## If You're Working on Borrowed Time

If you have moved your work office to your home office and you're still working for someone else, your employer may let you take your PC home for a while until you can get your own. If she offers, take her up on the deal.

Or perhaps you already have a PC in your home. Maybe it's not the coolest thing in the world, but it will enable you to get the job done until you can afford a faster, slicker model. Just offer to pay your daughter a few dollars a week rental fee and promise not to delete her favorite games. She may find it in her heart to let you use it for the short-term.

*For tips on buying that first computer, see* Discovering PCs, *by Katherine Murray (that's me!), or* PCs for Dummies *(4th edition), by Dan Gookin, which comes with a nifty little booklet entitled,* Computer Buying Tips for Dummies.[2]

If you know you need a computer and you're still clenching your teeth over it, it may help to plan out just how much you can spend. Use the following budget to help evaluate how much you want to spend—for what kind of power—in your first PC.

### PC Budgets: Wishes and Realities[3]

| Item | High End | Low End | Aim For |
|------|----------|---------|---------|
| Basic system[4] | $2,299 | $799 | _____ |
| Monitor | $1,699 | $249 | _____ |
| Printer | $5,999 | $179 | _____ |
| Fax/modem | $379 | $89 | _____ |

**Extras:**

Sound card _____

Speakers _____

Microphone _____

Backup tape drive _____

UPS power supply _____

Scanner _____

Graphics tablet _____

**Software**

Bookkeeping _____

Application programs _____

Internet/Web access_____

## The Softsoap on Software

Software is to a computer what a movie is to your VCR. A VCR is a great machine, but it's not worth much unless you have something to put in it. Likewise, the computer is just a heavy paperweight without the software programs to run it. No matter what goal you want to accomplish, there's a program to handle it for you.

| If You Want to Do This | You Need This Type of Program | Popular Examples |
|---|---|---|
| Write letters, compose reports, do anything that requires you to work with letters, words, sentences, and so on | Word processing | *Microsoft Word* *WordPerfect* *Word Pro* |
| Create a budget, design a balance sheet, do financial forecasting, create charts | Spreadsheet | *Microsoft Excel* *Lotus 1-2-3* *Quattro Pro* |
| Enter client information, print mailing labels, keep track of personnel data, design an inventory system, track your ordering | Database | *Microsoft Access* *Paradox* *FileMaker Pro* |
| Organize company bookkeeping, keep track of taxes, balance your checkbook | Financial manager | *Quicken* *QuickBooks* *Microsoft Money* |
| Publish newsletters, business cards, books, magazines, or brochures | Desktop publishing | *Adobe PageMaker* *Microsoft Publisher* *QuarkXPress* |

What you need in any PC is the ability to run the software you must use—probably a word processor and perhaps a spreadsheet program. If you've got room on your computer's hard drive, a financial program like *Quicken* or *QuickBooks* (both from Intuit) can help you keep the bookkeeping part of your business straight. Make sure you keep copies of important files you create—especially if you have borrowed the computer and have to give it back—so you've got safe backups of the work you've done.

Use this list to identify the software you need and how much you plan to spend on it.

| Do I Need This? (Yes/No) | Software Type | Which Program? | Cost |
|---|---|---|---|
| _____ | Word processing | _____ | _____ |
| _____ | Spreadsheet | _____ | _____ |
| _____ | Database | _____ | _____ |
| _____ | Financial program | _____ | _____ |
| _____ | Desktop publishing | _____ | _____ |

## Where Do You Get It?

The question of where to purchase a computer and the software to go with it is an important one. If this is the first computer you'll buy, go play with the computers at your local computer store, WalMart, or any other store in your area with PCs. There may be a used computer store in your town that carries lower-cost models you can try your hand at.

The point is to actually get your hands on a PC so you can decide what you like and what you don't. Do you like the models that sit horizontally on your desk or the ones that stand up like towers? Do you like big monitors or small monitors? Is there a certain kind of keyboard you'll be happy with? Experiment with different computers until you get an idea of what you like and dislike. Then check the prices and compare them with mail order houses like PC Connection to see who has the best deals.

The same issue applies to software. You need to see it before you buy it. In most cases, you'll find out about a program from a friend, a coworker, your ex-boss, or someone who does what you need to do with the program. Ask someone to show it to you. If that's not an option, go to a computer store and ask to see a demo of the product. You can then make an educated choice, whether you purchase the program from a retailer or a mail order catalog.

Many people purchase computers and software from mail order companies because they find it saves them money. If you don't know much about PCs and are buying your first one, ask a trusted friend and PC enthusiast (we all have at least one) to help you. Or check out some of the magazines devoted just to PCs. *PC World*, and *Family PC* are both good and include reviews. And *Computer Shopper* has just about every mail order house in the world listed! It's huge—something like 400 pages—and oversized! There also are a number of books that can help you with PC purchasing dilemmas: In fact, come to think of it ... oh yes, I remember now ... I wrote that one called *Discovering PCs*.[5]

## That Terrific Telephone

If there *is* a tool that's even more important than the PC, it's the telephone. We simply couldn't do without it, in everyday life or in business.

Yes, you're thinking, I already have a phone. Well, at least I've got *something* I need.

But you may want to think about adding a second line, if there's a lot of traffic on your house line. The second line is an additional cost—sometimes a pretty hefty additional cost—but it ensures that business is business and home is home, which can get pretty confusing when you're a work-at-home parent.

At first the benefits of having a second line might not be obvious. But about the third time your teenager answers a call with her Alice in Chains CD blaring in the background, you'll appreciate the professional perks of having your own business line. A second line also enables you to talk to clients on the phone and surf the Internet at the same time.

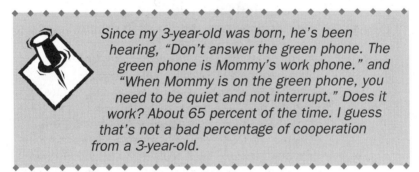

Since my 3-year-old was born, he's been hearing, "Don't answer the green phone. The green phone is Mommy's work phone." and "When Mommy is on the green phone, you need to be quiet and not interrupt." Does it work? About 65 percent of the time. I guess that's not a bad percentage of cooperation from a 3-year-old.

Your local phone company probably offers a number of phone features that can enhance—or detract from, depending on your personal preference—your professional appeal. Current phone features include these:

- **CallerID**: If you've got the right type of phone or box with a CallerID display, this feature shows you the names and numbers of your most recent callers. This is handy if you don't get to the phone in time and the person calling doesn't leave a message. (It's also great when your daughter's friends keep calling and hanging up and don't know you've got CallerID!)

**Double or triple rings**: You can get different numbers connected to your single line, so when a client calls, for example, you hear a distinctive ring. In my house, I've got a double-ring number that lets me know when clients related to a particular project are calling. That way I can make sure I hurry to the phone if I need to; or I can let the answering machine get it if I'm busy writing.

**Automatic callback**: This is the Star-69 (or *69) feature that automatically calls back the last person who called you. This is great when you get cut off while talking to a client who called you. My suspicion is that it's used more often for catching people who annoy other people by dialing a number and hanging up.

**Voicemail**: Some local phone companies offer their own automated voicemail systems; you simply dial a number on your phone that sends all your calls to your voicemailbox. When you return home (or when you're ready to receive calls again) you dial the number to turn off the voicemail interception. I've heard more complaints than kudos about this, but the feature must be successful or it wouldn't still be around. Many people claim that they forget to listen to their messages unless they see a little light flashing on their answering machine. That's me, too. Out of sight, out of mind.

**Call waiting**: Yes, this is the scourge of the phone features. And yet ... confessions are in order: I have call waiting on my phones. When you are deciding whether to get call waiting on your phone, think about how your clients will feel when you have to leave them to answer the beep. If you don't think they'll mind, go ahead. If you don't like the idea, skip the feature. If you have to get call waiting when you first set up shop because

### Been There, Done That

*"Technology is not just for the young, although our young would like us to think so. One day, when I was fixing dinner, my daughter was on our house phone talking to her best friend. She asked if she could use my computer—which means she wants to play on the Internet—since I was cooking, anyway. I said sure. When I went upstairs to call her down to dinner, she still had the house phone on her shoulder, with her best friend on hold, another beeping in, her fingers busy in a global chatroom on the Internet, and she was dialing my business phone to call and ask another friend about plans for Friday night. I pulled the plug on everything. I was afraid her brain was going to explode."*

—work-at-home mother of three

you're watching expenses and can't get a second line, resolve to get a separate line as soon as you can afford it.

 **Call conferencing**: Especially if your business relies on you getting people together to work on projects, schedule jobs, and the like, you may want to add a call conferencing feature to your phone line. This enables you to get two or more people on the line at the same time so you can discuss voice-to-voice the issues you need to iron out.

**Call transfer**: Some companies support this feature, which enables you to have calls forwarded to a second number. This is great if, for example, you want to have calls sent to your cellular phone while you're at your daughter's ballet class or you want to be able to get client calls when you're visiting your mother in Spokane.

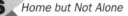

The features available in your area are easy enough to add: Just call your local phone person and ask what's available and what the monthly charges will be. Most feature run somewhere around $4.00 to $6.00 a month, which isn't an enormous cost for trying something that could help you manage your business better. And, if worst comes to worst and you're not happy with the feature you've added, a simple call can discontinue it as quickly as you added it.

### Professional Parent Panic!

*"I was running my business using my house phone, when my phone service was interrupted for six days. It was awful. Everyone told me if I had a business line, the phone company would have fixed the problem sooner. This past summer I had a business line put in, and when the phones went down after a bad storm, the phone company was out here within hours to fix it."*

—work-at-home mother of three

### What Kind of Phone?

So what kind of phone would be right for you? The following questions will help you see what you do—and don't—need in a phone. Circle true or false for each entry.

I spend at least one hour a day on the phone.     T     F

My phone calls average 15 minutes or more.     T     F

I often take notes while I'm on the phone.     T     F

I usually talk to the same people each day.     T     F

I need the flexibility to move from place to place while I'm on the phone.     T     F

What's your score?   # True: ____   # False: ____

If you checked more "Trues" than "Falses," you need a phone that is comfortable to use for long periods of time. (Which means you don't want a small flip phone or one with a short cord.) A speed-dial feature would be nice, because you wouldn't have to dial the same numbers over and over—you could just push one button and dial your customer or coworker. And if you write while you're on the phone, or you need to move freely so you can look up information, check on the kids, or let the dog out, make sure you get a portable phone that doesn't tie you to one spot in the house.

### Professional Parent Panic!

I learned the hard way the value of cordless phones: When my son Christopher was 2, we lived in a sprawling house in the country. Most of the time, he played with cars, trains, or blocks in my office—which was in the loft overlooking the family room—while I worked. One day he decided he just *had* to watch his favorite show and I had calls I just *had* to make, so I got him situated in front of the TV—which I could almost see when I peered out my office door—and went back upstairs to make my calls. One phone call turned out to be not so short and sweet (I was dealing with a fussy author), and by the time I was able to get off the phone, I was in a panic. Was Christopher still watching his show? I listened carefully. No sound. Not even the television. I skidded down the stairs and searched the family room. No Christopher. I started yelling his name, close to a full panic now. I ran through the house and finally found him, on the kitchen counter, smiling happily as he watched the water in the sink overflowing onto the kitchen floor, something it had apparently been doing for several minutes. He had pushed a chair up to the cabinet, climbed up, put the stopper in the sink, and turned the water on. I never did figure out what gave him the idea. But I did go right out—that very afternoon—and buy a cordless phone.

**What Kind of Phone Do You Need?**

Do you need a new phone?

What features do you need?

_____

_____

_____

_____

What brands do you like?

_____

_____

_____

_____

How much do you want to spend?

_____

One final note about phones: Keep an eye on your long-distance service. People who work at home seem to get a higher-than-average share of long-distance solicitation, and there is a big difference between carriers. Take a look at your phone bill and find out what you're paying per minute. Be very careful about the "special deals" the large carriers offer businesses—often they are set up to benefit large companies and small, one- or two-person operations wind up losing money on the deal.

In one horror story a work-at-home mom shared with me, a large long-distance company (one that should know better) literally hijacked her service. Apparently all she did was answer the phone, and when the caller asked, "Are you Mrs. Jane Doe?"

she said, "Yes." The long-distance salesperson then recorded her "Yes" and applied it in the recorded segment saying she wanted to change her long-distance service to their operation. As a result, she began getting charged .21 a minute—as opposed to her chosen carrier's .14—and she didn't even know it. So be careful what you say "Yes" to, and make those long-distance salespeople work for their money. If they don't convince you—truthfully—that they have the best rates for your needs, wait until you know what you want. And if you get tired of being contacted, ask them not to call you anymore. Legally, once you ask to be taken off their list, they are not supposed to solicit your business.

### What About Fancy Phones?

Well, the phone company wants you to think you need that $250 phone with the built-in CallerID display. Do you? Only you know for sure. If you're not adding a phone line, you can simply use the phone you already have. If you are adding a phone line, or you're working off an extension, get a phone that is comfortable to use, gives you portability (if that's important to you), and is in the price range you feel happy with.

Any number of different kinds of phones are available today, however, and more will no doubt be around tomorrow. Cellular phones can go with you anywhere; they can cost anywhere from $29 to $500 dollars, and you pay a monthly usage fee that is over and above your regular old house phone bill. Faxes often have phones built into them; so if you need a fax machine anyway, that might be an attractive option for around $200. And then there's the ever-popular multipurpose machine: a combination fax/printer/scanner/modem/phone (a great invention with an ugly name), which is the fastest-growing computer add-on and retails for about $500.

## Leave Your Message After the Beep

Answering machines are a part of everyday business in the '90s. If you are one of those people who hang up when they get somebody's answering machine, you probably hang up a lot. Even large companies now use voicemail to answer the phones. You may go through several levels of menus before you actually talk to a real, "live" voice, if you ever get one.

What do you need in an answering machine? Something simple enough that you can use it without taking a training course. Something with good-quality sound, so it doesn't sound like you're yelling out at people from inside the sink drain.

Just a few years ago, answering machines stored your outgoing message—"Hi, you've reached Masterpiece Painting. We're not in to take your call, but if you leave your name, number, and a brief message after the beep, we'll call you back as soon as we get in."—on a small tape. It was your basic tape recording scheme. Today, the outgoing message is stored on a small microchip. The great thing, the manufacturers tell us, is that this "digitized sound" is the best quality you can get. The downside is that every time you lose power, someone trips over the cord, a storm blows in, or there's an electric hiccup on the line, you have to rerecord the message. Ah, the things we suffer in the name of progress.

Most answering machines sold today also offer a remote messaging feature that lets you call in from a phone at another location to retrieve your messages. You may pay $5 or $6 dollars more for the feature, but it's a great help when you're waiting for an important call and you've got to take a sick child to the doctor.

You can pick up an answering machine for under $100, unless you want really complicated features that are geared for multiuser phones, features that let you leave memos and use the machine as an intercom system. Just a simple $49 answering machine suits me fine, which may be why I'm rerecording my message every time someone in my office sneezes.

## Do's and Don'ts for Answering Machine Messages

Don't have the dogs bark your message.

Remember that clients who don't know you will be calling.

Fun is nice, but "professional" is important.

Let the kids do your house message, not your business message.

If you use your answering machine for both home and business, just give the facts on the machine: "You've reached So-and-So business. Leave your name and number and I'll call you back."

Check your messages twice a day or whenever you return home.

Don't leave an old message on too long

Do use your message to communicate information that will help clients: "I'll be out of the office from December 2 through December 5; but if you leave a message, I'll return your call as soon as I can."

Do smile when you record your message. (I know, you'll feel silly—but the message will sound better.)

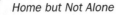

What does a business message sound like? Mine goes like this, "Hi, you've reached Katherine Murray at reVisions Plus. I'm not in to take your call right now, but if you'll leave your name and number after the beep, I'll call you back as soon as I get in. Thanks for calling!" For years, I cringed every time I recorded that message. I wanted to do something fun, creative, entertaining. I learned, however, that people generally don't like answering machines, and they rarely listen to the message, beyond making the mental note that the voice they hear is yours, which means they've got the right number.

---

### What Do You Want in an Answering Machine?

Do you need an answering machine?

Check the features you want:

_____  Digital recording

_____  Messages of any length

_____  Remote message playing

Other: _____

How much do you expect to pay? _____

---

## Supplies for the Sweet

Now we're coming down to the nuts and bolts of the home office. Supplies. The little stuff.

Finally, you're thinking, something inexpensive. Well, maybe.

You might be surprised at how much you can spend on file folders, accordion folders (my personal favorite office supply), disks, printer paper, toner, ink cartridges, paper clips, rubber bands, index cards, pens, pencils, highlighters, markers, write-on boards, clipboards, bulletin boards ... get the idea?

You've heard the phrase "nickel and dimed to death"? The person who coined that owned an office supply store.

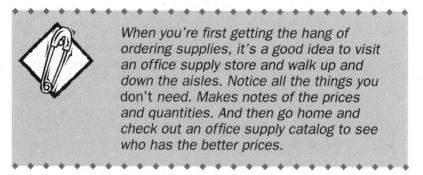

*When you're first getting the hang of ordering supplies, it's a good idea to visit an office supply store and walk up and down the aisles. Notice all the things you don't need. Makes notes of the prices and quantities. And then go home and check out an office supply catalog to see who has the better prices.*

The best way to get a handle on the kinds of supplies you need is to sit down with a pencil and paper and write down absolutely everything you can think of that you might possibly need to do what you do on a daily basis. If you're working at home for an employer, the company might give you the supplies you need or agree to reimburse you for the items you purchase that you would ordinarily receive free at the office. (Keep those receipts!) The nature of your business will have a lot to do with what supplies you need, but most businesses—just for the paper pushing part—need the following items:

 Computer disks

 Printer paper

 Printer ribbons, ink cartridges, or toner cartridges

 Pads of lined paper

 Pens, pencils, markers, and highlighters

 Folders

A stapler and staples

Yellow sticky notes

The where, when, and how of buying supplies are important factors in how much you spend on them. If you go out and get paper when you're down to your last few pages, you'll be more likely to pay for whatever's nearest—which may not get you the best deal.

The type of supplies you need will depend on the nature of your business. If you run a beauty shop from your home, you will need all the supplies related to the tasks you do on a daily basis. If you assemble children's furniture, you'll need a different set of supplies. Think about what you're most likely to need day by day—both for the business-management part and for the everyday tasks—and add those items to your list.

## Hold Everything!

Of course, it's not part of your ongoing expenses, but once you purchase those supplies, you need

somewhere to store them. The disks need disk holders, small clear or off-white storage boxes that protect them from dust and other environmental hazards. You need a place to put the printer paper, ribbons, and whatnot; shelves will do. What about a desktop container for your pens and markers? And if you don't have a filing cabinet yet, you'll need one or two to store those folders.

## Supply of the Year: Accordion Folders

Okay, so I'm plugging a product. I love these things. I use them for everything. Those little 12-pocket folders that open up to store whatever your heart desires are essential at my house. I use one for my home to organize all the bills as I pay them; I use one for my business to do the same thing and to store receipts for payables. At the end of the year, I just take the folder out of my file cabinet, give it to my accountant, and get a new folder for the next year. I used one to help organize the research I did for this book: one pocket for each chapter and one to keep all the notes, interviews, and articles together until I was ready to write. Simplicity. Heaven!

## To Bulk, or Not to Bulk?

There's also the question of buying in quantity. Should you purchase everything you need for six months at a time, or should you buy it as you need it? Check out the prices you can get both for large orders and piece by piece. You may be able to get substantial discounts if you order items you know you'll need in bulk. (And if you buy from a mail order company, you may be able to get shipping free.) Weigh out the plusses and minuses, and see whether (1) you are sure you'll need the same supplies you are using now in six months; (2) you can afford the investment; and (3) you've got room to store the extra supplies.

*If you know other work-at-home parents who are running small businesses, consider creating your own co-op for office supplies. Two or three or more business owners can go together on one large order—and get a large-order discount—then divide up their wares when the shipment comes in.*

### What Supplies Do You Need?

Make a list of all the supplies you need and indicate whether you will purchase them once, occasionally, or often within a six-month period. This will give you an idea of the supplies you can order in bulk—if you've got the money and the room—to save you from frequent shopping trips.

| Supply | One-Time Buy | Occasionally | Often |
|--------|--------------|--------------|-------|
|        |              |              |       |
|        |              |              |       |
|        |              |              |       |
|        |              |              |       |
|        |              |              |       |

## Postage Due!

Another variable cost is one you already deal with, to some degree: postage. Right now you use postage for bills and letters. If you will be sending paperwork, books, pamphlets, brochures, and so on through the mail, postage becomes a heavier burden.

The best advice when it comes to postage is this: *Don't pay it when you don't have to.* Here are a few ideas to help you cut postage costs:

**Send by e-mail** any letters, reports, or memos you can.

 **Use bank-by-phone** whenever possible to save postage paying bills.

 **Shop around for postage rates** and go with the best price. Overnight services like Federal Express and DHL are great when you've simply *got* to get something in a client's hands right away, but they will also cost you $10 or more per shipment. The U.S. Postal Service has an overnight shipping option that—for most packages to most places in the continental United States—costs $3. Sound like I'm fussing over nickels and dimes? These costs—which seem comparatively small—add up quickly, and it's a habit that's hard to break once you start.

 **Look for alternatives.** If your client needs to see a document right now, can you fax it? What about e-mail? Will you be in the area anyway? Don't just give up and ship something before you've investigated the options.

 **Educate yourself.** If you rely on a mailing company to do your packing and shipping for you, plan on paying a premium price. Investigate all your shipping options—who ships to that region the fastest, for the lowest cost?—before you commit.

 **Ask for shipping numbers.** No, really! If you work in a field that has you shipping projects back and forth (case in point: publishing), ask your project coordinator for the shipping account number. You may be able to ship their work back and forth on their dime. If they won't give it out, feel free to make your own decisions about the best carrier to use, whether they use a more expensive service or not.

*Even though I have a Federal Express account for my small business, I rarely use it. Costs have just gotten too high. Now I ask the publishers I work with to provide their shipping account information for me to submit my projects. If they don't want to give it out, I ship my books first class, U.S. Postal Service. The projects are there within three days and it costs me $3. Hey, it doesn't hurt to ask.*

## What's Your Postage Picture?

Will your business use a lot of postage? _____

Which aspects of your business will involve shipping charges? _____

How often will you pay postage? _____

Do you have alternative methods of shipping?

List them here:

_____

_____

_____

_____

_____

What will it cost to ship with

_____        Federal Express

_____        DHL

_____        U.S. Postal Service

_____        Other

## A Tiger in Your Tank

Another expense you may not notice right away is the one that goes into your gas tank. Are you using your car for business? If so, you can keep track of the mileage and write the expenses off.

Accountants advise keeping a journal in your car to record the mileage—before and after—for any business trips you make. This means training yourself to think about where you're going before you go: If you drive 60 miles to take your kids to the pizza-parlor-playground-place, and then stop by your accountant's office, it's not technically a trip to your accountant—which means you can't write it off. If you go to the accountant's office *first*, however, it's a trip to the accountant's office. A bit silly, I admit, but something to keep in mind.

You also can pay yourself a certain per-mile rate (companies pay anywhere from .12 to .21 or more a mile), which includes gasoline reimbursement, as well as oil, antifreeze, and normal wear and tear. You can use a sheet like the one below to keep track of costs and reimbursements.

### Keeping Track of the Car

| Date | Beginning Mileage | Ending Mileage | Trip Description | Per Mile Rate | Total Paid? Cost |
|------|-------------------|----------------|------------------|---------------|------------------|
|      |                   |                |                  |               |                  |
|      |                   |                |                  |               |                  |
|      |                   |                |                  |               |                  |
|      |                   |                |                  |               |                  |
|      |                   |                |                  |               |                  |

The easiest way to keep things straight, of course, is to have a car you use strictly for business purposes. But if you're working at home, and your commute to the office is all of 10 steps from the kitchen to the den, it's hard to justify a $26,000 luxury car.[6]

# There's No Such Thing as "Free" Time!

If you're a parent, you already know that time is one of your most precious commodities. If you're a parent and you work, your time is under even more demand. If you're a parent and you work at home, time takes on a whole new meaning.

Many people who *aren't* walking in your moccasins will think now that you're home, you have all kinds of time for things like chatting on the telephone, playing a morning round of golf, taking the kids to the park, and so on. Your kids will think you're accessible to get them snacks and help them fingerpaint the garage floor all day long.

You'll quickly find yourself trying to fit more than one minute's work in each minute. You'll try the "two-things-at-once" trick. You'll attempt to keep Rachael busy while you print a report. You'll try sewing the hole in Jason's pocket while you talk to a buyer on the telephone.

It's not going to work.

The fact remains: One of the necessities—the things you must have in order to start working at home—is the time to do it.

Best advice? Set a schedule for yourself. Define your work hours and stick to them, at least until you have enough data to revise wisely. If you are working at home part-time, think about when you can be most effective, how many hours you need, and what days you need to take those hours. Then make yourself a schedule.

If you are working full-time at home, block out the times you'll be working, and also schedule in breaks, lunch, kid time, and time for miscellaneous interruptions.

## Starting Out with a Schedule

Here's a schedule you can use to sketch out your intended work hours. Two guidelines apply:

1. Don't plan on working more than two solid hours without a 15-minute break.

2. If you absolutely have to work Saturday, vary your hours and give yourself some time to play. (And no, I didn't forget Sunday. As far as I can tell, for the last few thousand years it's worked pretty well as a day of rest.)

BEST &
**WORST**

*Worst:*
When the kids have snow days and I'm under a tight deadline.

|       | Mon. | Tues. | Wed. | Thurs. | Fri. | Sat. |
|-------|------|-------|------|--------|------|------|
| 8:00  | ____ | ____  | ____ | ____   | ____ | ____ |
| 9:00  | ____ | ____  | ____ | ____   | ____ | ____ |
| 10:00 | ____ | ____  | ____ | ____   | ____ | ____ |
| 11:00 | ____ | ____  | ____ | ____   | ____ | ____ |
| 12:00 | ____ | ____  | ____ | ____   | ____ | ____ |
| 1:00  | ____ | ____  | ____ | ____   | ____ | ____ |
| 2:00  | ____ | ____  | ____ | ____   | ____ | ____ |
| 3:00  | ____ | ____  | ____ | ____   | ____ | ____ |
| 4:00  | ____ | ____  | ____ | ____   | ____ | ____ |
| 5:00  | ____ | ____  | ____ | ____   | ____ | ____ |

There are also time-management programs and schedulers, like the electronic version of DayTimer, that help you stay on track for appointments and personal goals. You can use a scheduler to establish your work schedule and remind you of important checkpoints in your projects.

*Avoid the temptation to schedule every moment of your day. Give yourself time to breathe, to laugh, to have cookies and milk with your kids. It's one of the perks of working at home.*

There's another side to time-management beyond the now-I-work, now-I-don't issue. How will you keep track of your projects? Again, the type of projects you need to keep track of and the way you choose to do that will depend on the type of work you do. If you are selling advertising space for a local magazine, you might set a goal at making 30 contacts a day. If you are writing a book, you might want to write one chapter a week. If you are running a home-based daycare center, making it through the day with your sense of humor and no stitches is a pretty big accomplishment.

How will you track what you do? There are various computer programs—such as *Microsoft Project*—that can help you organize your work time electronically. But you might try other ways as well. I used the good old-fashioned 3"-by-5" card system for a while; I'd keep one for each project, along with what I needed to do and when I needed to have it completed. And I always included a place I could check off when I finished it. (That's the nice part.) Something like this:

*Project:* VanArsdall Annual Report

*100% Due:* 3/23/97

| Item | Date Due | Date Completed |
|------|----------|----------------|
| Rough draft | 2/23/97 | 2/21/97 |
| First final draft | 2/28/97 | 2/28/97 |
| Final final draft | 3/16/97 | 3/12/97 |

Another must-have is a friendly monthly calendar. You might get the big write-on-the-wall kind that you wipe off once a month and start again. I prefer the desktop version that I can write in and scribble up: this call to this person today, that meeting with that person tomorrow—vacation! I keep those calendars from year to year and file them with my tax items at the end of the year, and it's fun to look back through them from time to time. Makes me feel like I'm really getting somewhere. (And, even if I'm not, I can see that I've been busy getting nowhere.)

And down the road your write-in calendar can really come in handy. When you forget to log the miles you traveled to do research on that new program you're designing, your calendar will remind you. And when a client tells you that you promised to have the curtains finished on the 30th, you can look at your calendar and see—and show him—that he's mistaken: You agreed to the 10th of next month.

You'll soon develop a way to keep yourself moving with your deadlines in mind; and as you gain more experience working at home, you'll quickly weed out the methods that don't work for you and fine-tune the ones that do. Just remember to start writing things down and keep writing them down—someplace you'll remember to look for them—and you'll have the answers you need later when people start asking you questions about what you said, did, or planned on some foggy day in your past.

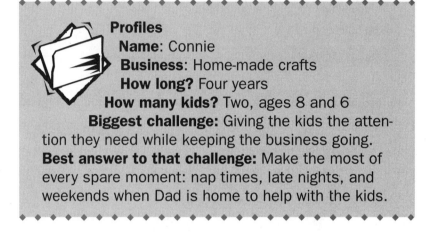

**Profiles**
**Name:** Connie
**Business:** Home-made crafts
**How long?** Four years
**How many kids?** Two, ages 8 and 6
**Biggest challenge:** Giving the kids the attention they need while keeping the business going.
**Best answer to that challenge:** Make the most of every spare moment: nap times, late nights, and weekends when Dad is home to help with the kids.

# It's a Family Affair

You are used to taking other peoples' needs and expectations into consideration. At the office, you didn't wear your bunny pajamas to board meetings; you didn't sing show tunes at the top of your lungs while everyone else was working; you tried not to cause other people discomfort or inconvenience them by making unrealistic demands.

You're really going to need those skills at home.

Because you will be tested and tried. Your friends and relatives—and especially your kids—won't understand the "home = working" part of your life. And home may be the one place in your life that you can get away with the "because I said so!" mentality.

*"Why do I have to do my homework now?"*

*"Because I said so!"*

*"Why can't I use your business phone? You're not using it!"*

*"Because I said so, that's why!"*

*"I don't see why you can't run me to the mall. You're home, aren't you? Wasn't that the whole idea, that you could be here for us kids?"*

*"No, I can't take you to the mall. Why? Because I said so!"*

The problem with "Because I said so!" is that it's a show of power with no education behind it. Yes, you did say so; yes, you are the parent. But no one is any better off than they were when the question was asked, which means it will be asked again ... and again ... and again. If you explain *why* those requests conflict with what you need to do, your kids (or friends or relatives) will grasp the reasoning behind your answer. And maybe the next time they are tempted to ask, they'll remember the why on their own.

Information and education can solve some of the challenges that will inevitably loom to greet you on your path to working at home.

## The Family Meeting Revisited

Back in Chapter 1, you were encouraged to have a family meeting to talk with your family about this working-at-home idea and to gather input from each person on what's important for the family. Giving everybody a say helps build the feeling that the family is a team pulling in the same direction.

Now that you've defined the type of work you're going to do, the space you need for your office, the hours you will work, and how much quiet and contact time you need, it's time for another meeting. This time, you'll do most of the talking, explaining not only what cooperation you'll need from the family but how they can help you and what you're offering them when they do.

It's proposition time.

In the last several sections, you've considered what you need for your work-at-home situation in terms of space, equipment, and time. Now you need to communicate the impending changes to your family members so everyone is clued in and enlisted. When they know change is going to come and how it will benefit them, they'll be more willing to help make the transition a smooth one.

Of course, you know your family better than anyone else, so set up your family meeting in whatever way fits you best. The following section gives you an idea of how and what to cover, in case you need some help planning it out.

## Explain the Change

If you have a spouse, we can assume that he or she has been part of the decision-making process that's brought you to your choice to work at home. Having both parents enthusiastic and clear-sighted about changes is a great reassurance to the kids.

As you and your spouse explain the upcoming change to your children, do it together. Be playful. Let your excitement show. If Dad is leaving the office to work at home and Mom sits there sullenly staring at the floor, the kids are going to know this is all Dad's idea and Mom doesn't like it one whit. If Mom is quitting her job to start an afghan-crocheting business and Dad is really worried about what that will do to them financially, the kids are going to pick up on it right away. Make sure you work out your differences with your spouse *before* you come to the family meeting, so you can present the plan to the kids as a team. Your kids will be reassured, and they'll be as optimistic about the change as you are.

## Explain the Business

Tell your kids what you're going to do at home, why it's important to you, and what you think it will mean for your family. If you're starting a chimney-cleaning business with your two best friends, tell your kids why you decided on that business, how great it will be to work with your friends, what kind of hours you think you will work, how many hours you'll be out on calls, and so on. If you have the equipment you'll use to do your job, walk the kids through the process so they know exactly what you'll be doing all day. Teaching them about the business, so they know more about what you do, cements that "our family business" feeling.

## Cooperation 101

Now comes the fun part. You need to communicate to the kids what you expect them to do to help as you begin working at home. This isn't the chore part (that comes later). You will simply list your basic rules for home operation (which means you've got to have them ironed out for yourself):

- My no-excuses work hours are 10:00 to 12:00, 1:00 to 4:00, and 9:00 to midnight.

- Don't interrupt while I'm on the business phone.

- If you need something while I'm on the phone, write it on the chalkboard.

- Don't use my office supplies without asking.

That was my first stab at work-at-home rules. My kids stared at me with that grumpy look that says they don't like to be ordered around. I tried revising the rules, hoping for a less dictator-like approach.

 I will work during these hours: 10:00 to 12:00, 1:00 to 4:00, and 9:00 to midnight.

 Please wait to talk to me until I am off the phone.

Use the chalkboard to leave me notes and reminders.

 I will gladly share some office supplies if you remember to ask me first.

That was better. Combined with a short explanation of why each of those rules was necessary, they seemed to take hold. It took reinforcement—it *still* takes reinforcement—but I had the basic groundwork for boundaries in my business life.

These rules are in effect while I'm working:

1. _____

2. _____

3. _____

4. _____

## Questions and Answers

Once you've covered the basic points—what this change means to your family, why the business is important to you, and how you want the kids to help—your young audience is bound to have some questions. Don't settle for shrugs: Ask your kids

what more they'd like to know. You might get
questions like this:

*"Can I help?*

*"Do I still have to go to school?"*

*"Can I answer the phone sometimes?"*

*"Is this kind of what Jake's dad is doing?"*

*"Does that mean I don't have to go to the
baby-sitter's?"*

*"Are you sick or something?"*

*"Can I get a puppy now?"*

*"Will we still get McDonald's?"*

If your kids ask a question you don't know the
answer to—like who will pick Matt up after soccer
on Thursdays or what Deirdre will do instead of
going to the sitter's house—write it down and let
them know you'll answer it as soon as you work
that part out. You don't have to have all the
answers today, but letting them know you're
working on it will help keep them from worrying
about unresolved issues.

You might be surprised at the level of enthusiasm
they show; then again, you might not. Most kids
are interested in what their parents are doing—
especially young kids—and they want to know
how it affects their lives. That means if you're
doing something really neat, they are excited ...
because they'll sound really cool when they tell
their friends. The older they get, the more
independent they are; what you do doesn't affect
them quite so much.

At least that's been my own experience.

The first time I did a television interview for my first parenting book, *The Working Parents' Handbook*, it was a pretty big deal to me. I was scared and excited. I wanted my kids to care. Finally, I asked them if they were going to watch. My son Christopher glanced up at me and shrugged, "Oh, it depends. If *Rugrats* is on, I don't want to miss it."

Pffffft (the sound of my ego deflating).

But that same child, when it suited him, happily brought up the success of the book in front of a roomful of parents and kids a few nights later. We were standing in a line at an open house, when he looked up at me and said, "Do these people know *you're* Katherine Murray, the author of *The Working Parents' Handbook*? Do they know you're *famous*?" By the time he reached the last word, he was nearly shouting. Parents looked at me strangely. I looked for a folding chair I could crawl under.

The moral? Don't be surprised by whatever response you get. Somewhere, deep down inside, my kids are pretty proud of the fact that their mom writes for a living—although they might never admit it to me. Somewhere down inside those small hearts, your children will be proud of the fact that you are working at home, too—that you made a decision to take hold of your life and create the working situation you wanted for yourself and for them. And someday, when it comes time for them to make the same choice, they will have a role model for doing that too.

## The Game Plan

Once you've answered your kids' questions, it's time to lay out specifically what's going to happen. If you're going to renovate a bedroom into an office, let them know when construction is going to start. If next Tuesday is Dad's last day at the office, tell them so. (And plan a party to celebrate!) If they will begin seeing new people at the house—prospective clients—make sure they know ahead of time that strangers will be coming to the door, and tell them how you want to handle it. The idea is to not pop any surprises on the kids. You want them to be prepared and excited about the business, not worried about the changes and insecure about their own responsibilities.

When I first started working at home, my game plan looked something like this:

  Monday A.M.: Ben comes to build shelves in the office.

  Tuesday P.M.: Ben finishes with shelves.

  Wednesday: Phone company installs new phone line for the office.

  Thursday: Mom starts new office hours.

Now take a few minutes and use the space below to write out your own game plan.

**The Starting Game Plan**
Here's the plan for the next few weeks, as I get started working at home:

_____

_____

_____

_____

_____

Letting your kids know what's going to happen when is an important part of a successful startup. You might want to keep an ongoing game plan posted on your family bulletin board, your fridge, or any other area where your family typically leaves notes and messages in your house. Letting your kids know on a weekly basis what's coming up during the week helps them make choices about things in their own lives. Then they can answer questions like these for themselves:

- When should I ask if Brock can come over and play?

- Will Mom be able to help me with my science project?

- I want to go to the pool. Maybe Tuesday?

- Arcade! Arcade!

## The Chore List

Ah, the family favorite. Are your kids doing chores around the house today? A chore list is a logical part of "what-you-can-do-to-help-us-run-this-household-smoothly" and communicates to the kids exactly what you expect from them. You don't have to go into assigning specific chores today—this meeting will be long enough as it is—but you do want to mention that you will need everyone's help to keep the family and house running well, so *everyone will have a job to do.* In Chapter 9, you will learn why it's important to let your kids do their chores and how to set up payoffs for when they achieve their goals.

## The Goals! The Goals!

As you wrap up your meeting, explain what working at home will mean to you and your family. What are your goals? A happier family? A more secure financial picture? More time together? Flexibility? Personal growth? Let your kids know why this is important to you and how it will benefit the family as a whole. End the meeting on an upbeat note, and make sure everyone knows that you'll meet again a few weeks down the road to talk about all the changes that are going on.

## Summing Up

In this chapter, you've taken some huge "Mother-may-I?" steps toward setting up your work-at-home environment. There are lots of things to think about: practical issues like where you'll work, what you'll need, and how you'll manage it. But there are emotional issues, too, perhaps even more pressing: Does your family understand what's going on? How can you help prepare them—and you—for the changes that are taking place?

Feel good about the moves you're making—this is important stuff. And remember: Disney World wasn't built in a day.

Now, who hid the chocolate chip cookies?

## Notes

1. *The Manager's Intelligence Report* (Chicago: Lawrence Ragan Communications), p. 5.

2. Katherine Murray, *Discovering PCs* (Foster City, Calif: IDG Books Worldwide, 1997); Dan Gookin, *PCs for Dummies, 4th Edition* (Foster City, Calif: IDG Books Worldwide, 1996).

3. Prices are based on the January 8, 1997, edition of *PC Connection* magazine.

4. A basic system includes the system unit, keyboard, and mouse. Monitors are sold separately.

5. Murray.

6. This is not as far-out as it sounds. A former coworker of mine (a rather corrupt individual) had a pretend "consulting business" in order to write off his $525-per-month lease payment on his car. Sooner or later, he'll be "consulting" with the IRS on that, I'm sure.

# What About Child Care?

*"Always let your conscience be your guide."*
—Jiminy Cricket, *Pinocchio*

Child care may be one of the biggest reasons
you want to work at home. Who can care for
the kids better than you? No one. Being home
when the bus arrives, being free to schedule
dentist appointments and go to teacher
conferences, is an important benefit—no doubt
about it. But if you're starting your work-at-
home experience with the expectation that life

will be smooth sailing with three kids under 5 at home—and that you'll find plenty of work time, phone time, and quiet time—you need to bring your expectations down a few notches.

**BEST** &
WORST

*Best:*
"The sense of accomplishment."

Life with kids is hectic. Wonderful, but hectic.

Life with kids and an at-home business is not going to be any less hectic. In fact, it will be worse. Now you've got the added pressure of earning an income from home. You've got a professional image to worry about. You've got deadlines to meet.

And your kids are still kids.

In this chapter we'll take a look at realistic options for child care. Will you need part-time child care? Most of us do. Do you plan to depend on your neighbor to fill in the gaps when you've got a meeting to attend? You'll have a chance to explore your options and to evaluate those choices in light of your priorities and work schedule.

# Do You Need Child Care?

Many people try *not* to have child care when they first start working at home. Depending on the personalities of your kids, your own personality, and the nature of your work, you might be able to get by with no child care or with very little care from an outside provider.

The key is to tune into your kids, your business, and your own needs—and to keep on tuning in.

When I first started my business 10 years ago, I had no intention of making daycare arrangements for my kids. I wanted to be home working with my kids—and that was that. If I had a meeting, I scheduled it when my husband was home. It seemed pretty simple.

My children have grown up in my office, playing Legos, My Little Pony, MicroMachines, and now Super Nintendo beside my desk. I gave them activities and projects to help break up the daily routine. This worked very well—almost blissfully well—for my two older kids. But Cameron, who is the most on-the-go and the youngest of the three, wasn't happy working on projects, coloring, or painting.

He'd bring a football in and stand in front of my desk. "Catch!" he'd say suddenly, and throw the football at my head—over several thousand dollars worth of computer equipment, phones, a fax machine, and whatnot. After righting the lamp, I explained that we don't play football in the house, much less in Mommy's office.

The next time it was the Frisbee. And I was on the phone with a client.

All of a sudden, after raising two and a half kids and working for almost eight years in my own business, I realized I needed child care. Cameron needed something I couldn't give him while I worked, and that was an outlet for his tremendous energy. Coloring I could help with. Puzzles we could do. Football wasn't something I could play while I wrote books for a living.

### Professional Parent Panic!

*"I had just put Jessica down for a nap when the phone rang. I had a conference call with a client and a supplier, and it went on for a long time. About half-way through the meeting, while I was still on the phone, I peeked into Jessica's room and ... no Jessica. I almost screamed. Just as my client asked me a question, I spotted my daughter—asleep in the middle of the stuffed animals on her sister's bed."*
—work-at-home mother of two

So today, $3\frac{1}{2}$-year-old Cameron goes to preschool from 9:00 to 11:30 three mornings a week. He comes home flushed, smiling, and ready for lunch and a nap.

If you ask him what he likes best about preschool, it's not the friends, the coloring, the painting, or the snacks. It's the gym.

## Identifying Your Needs

When you first begin working at home, you don't have a track record to rely on. You probably don't have any idea, really, of how this is going to go. You don't know how many hours you'll be working and which will be the most demanding hours. You don't know how your kids are going to react, whether they'll be happy all day while you work or get restless as soon as the morning cartoons are over.

Even if you decide not to have child care on a regular basis, there will be times when you need to meet with a client, do research at the library, go to a professional organization, attend a seminar, or simply have a cup of coffee with a friend. Answer the following questions to get an idea of the kind of child-care arrangements you need to make for both out-of-the-office and in-office times.

  Will your work take you out of the office?

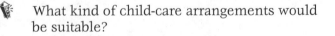  Will your children be able to go?

What kind of child-care arrangements would be suitable?

In the office, do you need a certain amount of time uninterrupted?

  If yes, how long?

  Can your children be doing an activity at this time or is child care a better option?

Most work-at-home enthusiasts suggest you have at least some kind of outside activity or sitter to use as a backup in case of sudden meetings or schedule changes. Your backup might be a neighbor, Grandma, a friend, or someone you know who watches children on a drop-in basis. Even if you decide not to go with a regular child-care routine during your work week, someone you can rely on in a pinch is an important part of your support team.

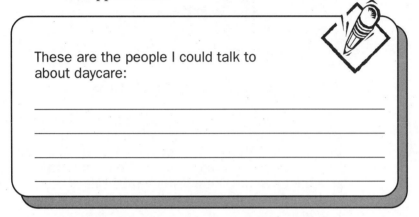

These are the people I could talk to about daycare:

_____

_____

_____

_____

*Of course, school—which for most of us occurs only nine months of the year—is a great help to work-at-home parents with school-aged children. You can easily schedule your meetings, have your coffee, and do all the research you need during the average school day. But preschoolers and toddlers offer a special challenge because they have shorter attention spans and more craving for interaction with Mommy and Daddy. It's for these little guys you've got to consider carefully what's best— both for you and for them—in terms of child-care arrangements.*

Several of the work-at-home parents I spoke with relied on trading child care—"I'll watch yours this Tuesday; you watch mine next Tuesday"—to get the focused work time they needed. This arrangement gives their children some much-needed socialization and gives them uninterrupted blocks of time to get their work done.

### Been There, Done That

*"I wanted everything to run as smoothly as it had, without the business interrupting our time together. I worked at naptime and after the kids went to bed at night, and then went to meetings and shows on Saturdays, when my husband was home."*

## Identifying Your Kids' Needs

You know your family best. Like the people under my roof, chances are the people under your roof are all a little different from one another. Your kids might be great at pretending for hours at a time, making forts and such, or they might need continual direction. "What do we do now? We're bored!"

Perhaps you have one of each.

Maybe your kids love to read and are happy working on projects, painting, working with clay, building rocket ships, and so on. Or maybe they go from TV to video games and back to TV all morning. Or perhaps you have a budding athlete, like Cameron, who always needs to be throwing, pushing, kicking, running, or climbing something (when he's not asleep).

You will know fairly quickly, simply from observing your kids, what their different needs are. You'll have a sense of whether they need experiences to challenge their brains, their imaginations, or their muscles. When you have that sense, ask yourself this question: Will they get everything they need if they are home with you while you work all day. You may decide that attending preschool or a co-op, or spending an afternoon across the street with a friend, is a good thing for Timmy emotionally and socially.

# Finding Good Child Care

Let's say you want to find some kind of child-care program to cover a set number of hours each week, giving you time to make important phone calls, work on focused projects, meet with clients, and get errands done quickly. There are a number of options to consider.

Just as children come in all shapes, sizes, and colors, there are all kinds of daycare arrangements out there. The trick is to investigate what's possible; then look around your area and see what's available; look even harder and see what's practical and feasible (in other words, what fits your budget and is close enough); and then ask the most important question of all: Which caregiver will give your child the love, support, and protection she needs when you are not there to give it to her?

## Important Considerations

As you are thinking about what kind of child care will work for you, several factors will weigh heavily:

- **Age**. It's no secret that children need care—and they need loving care no matter what age they are. Different ages bring different needs, however. An infant needs one kind of care; a ninth-grader needs another.

- **Hours**. Think about the hours you will need child care. If you need just one morning a week, you might be able to participate in a child-care co-op, where several parents share the responsibility of watching the children. If you need several mornings a week, you might look into preschools in your area. For full-time help, daycare centers are available. And don't forget the baby-sitter who will come to your house—usually on a full-time or established part-time schedule—or the neighbor who can help out in a pinch.

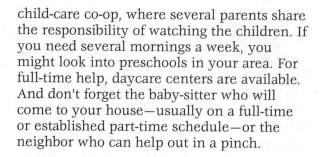 **Budget**. Some kinds of child care are more expensive than others. You might pay upwards of $35 a day for one preschool and perhaps $15 for a home-run daycare. Grandma might pooh-pooh your attempts to pay, and your best friend might accept token payment only grudgingly. Know what you can afford, as well as what kinds of child care best suit your child's needs, before you choose.

## What Are the Options?

If you've established that you need to rely on someone other than yourself, your spouse, or your family for child care at least part of the time, you'll be looking at the various options. There are several to choose from:

 You could arrange to swap baby-sitting time with another work-at-home parent.

 You could find a sitter to come to your house while you work.

 You could enroll your child in preschool.

 You could use a local daycare center.

In the next sections, we'll look more closely at these options.

The following sections take a look at different daycare alternatives you can try. Remember that there are pros and cons to each of these different options—the key is to do your homework and find the one that best matches what your child needs.

 *Spend some time talking to your child about why you need certain hours of uninterrupted work time. Would she be willing to watch a movie during those hours? Would she rather go to a friend's house? What does she think of preschool? A willing child is a happier child at the sitter's or at preschool. If she thinks you value her input, she'll be more likely to give it.*

## The Baby-Sitting Swap

Sounds like a good deal, right? Trent watches your kids on Tuesday afternoons, and you watch his kids on Thursday mornings. That arrangement works well for many people. It's the old bartering system, so no money changes hands. The kids get to play, and the work-at-home parents get a solid morning or afternoon to get things done.

Are there any special things to consider when you arrange baby-sitting swap time? Well, just a few:

- **Make sure you know the person you're swapping with.** What's he like with his kids? What will he be like with your kids? (Don't feel bad about checking him out—he'll be doing the same thing to you.)

- **Learn about the kids you'll be watching before you watch them the first time.** What do they like to do? Should you have special snacks on hand? Are there any allergies you should know about?

- **How will you both handle behavior problems?** By calling each other? Using time outs? Establish up front what feels comfortable for you. This will avoid any problems or hurt feelings later.

 **Agree that you will call and check in** at least once each time he is watching your kids, and ask him to call you on your day, as well.

 **Talk out any trouble spots the same day they appear.**

Before you start the swap routine, organize a day or two on which you all get together just to visit. Let the kids play, and you and your baby-sitting partner trade kid stories. Just get comfortable with each other. This builds recognition for the kids and creates a foundation of security for you so you can be effective during those precious few quiet hours.

## The In-Home Sitter

In-home baby-sitters are great if you're comfortable having someone else caring for your kids while you're home. The challenge, of course, is not jumping up each time a little voice yells, "Uh oh! I spilled it!" or wanting to go in and separate the twins each time they start wrestling for the remote control.

Depending on the number of hours you need a sitter, you may or may not have to pay a premium for in-home child care. Some sitters charge by the hour; others charge depending on the day and frequency.

Where can you find a good in-home sitter? Here are three places to look:

 Some colleges have placement services for their education or social service majors.

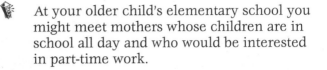 You might find a caring individual looking for part-time work at your church or synagogue.

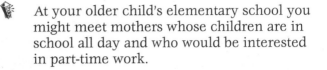 At your older child's elementary school you might meet mothers whose children are in school all day and who would be interested in part-time work.

Perhaps the most often-used sources of information about good in-home care are friends and neighbors. This friend had a sitter who was wonderful last summer and won't be needing her services this summer. Keep your eyes and ears open, and the right in-home sitter may come to you.

*Before you hire an in-home sitter, invite her over to "play" at least twice in an informal setting. Let her interact with your children and give them a chance to get comfortable together, with you nearby.[1]*

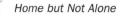
Make sure, when you find the sitter, that you
discuss how to resolve any issues that may arise.
Talk about discipline, stresses, financial situations,
and illness. Iron out the wrinkles up-front, as
much as possible.

Remember, too, that an employee you have in
your home is an employee nonetheless—so check
with your accountant and make sure you've got
the right paperwork filed with the IRS.

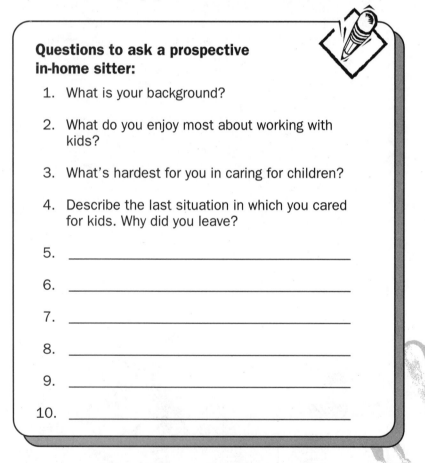

**Questions to ask a prospective
in-home sitter:**

1. What is your background?

2. What do you enjoy most about working with
   kids?

3. What's hardest for you in caring for children?

4. Describe the last situation in which you cared
   for kids. Why did you leave?

5. _____

6. _____

7. _____

8. _____

9. _____

10. _____

The best word of advice about an in-home sitter is
this: Get references *and check them*. It is possible
to do this without affronting or insulting the
prospective caregiver. Anyone who loves children

will understand your need to be thorough in making sure you've hired the best possible person to care for your child.

## The Preschool Prerogative

As a work-at-home parent, you have yet another freedom that parents who work full-time do not have: You can take your children to and from preschool several mornings a week. Most preschool programs run 2 to $2\frac{1}{2}$ hours at a time, and many are located in churches or local community centers.

Many preschools offer different schedules, including Monday-Wednesday-Friday and Tuesday-Thursday programs. Some have all kinds of activities, including field trips, parent fairs, music, and dance, in addition to age-appropriate letter and number recognition lessons.

When you've found a preschool you think will work, take your child on a visit. I wouldn't recommend doing this the first time you see the place: You want to know what the school is like before you take Jason along to see it. If you can, visit on a day when Jason's class is there, so he can see who his teachers will be, what kind of activities the kids are involved in, and what his classroom will look like.

Cost varies greatly from preschool to preschool. Check all the schools in your area and shop around before deciding. Remember, too, that many preschools have long waiting lists—so as soon as you decide on a particular school, make sure you get the paperwork turned in.

## The Daycare Center

Another option you have for child care, particularly if you need to make arrangements for half-time or more, is the daycare center. In a daycare center, teachers care for classes of children, and the number of children assigned to each adult depends on the children's ages and the requirements of the state you live in. Daycare centers usually are happy, busy places with many different ages of children and smiling, creative, and loving teachers.

## Evaluating a Daycare Center

Here are some questions you may want to ask the director of the daycare center when you visit:

 **What is the overall mission statement of the center?**

**Has a formal complaint of any kind ever been filed against the daycare center?** If so, what was the situation and how was it resolved? If not, what should a parent do if he or she has a question or concern?

**How accessible is the director of the center?** (Hopefully, she or he is the one who will give you the initial tour.) What is the director's background, and what does she or he find most challenging about running the center successfully?

**How does the enrollment at the center compare to the enrollment a year ago?** Is the enrollment growing? Have the necessary number of teachers and aides been added?

**How many adults are available for your child's class?** There may be one full-time teacher and a teacher's aide, depending on the age group and the number of children in the class. What is the adult-to-child ratio in the class?

 **Are there child-sized tables and chairs available for your child?** Most centers also have child-sized toilet facilities and are equipped for both small and middle-sized (school-aged) children.

**What does the staff do in the event of scrapes and bruises?** At what point do they notify you? Is there an accident report or some reporting policy they follow in case of an injury?

**What types of meals are offered?** Licensed daycare centers follow state guidelines for nutrition; most states require that lunch menus be posted weekly so parents can see what their children are eating during the day.

**What happens during a typical day?** Is there a balance between active and quiet times? How many times a day will your child be read to? Will he or she get to play on the playground? What happens on rainy or cold days?

**What does the general learning atmosphere feel like?** At preschool age, learning should be an exploration: You should see plenty of toys for "pretend"—dress up clothes, toy kitchens, and blocks, for example. While preschoolers are apt to learn things like colors, shapes, numbers, and maybe letters, there shouldn't be any pressure on learning at this age. Preschool should be fun.

**How is discipline handled?** If you don't see any signs of it going on around you, ask. Daycare centers usually use a "time out" method when they need to discipline. Get clear guidance on what's acceptable behavior and what isn't.

In the summer and during school vacations, the daycare center may provide short-term, drop-in

> *You do want to get your child's opinion of the daycare he likes best; you don't want to overwhelm him with choices. Narrow the decision down to your two or three favorite places; then take your child with you for a short visit to each.*

care for your school-aged children. If you are used to scheduling meetings while Jenny's at school all day, and suddenly you are faced with summer break, you could use a daycare center to give Jenny a day out in the world (they typically schedule field trips galore for the school-aged crowd) and give you the time you need to have your meetings uninterrupted.

## Daycare, Home-Style

Home-run daycares provide fun and interaction in a comforting environment: the provider's home. In a home-run setting, the care provider, usually a mother herself, watches several children in addition to her own. She is a work-at-home parent herself, earning a living and staying close to her children while she works.

How do you find a home-run daycare? Ask friends, family members, teachers, coworkers, and anyone else you can think of if they know of any great home-run daycare centers in your area. The best way to find a reliable home daycare situation is to ask your friends for referrals. If you don't know anyone who uses home daycare, start by looking for a child-care agency in your area. Look in the *Yellow Pages* under Child Care or even Preschools. You also might want to contact your local Child and Family Services Division (a segment of your local government) to find out about agencies and services.

## Evaluating a Home-Run Daycare

Once you've found a home-run day-care you want to check out, go and visit by yourself first. You may want to observe and ask about the following things:

 **Is the overall atmosphere of the home happy or harried?**

 **Is there a separate "children's area"** with easels, tables and chairs, toys, and blocks, where the children feel welcome to play with abandon?

**Does the daycare provider offer a set schedule** during which she does different activities with the children?

**How does she handle nap time?**

**What does she do when she has sick children at home?**

**How is discipline handled?**

**Is there an outdoor, fenced play area** with play equipment appropriate to the ages of the children?

Again, ask for references. The daycare provider probably can give you the names and numbers of the parents of some of her other charges. When you get the numbers, *make the calls.* The provider won't mind you checking, and the parents won't mind giving their input: Everyone understands your need to make sure your children are protected and cared for.

### Home Safe Home

One of the biggest differences between a daycare center and a home-run daycare center—besides the number of children—is the adherence to health and safety guidelines. In order to be licensed, daycare centers have to meet strict state requirements.

If you are electing to use a home-run daycare, you need to think about and ask about some safety issues yourself. Does the daycare provider have an adequate number of fire alarms and extinguishers? Does she have an emergency plan that she explains to the children about where to go and what to do in case of fire. Does she teach the children how to call 911? Where do they go in case of inclement weather? These are not issues you need to resolve on your first visit, but they are important things to address before you begin dropping your child off in the morning.

## Ready for Anything!

Hopefully it's not something you'll have to deal with, but you're better off safe than sorry: You need to be prepared in case your child is injured while he's away from you. Caregivers—whether they simply watch Kimberly in their home two mornings a week or she is enrolled in a preschool—need permissions so if there is an emergency and you are unreachable, they can get medical help for your child immediately. This means you give the caregiver the right to authorize emergency medical care until you arrive on the scene.

**Profiles**
**Name**: Tina
**Business**: Baby-sitting
**How long?** Three years
**How many kids?** Three, ages 8, 6, and 4
**Biggest challenge:** Parents who change their schedules from week to week.
**Best answer to that challenge:** Being clear with my hours, telling parents "These are the hours I'm available."

You can take care of this by writing out a simple consent form. Something like this will work:

*While* << caregiver's name >> *is watching my children,* << list your children's names here >>, *I give her permission to authorize emergency medical care in the event that I am unreachable and an accident occurs involving one of my children. I wish to be contacted immediately at* << list your number here >> *in case of such an emergency, but would ask that medical help not be postponed if I am not available.*

Sign the note and date it, and keep a copy for your records. Make sure the caregiver understands the importance of the permission sheet and keeps it in a place she can get to easily if an emergency happens.

## Summarizing Your Child-Care Choices

So, now you've been through the most popular child-care choices:

   No thanks, I'll do it myself

   A little sitter swapping would be nice

   The in-home sitter

Preschool, if you please

 Daycare, home or center

To find the best possible circumstance for your child, investigate all the options in your area. Talk to other parents: Find out what they like and don't like about different preschools and centers. Take the time you need to make a decision you'll be comfortable with, and don't allow yourself to be rushed into anything. And *always have a backup—* a friend or relative—in case your original daycare plans fall through.

---

What kind of child care would work best for our family?

First choice: _____

Second choice: _____

Third choice: _____

Alternatives/Comments:

_____

_____

_____

_____

_____

---

# Keeping Child Care Working

Once you get set up at home, find child care, and begin moving into a regular routine, what can you do to keep things running smoothly? Here are a few tips that will help you anticipate and perhaps bypass problems with your caregiver:

Establish your schedule, as much as
possible, and stick to it. Don't vary your
drop-off time every day; and, especially after
a long, harried day, call if you're going to be
more than 15 minutes late.

When you think your schedule will
change, let the caregiver know. If you
know you have a change coming up—say the
meeting you had scheduled for Thursday was
rescheduled for Monday—let your sitter
know as soon as possible. This allows her to
plan anything that needs to be rearranged to
accommodate the change.

If you have a flexible schedule, give your
caregiver a copy of your schedule as
soon as you have it. Telling her is okay, but
having it in black and white lets her refer
back to it later.

If "drop-ins" are okay with your
caregiver and you think you might need
her services on a stray day here and
there, talk to her about it first. Call and
ask whether it would be okay, or ask a week
or so in advance. This lets her know how
many children she'll have, so she can plan
activities for the day.

When you have questions or concerns,
express them in a respectful, caring way.
Even if you're upset because Kayla said one
of the babies bit her, don't call the sitter up
and read her the riot act. When you drop
Kayla off in the morning, explain what Kayla
told you and ask the caregiver if she is
having a problem with one of the babies
biting. Talk about the situation
constructively: What can you do? What's
being tried? How can you help? What can
you tell Kayla to do if she's afraid it will
happen again?

Look at how you can help the situation and fight the impulse to explode. (And if your child has been hurt, that impulse is probably strong.) Remember that the relationship you establish with your child's caregiver is an important one both for your child and for you, and preserving it with open communication and respect is vital to keeping it healthy.

 **Ask the caregiver questions to show you're interested in her day.** "How are things going?" or "Is there anything you need me to bring?" lets her know you are interested in how things are working out and are open to hearing about any ways you can improve the situation.

**Basic friendliness and appreciation go a long way.** Gifts on the holidays, thank-you notes as appropriate, and little expressions of concern and caring for a special caregiver go a long way toward establishing a good and lasting relationship.

# The Do-It-Yourself Child-Care Guide

There are those of you who will insist on handling all the child care yourselves. In spite of what other work-at-home experts say about child care being a necessity, you are determined to do it all: start the business, raise your kids, take care of the house, even brush the dog once in a while.

I've been there. I understand. And, if that's what you want to do, then that's what you should do.

Of course, you must do everything you can to make sure your work-at-home business succeeds; but above all, you should trust your own instincts, at least until your 3-year-old throws a football at your head. Both of my older children grew up with Mom working at home, and although both of them started part-time preschool at the age of 4, we did quite well at home together all day, every day.

If you want to do the child-care thing yourself, there are several ways to keep your expectations realistic and your experience a pleasant one:

 **Think like a child**. Remember that 30 minutes seems like a lifetime to a child. Don't expect Sean to sit quietly watching the Discovery Channel while you finish writing that report. Make sure he's doing something riveting, and then finish the report while he's engaged.

**Vary activities**. Repetitious activities get boring quickly when you're little, so vary what you plan to do. One half hour, get out the crayons and the coloring book; the next half hour, suggest a computer game. After a snack, maybe it's time for a movie, followed by a trip outside to get the mail. Then it's time for toy trucks, followed by lunch, and— ah!—nap time.

**Take field trips**. A trip to the post office can be a real thrill when you've been cooped up inside all day. And if you let Zach put the stamps on himself (the postal worker won't care that the angels are upside-down) and put them down the mail chute, he'll feel like he's done something significant.

**Talk, talk, talk**. It's easy to get lost in thought and forget to make contact with our small officemates on a regular basis. Cameron doesn't let me forget this. When he notices he's been carrying on a monologue, he starts asking me questions: "What do you think, Mommy? Do you think I'm right? Do you like the color of his hat?" He always drags me back into the moment (sometimes unwillingly), but he gets my attention. (He has the makings of a great market researcher.)

**Put on a little mood music**. For a small investment, you can own all the Disney soundtracks ever made, plus read-along books for just about every story ever written. This has been a great addition to our home. Cameron loves to listen (a good skill to learn early), and he now has several of his favorite books memorized, much to the amazement of his older siblings.

**Let her help**. Especially if you've got a preschooler at home, you're going to get lots of help offers. Whenever possible, accept them. Envelopes can be licked carefully. Stamps can be stuck. Papers can be straightened, magazines put away. Once in a while, you can give little Paige a document to "type." There are other helpful opportunities, too, that aren't obvious to most adults: One of Cameron's favorite pretend games is Mister Fast Food Guy, for which he uses one of my steno pads and a pen. He asks me what I want for lunch, writes down my order, then rides his imaginary motorcycle to the fast food restaurant. He returns with lightening speed and a low-calorie, surprisingly light meal.

## Summing Up

So now you've looked at your child-care options from A to Z. You've asked yourself whether you need child care at all: Your children's needs, your business, and your time commitments will determine the answer to that. If you opted for child care, you thought about what type of care works best for your family. If you decided you want to take care of child care yourself, you thought about how to approach the responsibility realistically. Now don't forget to enjoy yourself, too—it's good to be home!

# Notes

1. There's no question that both men and women can be great caregivers: I say "she" here in referring to a caregiver because it's easier and more personable than either "s/he" or "he or she." (No offense, dads.)

# Getting to Work

*So much to do, so little time! Now that you've explored some of the possibilities— What can you do at home? What do you need to get started?—you're probably eager to put your ideas into action. Whether you are a self-employed work-at-home parent or a parent who is working at home on someone else's payroll, you can bank on the fact that you'll have new stresses to face, new challenges to master, and new obstacles to overcome. This part of the book focuses on the startup issues and helps you put a system in place to keep yourself from drowning in disorganization.*

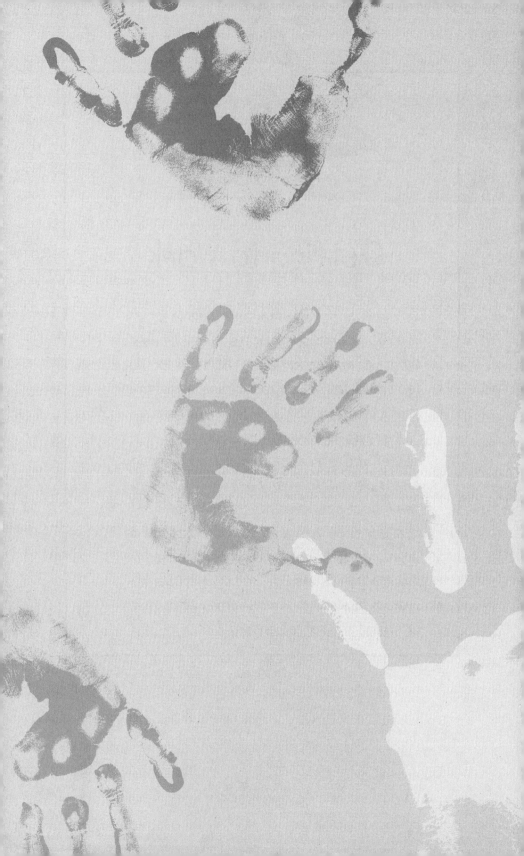

# The Self-Employed Parent

*"Don't give in! Make your own trail."*
—Katharine Hepburn

It's a fact of life: If you plan on being self-employed, you've got to have a head for business. And if you plan to work at home, you've got to have a heart for family. Of course, no one says the head for business has to rest on your own shoulders: You can rely on the expertise of a number of business professionals in your community. People like accountants, lawyers, business advisors, and insurance agents can fill in the gaps in your knowledge as you get started in your new undertaking.

**BEST** & WORST

**Best:** "The freedom to control my own schedule."

Of course, the heart part is up to you. As a self-employed parent, you have a unique task with unique stresses. Not only are you working at home, but you are the only person on your payroll: You're the one who earns the income, writes the check, and pays the taxes. You're the one who gets the work, does the work, and looks for more work.

So much for glamour. One writer puts it this way: "Small business owners (at least at first) do not delegate and supervise—they *do*."[1]

Much of your success in your work-at-home endeavor will depend on the amount of thought and realistic planning you put into it. Taking some time to stop and think about what you're doing before you do it can save you from the missteps and mishaps that occur when you let the flow of life take you where it will.

## Before the Plunge

Being self-employed and working at home for someone else are two very different things. Both parents work at home. Both parents have joys and stresses to deal with. Both parents have home and family to balance as they learn to build their careers right there on the premises.

Although the work-at-home parent has a number of challenges to meet as he arranges his work situation to suit those he answers to, the self-employed parent is doing her act without a safety net. There's no one in charge—except her—to gauge whether she's making the right decisions.

There's no one there—except her—to account to for her time, to tell her to watch her phone bills, or to suggest that she needs a day off.

Because so much responsibility falls squarely on your shoulders if you are a self-employed parent, there are a number of things you should do right off the bat to make sure you get your business started on solid ground.

## Create a Family Budget

If you didn't have a budget before you decided to go into business for yourself, you'll certainly need one now. Before you make any other plans, you need to know exactly how much you've *got* to have in order to keep your household running smoothly. Then, if your income drops in the early stages of working at home, you can see where your budget is suffering, and you'll know where to cut back.

   That may mean fewer trips to the drive-through window.

   That may mean a trip to the park instead of to the Bahamas.

   That may mean no diamonds for Christmas, no new car this year, and fewer nights out on the town. (Oh, I forgot—we're *parents!* We don't get nights out, do we?)

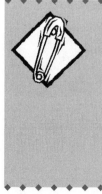

*Even if money isn't an issue in your household, it's a good idea to have a budget. That way you can see where your money goes, which helps you make educated decisions about where you want it to go. You may be unknowingly supporting your local phone company, thanks to your teenager and her phone line, but you won't discover that until you take a good look at your bills.*

Your family budget will show you where the belt needs to be tightened, or simply where it *can* be tightened if necessary.

When you're starting out, it's important to get your personal finances in order. If you attempt to borrow money from a bank or a commercial lender, they aren't going to give your business money simply because you say it's a business. They will want proof that you're good for the loan. They will want to see your credit history, your paying record, your current cash flow, and so on. You'll need to have a clear picture of your personal situation because, most likely, you'll sign for that first business loan yourself as a regular person, not as a business owner. Once you have established a payment history with that lender, you'll have a better chance of getting a business loan in the business's name next time.

## Rules for Discussing the Budget

- Parents only—no kids allowed!

- Plan it ahead of time, with quiet time before and after.

- Agree to a "no blame" rule.

- Look constructively at the budget; it's your starting point.

- Make a date to look at the budget again in three months.

- Set a goal you both want to achieve.

- Decide to work together to improve your financial situation

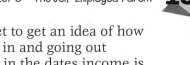

Use the following budget to get an idea of how much you have coming in and going out financially. If you write in the dates income is received and payments go out, you'll also get a picture of any "slim spots" in your month.

## Monthly Family Budget

**Date:** _____

| Income | Amount | Date Received |
|---|---|---|
| Salary 1 | _____ | _____ |
| Salary 2 | _____ | _____ |

*Monthly Total Income:*

| Expenses | Amount | Date Due |
|---|---|---|
| Mortgage or rent | _____ | _____ |
| Homeowner's/ Renter's insurance | _____ | _____ |
| Electricity | _____ | _____ |
| Gas | _____ | _____ |
| Water | _____ | _____ |
| Phone | _____ | _____ |
| Cable | _____ | _____ |
| Car payment 1 | _____ | _____ |
| Car payment 2 | _____ | _____ |
| Car insurance | _____ | _____ |
| Groceries | _____ | _____ |
| Gasoline | _____ | _____ |
| Clothing | _____ | _____ |
| Entertainment | _____ | _____ |

Health insurance    _____    _____

Life insurance    _____    _____

Miscellaneous    _____    _____

_____    _____

_____    _____

_____    _____

_____    _____

### *Monthly Household Expenses:*

| **Debt** | **Amount** | **Date Due** | **Balance** |
|---|---|---|---|
| Credit card 1 | _____ | _____ | _____ |
| Credit card 2 | _____ | _____ | _____ |
| Loan 1 | _____ | _____ | _____ |
| Loan 2 | _____ | _____ | _____ |

**Monthly Credit/Loan Payments:** _____

**Monthly Total Expenses
(Household + Credit/Loans):** _____

Most of the items on this budget are beyond your control. After all, you don't get to decide how much your mortgage payment is; you simply pay what the lender says is the monthly payment. The same goes for your cars, your utilities, and your credit card bills. Groceries, gasoline, clothing, entertainment, and miscellaneous—which covers everything from a new basketball to the dog's vet appointment—are variables that you exercise some degree of control over. In those variable categories, write in not only how much you currently pay a month but how much you *want* to spend in the coming months.

Your budget will show you how much you're spending now, whether you're ending up each month with money left over, or if you're living from paycheck to paycheck, perhaps robbing Peter to pay Paul.

Although budgets aren't a whole lot of fun, they do give you some important information about your financial picture, something you need to grasp before you start up your own work-at-home business. Once you plug in all the numbers and find out exactly how much you've got coming in and going out, you can use your budget to discover these things:

- How much you're spending frivolously

- How much you carry in credit card debt

- How much you bring in and when it arrives

- Whether any expenses are out of proportion (the phone bill, the water bill, the gas bill; a discrepancy may reveal billing or service errors)

- Whether you could make payments easier by using the company's budget system (for electric, water, and gas bills) or by changing the due date

- When the tight spots in the month are (which will help your whole family know when *not* to ask for unnecessary things)

- Where you can look for opportunities to save money

The family budget will tell you one other very important thing: how much you need to bring in every month to keep your family afloat. If you earn the second income in your family, you have the reassurance of knowing that a significant portion of your family's income will continue even though you are starting a new venture. In that case, having a budget, and sticking to it carefully, will help you stay on track during the lean first months.

If you are a single parent, sole provider, or primary breadwinner, it's even more important that you plan the financial security of your family very carefully. You may have a good idea, a huge potential market, and all the opportunity in the world, but even great ideas take a while to catch on. Most experts say you should have at least six months' worth of income in savings to tide you over while you get your new business off the ground. Many of us don't have that kind of safety net—but we're able to navigate the high wire anyway.

*It's a good idea to call your accountant at this point. Tell her what you're planning to do, and ask her advice on how you can get a good idea of the average income and expenses in startup businesses like yours. If you don't have an accountant, get the name and number of someone from a friend or associate (or use the Yellow Pages), and ask a few simple questions about business startups. Most accountants are glad to answer a few questions from a prospective new client. It's good for their business.*

## Plan What You Expect to Make and Spend

Now that you've got an idea of how much your family needs to stay afloat, you can start thinking about the future of your business—the immediate future. How much will you spend, starting out? (Use the worksheets you completed in Chapter 3 to get an idea.) Where will that money come from? Do you have it, or do you need to borrow it? Who will you borrow from? What do you need to get that first contract? Make a list of expenses, equipment, people, supplies, anything you'll have to invest in before you can start recouping your expenses.

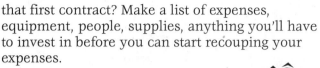

**My immediate needs to get the business started:**

| Item | Cost |
| --- | --- |
| _____ | _____ |
| _____ | _____ |
| _____ | _____ |
| _____ | _____ |
| _____ | _____ |
| _____ | _____ |
| _____ | _____ |

If you are starting out at home with a desktop publishing service, for example, you might have the personal computer but still need the software. And perhaps you need a better printer, a scanner, or a modem. These are all items that can affect whether you get the contracts you need from major clients.

If you are starting a window-cleaning business, you need the basic equipment and a vehicle to reach customers. If you are doing telemarketing from home, you might need only a script and a telephone. If you are baby-sitting in your house, you need toys, child-sized tables, an extra highchair, and maybe extra blankets. If you are starting a consulting business, you might need a separate phone line, business cards—or perhaps only the phone and a few good contacts.

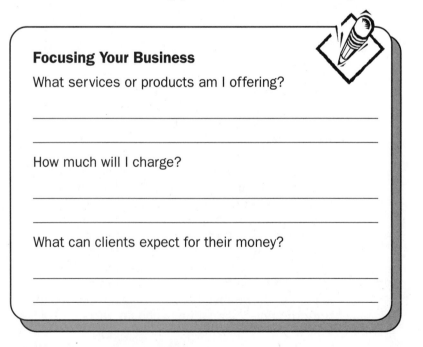

When you "guestimate" your income, think low. And plan your expenses high. Then, when the real numbers start rolling in, you will be pleasantly surprised.

Now, it's time to start dreaming and planning your first attack in your new venture. How much will you charge for your service? What kind of hourly rate do you need to make in order to recoup your expenses and earn a living? What is the going rate for services or products like yours in your area?

And don't concentrate only on the money issue: Get a clear picture of your business in your mind. See yourself performing the service or selling the product. Imagine interacting with your customers. Think about the quality of work you are offering, the guarantees you stand behind, and the mission statement of your business. Determining these things now will help you believe in your business, which will help your customers believe in you.

**Focusing Your Business**

What services or products am I offering?

_____

_____

How much will I charge?

_____

_____

What can clients expect for their money?

_____

_____

What kind of guarantee do I give?

_____

_____

_____

What is my company mission statement?

_____

_____

_____

_____

_____

_____

_____

_____

With all that information in place, think of a dozen people or companies you can contact to offer your new service or product. Know how much you will charge and guestimate how much you will make from each job. Remember, however, that you will hear "No thanks" or "We'll get back to you on that" more often than you will hear "Yes." So be prepared to contact many people in order to work with a few.

There still is a big question you need to answer: "Can you afford to go full-time in your new home business, or do you need to begin part-time?" Nationally, 50 percent of home-based businesses are part-time efforts; many people begin their new ventures in their spare time and on weekends until they have built up enough of a client base to support them at their current rate of income.

**My Contact List**

| Companies or individuals I can contact: | Estimated earnings for job: |
|---|---|
| _____ | _____ |
| _____ | _____ |
| _____ | _____ |
| _____ | _____ |
| _____ | _____ |
| _____ | _____ |
| _____ | _____ |
| _____ | _____ |
| _____ | _____ |
| _____ | _____ |
| _____ | _____ |

## Family Meeting! Family Meeting!

You've done a lot of work with your spouse and on your own. Now you need to clue the rest of the family in on the financial changes that may be coming. Call another family meeting and explain the dynamics of starting the new business. Talk about the need to start out with the necessary equipment, about the slow but gradual build-up of clients, and about your plans for success and living happily ever after. You don't need to mention dollar amounts or frightening scenarios— like what happens if nobody wants to buy your product—but you do want to explain the basics of what's happening as you start the business and how it will affect the family.

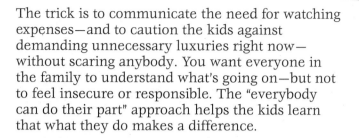

The trick is to communicate the need for watching expenses—and to caution the kids against demanding unnecessary luxuries right now—without scaring anybody. You want everyone in the family to understand what's going on—but not to feel insecure or responsible. The "everybody can do their part" approach helps the kids learn that what they do makes a difference.

For example, if you need to call for a group tightening of the belts, ask what each person is willing to give up for one month. (It's like giving up something for Lent; if everyone does it, it doesn't seem so bad.) Of course, with kids, the answers you get may vary wildly:

   Curtis, age 9, "I'll give up taking out the trash!"

   Julianne, age 4, "Peas!"

   Kristin, age 15, "Anything except my Internet time!"

   Mom, age 40, "Bubble bath."

   Dad, age 42, "My weekly trip to the hardware store."

You may want to set a family goal to mark the end of the belt tightening, as well. "When Mom's business makes its first thousand dollars, we'll go camping to celebrate." (Okay, maybe camping's not your thing, In that case, you can go stay at Grandma's for a few days. The idea is to do something special that doesn't cost much.)

# What Kind of Business Are You, Anyway?

One of the key decisions you'll make as you start your new business is what form your business will take. This is, by and large, a legal decision, and one that your attorney or accountant can help you make. Briefly, however, here are the different forms of business.

**Sole Proprietorship.** If you are the single owner of your business, you can be a sole proprietor. This means you don't have to incorporate (which saves you money and paperwork), but you are subject to self-employment tax, which takes a significant chunk out of each check you earn. (Remember, when you were employed by another company, the employer matched your FICA contribution. Now you'll be responsible for paying both halves of that tax.) The sole proprietorship is the most common form of business; it doesn't require any special tax returns, and the owner retains complete control of the business. As the owner, however, you are liable for all debts; and, in the event of a lawsuit, your personal holdings are not differentiated from your business holdings, which means you could lose your savings, possessions, and even your home in a sticky legal situation.

**Partnership.** If you are going into business with at least one other person—and you are sharing the decision-making power, the income, and the liabilities—you could be a partnership. Most experts say you should contact an attorney early on in the process when you begin investigating a partnership agreement: Partnerships can be complex and need to be planned out carefully.[2] Almost like choosing a marriage partner, the choice of a business partner will affect your life in a big way, so you need to discuss and decide on many different issues before you set up shop together. Legally, a partnership requires no different tax returns; each partner reports the income on his or her personal income tax returns. Both partners are equally liable for all debt in the company; and, in the event of a lawsuit, both partners are held personally responsible.

**A limited partnership** *is one in which the control of the business is given to general partners, and limited partners are given a share of the decision-making power and liability, equal to the amount of their investment. For example, if Joe invested 15 percent of the startup costs, he gets 15 percent of the decision-making power and 15 percent of the liability should the business fail.*

**Corporation.** The corporation is a unique business form: It is an entity separate from its owner. If you incorporate your business, it is no longer you offering a service; it is a business that exists separate from you. Corporations do require corporate tax returns—something you will want your accountant to handle—and must follow strict guidelines about issuing stock, holding annual meetings, assigning a board of directors, and more. If you are the single owner and sole employee, you may feel a little silly following all the seeming pomp and circumstance of a large corporate structure; but it's vital that you do so. The corporation provides you with protection for your personal holdings: If you are sued, you are liable only up to the amount your invested in your stock. In order to incorporate, you must file for articles of incorporation; again, you will want an attorney or accountant to do that for you.

Lawsuit protection isn't your own perk as a corporation—you also get a tax advantage sole proprietorships don't have. The self-employment tax you pick up as a sole proprietor (when you are employed, your employer pays half and you pay half of your Social Security percentage) isn't an issue for the corporation. But as a trade-off, corporations must file corporate tax returns—separate from personal tax returns—which means additional accounting fees and more paperwork to track.

**A subchapter S corporation** is a special kind of small corporation in which your business income flows directly onto your personal return. This can save you tax dollars and simplify your life. Talk to your accountant to determine whether you'd be better off as a Subchapter S corporation if you plan to incorporate.

**Professional Parent Panic!**

"One time when I was on the phone with the owner of a company, one of my kids came walking in asking me for 'bathroom assistance.' When duty calls, someone has to answer!"

**Profiles**
**Name:** Kevin
**Business:** Computer consulting
**How long?** Three years
**How many kids?** One, age 5
**Biggest challenge:** Finding long stretches of uninterrupted time.
**Best answer to that challenge:** Accept things as they are. Make the most of available blocks of time.

# Are We Having Fun Yet?
# Four Self-Employment Stresses

And you thought your old day job was hard. Working for yourself is, as the writer said, "the best of times, the worst of times." On good days, you'll want to do cartwheels in the front yard. On bad days, you'll want to pull the covers up over your head and pretend you never heard the words "self-employed."

BEST &
**WORST**

*Worst:*
"Feeling guilty
when the kids
say I work all
the time."

You can't ignore the stresses, but you can look at them as opportunities. In fact, those points of pressure are there for a reason: They are telling you there's something in your life that could be worked a little better, or your shoes wouldn't be pinching quite so much.

This section takes some of the most common stresses and turns them around to give you ideas of ways to work through and resolve them.

## Finances

Remember the budget? That's one of your best tools for battling financial stress. Get a clear picture of what's going on. Know what's going out and what's coming in. Keep an eye on your checkbook—or, better yet, two eyes. There's nothing wrong with knowing exactly how much you've got in the bank every day. There's no reason not to comparison shop.

*STRESS***BUSTER**

**#1**

Know what
you're
dealing with.

When you're worried about money, the best thing to do is to research what you're worried about. Look at the checkbook. Look at the bills. Look at the jobs you've got scheduled. See what needs to be done. Ask yourself these questions:

 Am I worried about something real or something that may happen in the future?

 What, specifically, is stressing me out?

 What can I do about it?

If you spend a few minutes thinking in a focused way about what's bothering you, the answer will come. If it's one of those vague, "What-have-I-*done*?"

fears, cast it out of your head and resolve to do everything you can with the information you've got to make your business work. If it's something concrete that you need to address—"I should have told my client I need that check by Friday" or "I know I overbid that job and now I feel guilty"—you can take specific action to clear up the situation.

STRESS**BUSTER**

**#2**

Never balance your checkbook in bed.

How many times have you tossed and turned in bed while visions of checkbook registers danced in your head? If you haven't yet, you will. This one was a difficult lesson for me, but one I now adhere to religiously: I spend all the time I need in my business accounts on Monday mornings. The rest of the week—including the middle of the night—is reserved for other things. Financial worries make lousy bedfellows. And little daytime fears become huge business-eating monsters around 2:00 A.M.

## Time

If there was one big bumper sticker we could slap on the '90s, it probably would be, "We don't have enough time!" Time for what? Time for anything! We don't have time to take a vacation, to watch the kids play soccer, to fix a big dinner, to sit and do nothing, to start a new business. And when we do carve out the time to do something we really want to do—like get that business started—it seems impossible that we will be able to keep things running successfully for any length of time.

Personally, I think time is overrated. I prefer the now. But when you're in business for yourself, time can be either an asset or a liability: You can either make something of it or waste it. And how you spend your time is critical to how your business develops.

So how do you keep from getting stressed about time? The best answer I've found is to keep your priorities in mind. Write them down. Stick them on the front of your computer. On your mirror. On the phone. Then, when the pace of life accelerates and you start reacting to everything around you, you will see those notes and remember why you're doing what you're doing. And you can reevaluate whether what you were trying to do was really in line with your priorities.

Why am I doing this?

1. *I've always wanted my own business.*

2. *I want to raise my own kids.*

3. *I love selling band uniforms.*

**STRESSBUSTER**

**#3**

Create a schedule and stick to it.

It goes with the territory for self-employed people: You rarely (if ever) feel as if you're "done." There's always more to do. One way to get a handle on time is to be more realistic with yourself. Start out the week with a list of things you need to accomplish by Friday. Then divide the tasks into days. Then create a schedule for the week and follow it. At the end of the day on Friday, review the week and see how you did. Need to revise? Okay, so revise. But don't throw the schedule out on Tuesday, when things start hopping. Stick with your schedule and meet your original goal. Over time (there's that word again), you'll learn how to anticipate the ebbs and flows and learn to get your work done without pushing yourself (and your family) to the max.

*Another thing a schedule must include is time when you don't work. Your family needs you present—emotionally as well as physically—and you need the break from business tasks.*

STRESS**BUSTER**

**#4**

Keep moving.

Some of us react to mounting time pressures by getting stuck in quicksand. There's so much pressure we just don't know what to do. The bank *must* get a report by 2:00 P.M. No matter what you try, it won't print. You can't remember the number of the technical support person you usually call. Your 3-year-old fingerpaints your fax machine.

You feel the quicksand up to your knees, and you're sinking fast.

On days like this, it's important to keep moving. Be thankful for small successes, but keep moving. Get anything done you can and fight the temptation to turn everything off and go sit in front of the television. Soon the stars will realign themselves and things will begin working again.

*"Success seems to be connected with action.
Successful people keep moving.
They make mistakes, but they don't quit."*
—Conrad Hilton[3]

## Growth

Most people think that business growth is a good problem to have. But I've seen several businesses fail in their first year because they grew too big too quickly. Thinking about and planning for the growth of your business is an important part of making sure it grows in the direction you want it to.

You may have dreams of a large operation you run from your home. You might want several employees, a fleet of vans, a herd of service personnel, and more. Or you might want to work quietly in your office, with your baby at your feet and the dog in the backyard.

**STRESS BUSTER**

**#5**

Whoever said "bigger is better" was wrong.

Each of these scenarios is a success, *if it's what you want.*

The key is to know what you want your business to become. You may just want to supplement your spouse's income. You may want to earn enough money that your spouse can leave his job and join you in the family business. You may want to turn your small home-based business into something big when the kids are old enough to be in school all day. But you need to plan your business's growth before it grows out of your control.

One important document that will help you determine a growth plan for your business is *the business plan.* Every business needs a business plan: It's like a starting point, a road map for the future of your business. If you go to the bank to apply for a loan, they'll want to see a business plan. If you talk to a business advisor, she'll insist that—and possibly help—you create a business plan. Even if you don't need a business plan to take to the bank, it's a good exercise to help you get focused on what you want and don't want in your business. Writing a business plan gives you the opportunity to think about how you will do things (like run your business on a day-to-day basis) and to see areas where you aren't fully prepared (such as checking out the competition or thinking about operating expenses, for example).

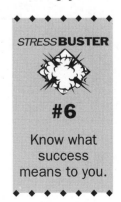

**STRESS BUSTER**

**#6**

Know what success means to you.

## Creating a Business Plan

Your basic business plan lays out your business idea; the basics of the business; how you will handle marketing; what competition you've found; how you will design and develop your idea, product, or service; how you will manage the business; and how you have arranged for the financial success of your business. Most business plans include these sections:

- **Summary.** The summary section introduces you and states the intent of the plan.

- **Description of business.** This section addresses the need for your business, then shows how your business meets that need.

- **Marketing plans.** Here you discuss how you will get the word out about your business.

- **Competitive analysis.** Who are your competitors? How are they doing? What will you do differently?

- **Plans for development.** How will you develop your idea, service, or product? What stages are involved? What people and resources do you need?

- **Business management.** How will you operate your business on a day-to-day basis? Will you do everything yourself, or will you need help? What are your operating expenses?

- **Financial documents.** Important financial documents you should have (your accountant can help you with these) include an income statement, a balance sheet, and a cash flow statement.

Check the business section in your local library or bookstore for more help. Many good books are available to help you create a detailed plan for your business.[4]

STRESS**BUSTER**

**#7**

Always
be the
nice one.

## People

Wherever you find people, you're going to find disagreements. Maybe your supplier is having a bad day. She promised you last week that you'd have the new shipment of dried flowers by today. They're not here. Now she's denying having made the promise.

You could rant and rave. You could let your blood pressure climb and try to convince her she's wrong. But it's better for your health, and better for your business, to let go of the things you can't change.

Ask yourself what you can learn from the experience. Perhaps you'll use a different supplier. Maybe next time you order from her, you'll order a week before you need the shipment, to give her time to lose the order.

One of the great things about working for yourself is that you are in the ultimate decision-making position. You have the power of the dollar: You can take your business elsewhere. That, in itself, is the only decision you ever have to make—whether to do business with that person or not. You don't have to pull someone else around to your way of thinking.

STRESS**BUSTER**

**#8**

Don't try
to change
difficult
people.

But what happens when the difficult person is an unsatisfied customer? Most healthy companies agree that when you make customer service your top priority, your business grows. People want to be treated right, and—since your customer is the one with the buying power, as you are in the case with the supplier—it's your job to make sure he gets what he is paying for.

When you hit one of those unreasonable people— and they are out there—try to remember he has a mother, too (and don't call her names!). Try to hear what the customer wants—through all the negativity and perhaps even disparaging comments—and do your best to deal with the situation fairly and get it over with. Sometimes grinning and bearing it gets you through customer conflicts much faster—and with more dignity and peace of mind—than waging a battle over inconsequential issues.

There is a limit, however, and of course you should never let a customer persuade you to do anything unethical in order to keep his business. You need to know where your lines are: How far are you willing to go for customer satisfaction? Know where your line is and stick to it.

What if the difficult person is a member of your family? The most important thing is to communicate. Sit down together and talk it out. Don't try to change her opinion. Just find out what the issue is. Listen. Decide together to work through whatever it is that's causing the problem. It's important to remember that your "difficult person" isn't really a difficult person at all—she's just having a difficulty you can help her resolve.

### Been There, Done That

*"When you're thinking about going full-time in your business, talk it over with your kids and your partner. I don't think my business would be as successful if my husband were not as supportive as he is. He encourages me when I falter, and gives me good advice—and only when I ask for it!"*

—work-at-home mother of one

# Someone to Watch Over Me: Getting the Help You Need

It's a good thing we don't have to keep everything we learn in our heads. Today we've got personal computers with CD-ROMs, the Internet, hundreds of business books, and more to help us learn the basics of business. None of these avenues, however, can replace the personal help you will get from professionals who make their livelihoods providing services for people like us. In the best-case scenario, you'll find great people who specialize in each of these areas to help you with the different needs of your business:

 Accounting

Law

Insurance

Business advising

## Getting—and Keeping—Good Help

It took me a long time to realize that the professionals who helped me with various business services weren't just strangers who did accounting, or practiced law, or sold insurance for a living. These were people I had relationships with, who laughed with me, who helped me figure out trouble spots, who taught me how to make my business stronger and more successful. Here are a few tips to help establish and grow those business relationships.

> **If you don't understand what's being said, ask for clarification.** Especially when we talk accounting, my eyes start to glaze. It took me years to stop acting as if I knew what my accountant was talking about and say, "Could you explain that again? I have no idea what that means."

> **Take notes.** Go to your meeting with a notepad and a pen, and write down the main points of your discussion. The service professional isn't the only one getting paid for this meeting: Your time is money, too. Make the most of it by writing down what was discussed and highlighting any items you need to take action on immediately.

> **Ask questions at the end of the meeting.** Before you leave a meeting with your accountant, lawyer, insurance agent, or advisor, look back through your notes and recap. "Okay, we talked about the petty cash thing, and we covered the quarterly amounts. I'm supposed to mail those in by the 15th. Is there anything else I missed?" This replay of the discussion brings up any unanswered questions either of you has. It also cements in your mind what you need to do as soon as you leave.

> **Pay promptly.** Who knows better than your accountant when your money is tight? But it's part of a mutual respect issue: *Pay as*

*promptly as you can.* If funds are too tight and you can't pay on time, send what you can or call. The professional will appreciate the contact, and it will further strengthen your relationship.

 **Be personable.** To me, this is the best part of being in business. I love the people behind the businesses. I talk to my accountant about his kids, to my lawyer about her mother, to my insurance agent about her new baby. Life isn't about business; life is about life. Business is one of the things we do with our time while we're living life. (How's *that* for a renegade philosophy?) When people you work with and for know you care about *them*, not simply about what they can do for you, it adds a whole new dimension to routine business interactions.

# An Accountant to Watch Your Pennies

Every person starting a business needs to talk to an accountant. Not everyone does, of course. But everyone *should*. When you are in the startup stages, an accountant can ...

 Help you determine the feasibility of your idea

 Help you develop a budget

Help create a business plan

Do your first income statement

Prepare financial reports for the bank so you can apply for a business loan

Help you decide what business form to choose

Later, when things are really cooking in your business, your accountant can ...

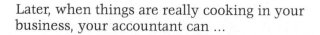 Help you set up payroll for yourself, your employees, and your contractors

Do monthly or quarterly balance sheets

Prepare financial reports

Take care of all your tax issues: advising, figuring, reporting, filing, and representing

Help you choose and establish an IRA

This is only part of what your accountant can and will do for your business. You'll ease into these needs slowly, as your business grows and you are faced with new challenges and opportunities. When you begin thinking about securing a business loan, for example, your accountant can be invaluable in preparing reports in a professional manner—just the way the loan officer will want to see them. When you have a discussion in the works with the IRS, your CPA can represent your business and answer questions with professional aplomb.

There are a number of accounting programs on the market, of course, that can help you do your own bookkeeping right there on your PC. Popular programs include *Quicken, QuickBooks for Windows,* and *Simply Business.* These enable you to balance your checkbook, do a number of reports, and track your expenses accurately. But while it makes bookkeeping at home easier, software accounting help does not replace the professional expertise your accountant can offer you. Even if you see him only once a quarter or once a year, having established a relationship with a real, live accountant gives you a resource that can never be surpassed by information on a CD-ROM.

```
QuickBooks - C:\QBOOKSW\SAMPLE.QBW - [Checking]
File  Edit  Lists  Activities  Reports  Graphs  Preferences  Window  Help
Invoice  Check  Bill  Reg  Accnt  Cust  Vend  Item  MemTx  Rmnd  Calc  Backup  Qcard  Help
```

| Date | Num | Payee | | Payment | Clr | Deposit | Balance | |
|------|-----|-------|--|---------|-----|---------|---------|--|
| | Type | Memo | Account | | | | | |
| 06/01/94 | 667 | State Bank Mastercard | | 104 81 | | | 7,055 85 | |
| | BILLPMT | | Accounts Payable | | | | | |
| 06/01/94 | 668 | Vito Insulation | | 1,024 00 | | | 6,031 85 | |
| | BILLPMT | | Accounts Payable | | | | | |
| 06/08/94 | 554 | Boy Scouts of America | | 36 98 | | | 5,994 87 | |
| | CHK | Light bulbs | Contributions | | | | | |
| 06/30/94 | 555 | Koepplinger Landowners | | 375 00 | | | 5,619 87 | |
| | CHK | July rent payment | Rent | | | | | |
| 07/01/94 | 556 | Nation Bank | | 300 00 | | | 5,319 87 | |
| | CHK | | -split- | | | | | |
| 07/02/94 | 557 | Bartel Insurance | | 3,332 00 | | | 1,987 87 | |
| | CHK | JAS quarter, worker's | Worker's Comp | | | | | |
| 07/31/94 | 558 | Koepplinger Landowners | | 375 00 | | | 1,612 87 | |
| | CHK | August rent payment | Rent | | | | | |
| 08/01/94 | 559 | Nation Bank | | 300 00 | | | 1,312 87 | |
| | CHK | | -split- | | | | | |
| 08/30/94 | 560 | Koepplinger Landowners | | 375 00 | | | 937 87 | |
| | CHK | September rent payme | Rent | | | | | |

```
Record   Restore   Q-Report   Edit/Split   □ 1-line view          Ending Balance:   16,753 87
```

```
Start   QuickBooks - C:\QB...                                     2:42 PM
```

*QuickBooks for Windows* makes it easy to set up your business, pay checks, balance your business checkbook, and more.

## A Story of Three Accountants

Once there were three accountants. The first was a short, squat little man with a pointed head. I went to him about the new business I was starting. "Ah," he said, "Pszzthka wif denaf elim!" I stared, dumbfounded. "Rightza nichoff sardoff elski ... " And he jabbered that way for the entire $75 hour. For months afterward, every time I looked in my checkbook, I felt sick. I had no idea what the man had said. He didn't speak my language.

The second accountant was a handsome, jovial fellow. Great handshake. A laugh that shook the walls. I was dazzled. I listened to him talk for an $80 hour, and I had no idea what he'd said afterward.

The third accountant was a nice-looking, intelligent man. He spoke softly. He carried a big notepad. He drew me pictures. He underlined words. Aha! The lightbulb went on and *I understood him*. And we've lived happily every after.

The moral? Finding the professional who relates to you in a way you can understand is an important part of making a successful relationship. Don't stop with your first choice if he's not helping you learn the ropes of your business.

# A Lawyer to Watch Your Ps and Qs

A lawyer in the wings is worth two in the courtroom. When you're first starting your business, it's a good idea to contact your lawyer—or to find one if you don't have one already—and use her as a sounding board for legal issues. There's no need to hire a $500-an-hour attorney to answer a few simple questions, but you should have legal counsel in some form so you know you're setting things up the right way.

Part of your lawyer's responsibility will be to help you incorporate, if that's the form you want your business to take. She also can answer questions about legal names, copyrights, permissions, forms that need to be filed with the state, and so on.

One thing your lawyer can help you do is determine what kinds of licenses and permits you need to start your business on the up-and-up.

The involvement of your lawyer may be next to nil, but she's an important part of your support team. Make the connection and start the relationship now, so if you ever need to be advised or represented in a full professional capacity, you will have an attorney who knows the basic history and vision of your business.

## The Scoop on Software

Your help doesn't have to come in the person-to-person form; there are a number of software programs specifically created to help you start that new business.

Three top CD-ROMs for startup entrepreneurs are *Start Your Own Business*, from NEBS software; *The Start-Up Guide*, from Dearborn Multimedia; and *Small Business Start-Up*, from Adams Media. For $50 or less, these programs will help you learn basic business concepts, test your idea, create a business plan, figure out how to market your business, and much more.

For law advice, you can turn to *Quicken Business Law Partner*, by Parsons Technology; *Kiplinger's Small Business Attorney*, by Block Financial; or *Small Business Legal Pro*, by Nolo Press.

## An Insurance Agent to Watch Your Back

Oh, come on now. Insurance agents are people too. In fact, I really like my insurance agent. She's a work-at-home mom.

Someone once said, insurance is a difficult business because "you're selling a negative intangible." When you buy insurance, you're paying for something you hope you never need. So you're throwing money away, gladly, just in case the dreaded thing (which is worse than spending the money) ever happens.

 We're afraid we'll get sick, so we buy health insurance.

 We're afraid we'll die and our families will be stuck with the bill, so we buy health insurance.

 We're afraid our houses will burn down, so we buy home owners' insurance.

 We're afraid we'll be incapacitated, so we buy short-term disability insurance.

We're afraid we'll be sued if someone falls on our steps, so we buy liability insurance.

When you're setting up your home-based business, you really need to talk to an insurance professional. What kind of coverage you need depends on what you do, whether customers will come to your home, your current health, and the health of your family members.

A good insurance agent—either an independent agent or one representing a company—should be able to present you with a number of different options and should be able and willing to advise you as to which policies would be best for you, in terms of coverage and expense.

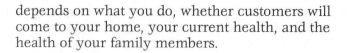

*Several associations for self-employed professionals offer group health care at discounted rates. I've been contacted by two different agencies and, although both promised lower premiums than the single policy I now have, neither was able to deliver those rates. Check out all offers—especially phone offers—very carefully. In the long term, I think it's better to develop a relationship with an agent you can call on the phone and see face-to-face once in a while, so you can resolve any policy issues and get answers to your questions.*

## What Does a Good Insurance Agent Do?

Good insurance agents are like good mechanics: You need to keep them when you find them. Here's a list of things a good insurance agent does:

- Keeps up-to-date on changes in the insurance industry

- Knows about your rate changes before you do

- Is always looking for the best rates, even if it means a company change

- Can advise you on insurance issues that affect your business, your clients, and your family

Meets with you one-on-one as needed to answer questions and explain policy changes

 Can propose policies tailored to your needs

 Is able to offer a variety of different policies so you don't need more than one agent

 Will work with an agency on your behalf if there's a problem with your policy

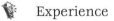

# A Business Advisor to Watch Your Growth

What's a business advisor? A mentor. Maybe even a friend. Someone who's been where you are. Someone who is successful doing what you plan to do. Someone who's been around the block a few times, taken a few wrong terms, and lived to tell about it.

A business advisor can save you from making mistakes you'd otherwise walk into blindly. With invaluable "been there, done that" information, your business advisor can give you advice, respond to your suggestions, evaluate your proposals, even connect you with people in the industry who can help your business succeed.

The key to finding a good business advisor is threefold. Look for these three qualities in an advisor:

Experience

Encouragement

Insight

*Experience* speaks for itself. You wouldn't go to another novice to learn real-life lessons on what to watch out for in your line of work. Someone with experience will have made mistakes and learned from them. You can benefit from their experiences, if you listen carefully.

*Encouragement* is crucial in an advisor. You'll need a "can-do!" attitude yourself, and you should surround yourself with people who have that attitude. If you propose a number of ideas to your advisor and he keeps answering, "That'll never work," get yourself another advisor. If the second opinion is the same, you may need to rethink your ideas. But make sure you're not just encountering the "Eeyore attitude" toward life.

An advisor with *insight* has been wizened by her experiences. She's thought about why things work as they do, and she's willing to share some of her understanding with you. The insights she's gained from her own business won't necessarily be the same you learn from yours, but having an insightful advisor will remind you to be looking for the lessons you should be learning from your own entrepreneurial adventures, whether good or bad.

*For a work-at-home parent, there's another quality that will make your advisor a perfect fit: She's done what you're doing. If she's raised three kids while growing her business, you know you've got similar issues to talk about. Even if she did it a generation ago, the basic tenets of love, fairness, and hard work carry through to today.*

How much time should you spend with your business advisor? Not much. You might arrange to talk monthly, perhaps over lunch if you enjoy each other's company, or maybe you can touch base by phone on an as-needed basis.

Here are some organizations you might contact to find a business advisor with the experience, encouragement, and insight you need:

- **SCORE:** The Service Corps of Retired Executives is run by the Small Business Administration and offers free business consulting for startup businesses from the people who've been there. Contact your local SBA or Chamber of Commerce for more information.

- **SBDC:** Small Business Development Centers offer startup and support services to beginning business. Run by the Small Business Administration, SBDCs often offer business incubators: small, on-site business locations with support services. As a home-based business, the low-cost office space won't help you much, but the services, seminars, publications, and advice can help you start your business on the right foot.

- **Chamber of Commerce:** Your local Chamber of Commerce is a good source of information for startup businesses. You can find out who else in your area has begun something similar and perhaps get a few names of professionals who are willing to help in an advisory capacity. The Chamber can help you link up with other professionals in your area of interest, and you can do some valuable networking at monthly Chamber meetings.

- **Your church or synagogue:** You might be surprised at how much help is available in your faith community. Often, men's or women's groups have advising services from which you can request help on a variety of topics. Talk to others in your congregation to find out who else is self-employed and discuss the possibility of starting a business owners' group, if you don't already have one.

- **Universities and colleges:** The business department of your local university can give you some direction on startup resources for small businesses. You may be able to hook up with a professor who'll let you audit a course or two (or take them for credit, if you need the hours).

 **Your business community:** There's nothing wrong with contacting someone who does something similar to your business in your community and saying, "I'm just starting out, and I was wondering if I could ask you a few questions." It's one of the golden rules of good business: When you move up a rung, help the person coming up behind you. With luck, the person above will do the same for you.

**SBA:** The Small Business Administration is a federal agency created to help small businesses in America. Through SCORE and SBDCs, the SBA helps small businesses gather the knowledge and experience they need to succeed, and, through a variety of lenders, it makes special loans available for qualifying small businesses. If you have World Wide Web access, you can visit the SBA at its Web site: http://www.sba.com.

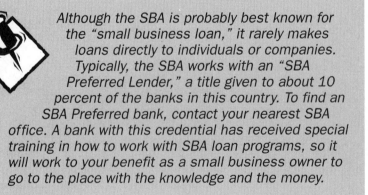

*Although the SBA is probably best known for the "small business loan," it rarely makes loans directly to individuals or companies. Typically, the SBA works with an "SBA Preferred Lender," a title given to about 10 percent of the banks in this country. To find an SBA Preferred bank, contact your nearest SBA office. A bank with this credential has received special training in how to work with SBA loan programs, so it will work to your benefit as a small business owner to go to the place with the knowledge and the money.*

### Help on the Net

There are several resources for home-based businesses on the Internet; you'll find a partial listing of them in Appendix B. One site you may want to visit on the World Wide Web is the Home Office Association of America's home page. The address is http://www.hoaa.com/. The HOAA lists all kinds of startup ideas and provides advice on how to spot work-at-home scams. It's worth checking out.

## Summing Up

In this chapter you've taken a look at the various issues you face as a work-at-home entrepreneurial parent. It's not an easy task, but one with incredible rewards on a number of different levels. The good news is that, with a good support team of professionals, you've got the game half licked. It's all about finding—and then using—your resources. And what a great lesson that is to pass on to your kids!

## Notes

1. Andrew A. Caffey, *Franchise and Business Opportunities 1997.*

2. *The Entrepreneur Magazine Small Business Advisor* (New York: John Wiley, 1995), p. 68.

3. *The Manager's Intelligence Report* (Chicago: Lawrence Ragan Communications), p. 5.

4. LaVerne Ludden and Bonnie Maitlen, *Mind Your Own Business* (Indianapolis: JIST, 1994) and Marcia R. Fox and Connie Cordaro (eds.) *Be Your Own Business* (Indianapolis: JIST, 1997).

# The Home-Working Parent

*"Whenever you are asked if you can do a job,
tell 'em, 'Certainly I can!'—and get busy and
find out how to do it."*
—Theodore Roosevelt

If you're working at home but on someone
else's payroll, some people will say you've got
the best of both worlds. You're enjoying the
freedom of the work-at-home life. You've got

the security of a regular paycheck. There are benefits you don't have to worry about. The work keeps coming, the checks keep coming, and you're home when the kids come home.

Pretty good arrangement, right?

And yet, you'll face some challenges too. Perhaps you've convinced your employer to allow you to work at home during your maternity leave. Maybe this is a part-time gig you want to extend to full-time. Maybe your company is having financial troubles and has closed a regional office and asked workers to move their offices home. In that case, you have security, but it might be only a temporary thing.

**BEST** &
WORST

*Best:*
"The flexibility
to do what
I feel is
important."

In any case, your success working at home—staying there and liking it—will depend on how well your employer and your clients acclimate to your new arrangement. If your boss didn't particularly like the idea to begin with, she might be swayed by the comments of a few jealous coworkers, and you might find yourself back in the office in a fortnight. And if people in the office suspect you're out playing in the yard with the kids or shopping at the mall when you should be working, you're always going to feel you've got to justify your actions, which is no fun and doesn't create a productive work environment.

In Chapter 2, you thought about what kind of work you could do at home for your employer and you learned how to approach the boss. This chapter picks up where that one left off: The boss said "Okay," either with or without enthusiasm, and now it's up to you to get the situation rolling.

## First Things First

When you are working at home for someone else, you've got a unique set of circumstances. You still are in the business of making people happy.

You've got to make sure that your at-home performance meets—or, better yet, exceeds—the expectations of your employer. You don't just want him to admit begrudgingly that the work-at-home idea has some merit. You want him to be so enthusiastic about the idea that he recommends that other parents in his office consider the same arrangement.

◆ ◆ ◆ ◆ ◆ ◆ ◆ ◆ ◆ ◆ ◆ ◆ ◆ ◆ ◆ ◆ ◆ ◆ ◆ ◆ ◆ ◆ ◆ ◆ ◆

*"Trust is the thing. If I trust him here in the office, I can trust him at home."*
—office manager with work-at-home employees

◆ ◆ ◆ ◆ ◆ ◆ ◆ ◆ ◆ ◆ ◆ ◆ ◆ ◆ ◆ ◆ ◆ ◆ ◆ ◆ ◆ ◆ ◆ ◆ ◆

How do you make sure your work-at-home arrangement gets off to the best possible start? You follow these five steps:

1.  Set your priorities.

2.  Set your schedule.

3.  Set up a reporting method.

4.  Set up a way to resolve difficulties.

5.  Make arrangements for emergency situations.

## Getting Your Priorities Straight

You're probably thinking, "I've already done this." And you have. (Remember Chapter 1?) Priority setting is an important part of knowing where you're going. Although you've determined, with your spouse and your kids, what's important for you as a family, you still have to do the employment part—the place where work meets family, right in the living room of your home.

You need to come up with ideas you can communicate to your boss as you get your work-at-home situation off the ground. The priorities you list might look something like this:

1. To be more productive at home than I was in the office.

2. To be accessible to my children during the day.

3. To give myself more time each day by eliminating the commute to work.

4. To reduce the number of personal days I take to care for my children when they are sick.

Notice that these are all related to either work or family; they indicate how you prioritize things where the two meet, one of the most important aspects of being a work-at-home parent.

What are my work-at-home priorities?

1. _____

2. _____

3. _____

4. _____

## Setting Your Schedule

The next step is deciding when you're going to work. Remember that the biggest complaint or concern employers have is not that you're taking advantage of them but that others are inconvenienced by your work-at-home status. If a client can't reach you during normal business hours or a coworker can't reach you to schedule a meeting, your employer is going to be less than thrilled with the arrangement.

As you think about your schedule, answer these questions:

 When is the most important time for you to be accessible to your employer?

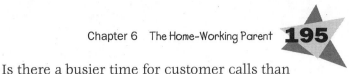

 Is there a busier time for customer calls than others?

 Do you have a quota to reach during specific hours?

Is there a time when it's unlikely you can be reached?

Will you be taking your kids to or from preschool at a specific time, fixing lunch, or putting the baby down for a nap?

Is there a specific time during the day that you can plan your calls?

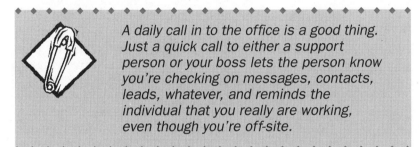

*A daily call in to the office is a good thing. Just a quick call to either a support person or your boss lets the person know you're checking on messages, contacts, leads, whatever, and reminds the individual that you really are working, even though you're off-site.*

You will do three things with this schedule:

1. You'll give a copy to your boss.

2. You'll keep a copy above your desk.

3. You'll put a copy on the fridge or the family bulletin board so everyone knows when you're doing what during the week.

## What Hours Will You Work?

If the work you do is an independent kind of thing—like writing a book—there aren't a whole lot of people depending on you daily to complete tasks so they can do their jobs. Other kinds of work, however—such as sales, appointment setting, and banking—rely on a close interchange of information among coworkers. (For example, I set the appointments; I give my list of appointments to you; you assign sales team members to carry out the appointments.)

If you are working in a solo occupation, you are in a better position to work whatever hours fit your life the best. For almost a year I worked from 9:00 P.M. to 1:00 A.M., doing most of my work after my children were in bed. If I were working in a sales job, that schedule would be impossible: Clients wouldn't be happy with me if I called them at midnight to set appointments!

## Checking In with the Chief

It's important that you and your employer come up with a way to document that you are, in fact, doing your job and that your performance has increased (you hope) since you started working at home. Reporting can take care of that. The way you report your progress will depend on what you and your employer are comfortable with, the kind of work you do, and whether there are systems in place already to monitor your work-at-home tasks.

 **When the Shoe Is on the Other Foot**

There's quite a bit of trust involved in working with someone you can't check on easily. I once took on a project that required the outsourcing of some design work. I contacted a person referred to me by a coworker. He was a designer of some reputation, very busy and in demand. He agreed to take my small project and fit it in during the following two weeks. I asked him when I could see the draft; he said, "I'm not sure." When I asked him what day he thought he'd have the proofs ready, he said, "I don't know." My ability to meet my deadline rested on his shoulders, and he was vague about the whole thing. He did get the project done on time—the day before my two-week deadline—but I spent a nervous period biting my fingernails in anticipation.

**My Work Schedule: Week of** _____

| Task/Comments | Mon. | Tues. | Wed. | Thurs. | Fri. |
|---|---|---|---|---|---|
| 8:00 | | | | | |
| 9:00 | | | | | |
| 10:00 | | | | | |
| 11:00 | | | | | |
| Lunch | | | | | |
| 1:00 | | | | | |
| 2:00 | | | | | |
| 3:00 | | | | | |
| 4:00 | | | | | |
| 5:00 | | | | | |

*You can use the Task/Comments column for specific times (as shown here), or to arrange your work day by tasks (Manager's report, Sales calls, Appointment setting, and so on).*

Your reporting might be a simple phone call:

> *"I'm not quite done with Chapter 6, but I'll be able to finish it in the morning."*

> *"I set seven of those eight appointments for you. They are all set for Cincinnati next Monday and Tuesday."*

> *"I put together four kits today. I'll need another load of parts by the end of next week."*

Or you might use e-mail:

```
To: Ed

From: Kathy

Re: Work progress

Date: 12-5-96

Ed,

Still working on 6. I'll send it in
tomorrow.

—Kathy

km/iHn
```

Or you could use a Weekly Report sheet like the one on page 199 which could show contacts made, appointments set, tasks accomplished, and so on.

Whatever you decide on, make sure it's clear, can be read at a glance, and gives enough information so you can accurately reflect what you're accomplishing. When someone calls you in January about something you did in October, you can look back through your files, find your copy of your Weekly Report, and go right to the task in question.

## Weekly Report: Week of

| Date | Task Comments | Time Started | Time Completed | Total |
|------|---------------|--------------|----------------|-------|
| 12-6 | Chapter 6 | 8:30 | 4:30 | 8.0 |
| | | | | |
| | | | | |
| | | | | |
| | | | | |
| | | | | |
| | | | | |
| | | | | |
| | | | | |
| | | | | |
| | | | | |
| | | | | |
| | | | | |

**Total Hours** _____

## Whose Employees Are Working at Home?

The last few years have brought increased awareness of the benefits of working at home. Many large corporations have begun work-at-home programs that include at last part-time work-at-home hours for certain divisions in their companies. Here are some of the big names[1]:

- Allstate
- American Express
- AT&T
- Blue Cross/Blue Shield
- Citibank
- Digital Equipment Corporation
- DuPont
- Hewlett-Packard
- Honeywell
- Hughes
- IBM
- J.C. Penney
- Journal Graphics
- New York Life
- Xerox

# Conflict Resolution 101

The best time to iron out conflicts is before they happen. Put a system in place so the lines of communication are open, just in case somebody misunderstands something. When you discuss your plans with your employer—complete with your priority list, your schedule, and your reporting method—explain how you will handle it when and if you two misunderstand each other or if one of you is unhappy with the way things are going. Here are some questions to get you started:

🖐   How often should we meet to discuss how the arrangement is working for both of us?

🖐   Can we agree to have an open-door policy so each issue is addressed as it comes up?

🖐   Can we agree on a specific length of time to try the work-at-home arrangement, no matter what?

🖐   Should we include an objective third party or simply resolve issues between ourselves?

## Conflict? What Conflict?

What kinds of conflicts can happen? A file gets lost. "That wouldn't happen in the office," your boss says. Your 3-year-old is throwing a fit in the background while your boss is on the phone trying to explain a change in the schedule. "The benefits of working at home," she says sarcastically. Is this conflict? It's the beginning of one. Talk about the attitudes now, before they get ingrained. At the next opportunity, you could open the door with, "I've noticed a couple of comments you've made lately about my working at home. Is there something we need to address here? Are you unhappy with my work?"

Yes, it's scary to ask for any criticisms that are building up. But it's much better to clear the air now, before problems start festering. And once you know what's causing the problem, you can start solving it, which will further strengthen your position at home.

## Making Arrangements for Emergencies

No matter how good it looks in our heads, or on paper, things never work out exactly the way we plan. There will be days when you simply *have* to go into the office to straighten things out. Your job may not depend on it, but your reputation as a work-at-home employee might. Perhaps there's an important meeting with a big client and your in-house team needs your help. Or maybe the department managers are meeting to plan the budget for next year; you'd better be there, or your salary might be the expense that gets cut. Or there's revolution brewing in your department, and your boss has called a departmental meeting—be there or else.

What will you do with Jason and Bryanna? Your sitter is lined up for Tuesday and Thursday, but here it is, Wednesday morning, and they want you in the office first thing after lunch.

Sure, if Grandma is close and doesn't work, that's a perfect fix. Or perhaps a neighbor can help in a pinch. The point is, you need to think about it *before it happens*.

Here's a plan for getting emergency backup in place:

- **Identify two or three different people you can call for emergency child care.**

- **Talk to each of those people** and find out how much notice they need, what they charge, and what they want you to bring.

- **Explain to your kids that there may be times when you must go into the office for meetings.** Make sure they know you have taken care of arrangements and they will be safe and cared for, no matter what.

**If your child doesn't know the sitter, make sure you introduce them soon.** Go over for an afternoon visit so Bryanna will recognize both the person and the house when she goes to visit for the first time.

 **Post the sitter's numbers** and make sure your spouse knows about the possibility of in-house meetings, so when she comes home and finds neither you nor the kids (did you forget to call again?), she won't panic.

 **Create an emergency plan.** Write a list of steps explaining what will happen if you have an emergency meeting and you must go in to the office with little or no notice. Here are a few ideas for the plan:

---

### Emergency Plan

*If I must go into the office suddenly, here's what we'll do:*

- *I'll call Donna (555-8899) to see whether Tiffany can come over. If she's not home, I'll call Teresa (555-3111).*
- *Take Tiffany to the sitters with her blanket, a sack lunch, and a movie.*
- *Call Roger at work and let him know Tiffany is at the sitter's. (Be sure to tell him which one.)*
- *Call the sitter and/or Roger from the office as soon as I know how long the meeting will last.*

If you have a school-aged child who needs child care—or at least looking after—you have another set of considerations for emergencies. Will your child need a ride home? Will he come home to an empty house? Think through the way you will resolve after-school issues for your school-aged child:

- You can have him go to a neighbor's house after school until you get home. (Be sure to talk to two or three neighbors and ask their permission. And on a day when you are suddenly called in, you'll have to call both the neighbor and the school, so both Philip and your neighbor know where he's going after school.)

- You can allow him to stay home alone, if you feel comfortable with his age and his responsibility level. If you allow your child to be home alone, make sure he has clear guidelines for what's okay and what's not: No cooking; No answering the door; No telling people on the phone, "Mom's not here right now." And write out a list of emergency phone numbers—a close neighbor, your number at work, Dad's number, the police, and the fire station—and post them on your family bulletin board.

*One of the most important thing in preparing for an emergency trip to the office is explaining to your kids that it might happen someday. That way, when they come home from school one afternoon and find you gone, they won't worry. They will know you have simply been called away for a little while (leave them a note inside so they know for sure), and they will know what to do until you get home. If you can, call from your meeting when you know how long you'll be there, to reassure yourself and your kids that everyone is safe and cared for.*

**After-School Rules**

If you get home and I'm not here, follow these rules until I get home:

_____

_____

_____

_____

_____

**Emergency Phone Numbers:**

Mom's #: _____     Dad's #: _____

Neighbor: _____     Neighbor: _____

Police: _____     Fire: _____

# The Kick-Off Meeting

Okay, you're ready for the sit-down meeting with your employer at which you will show her specifically what you're planning on the work-at-home front. Take along the following things, _in writing:_

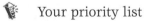   Your priority list

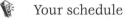   Your schedule

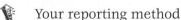   Your reporting method

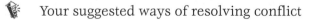   Your suggested ways of resolving conflict

   Your planned method of handling emergencies

   A list of questions you need answered

Go into your meeting prepared, with a copy of each of your documents printed, so your employer has one to refer to during the meeting.

As you discuss each of the items you've prepared, be ready to make changes—nothing is set in stone yet. The successful work-at-home arrangement will be a synergistic creation you and your employer create together. Your plans may meet with 100 percent approval, but there probably will be at least a few things your employer wants to change.

Although you don't need to take your emergency plan in to show your employer (or the list of home-alone rules for your older child), you should let people at the office know that you have made arrangements in case that "emergency" ever happens. This raises another issue, however: What do you—and they—consider an emergency? It's something worth talking about. If your boss thinks you should drop everything and run in each time there's a question about a report you did, he may be missing other ways of resolving the problem: for example, faxing it to you or calling you and asking you to read through it with him on the phone. Define an emergency situation—and how rarely you hope to use your emergency plan—and iron out any wrinkles before you leave.

You'll also want to come up with a list of questions about who pays for what, how specific parts of your projects will work, and so on. Use the following checklist as a starting point for your list of questions:

### Questions for the Boss

1. Do you want me to tell clients that I'm working at home?

2. Do you want clients to send proposals directly to your office, or should I have them come to me first?

3. Do you want me to use supplies from the office or to purchase my own and send you the invoice?

4. Will I be paid salary, hourly, on commission, or by the piece?

5. Will my benefits stay the same?

6. How will we arrange sick days?

7. Will you provide the equipment?

8. Will you continue to cover liability insurance and worker's compensation?

9. Will I still be able to participate in training opportunities?

10. When will my next review be?

11. _____

12. _____

13. _____

14. _____

You also should find out about options for career advancement. Does working at home mean that when they are looking for someone for a middle-management position, you'll be out of sight and out of mind? If you want to continue the corporate ladder climb, make sure your employer knows that your decision to work at home doesn't mean you want to get off the ladder. People on all rungs are working at home, so your decision to do so shouldn't mean you have to give up the possibility of moving to the next level in your career.

### And the Band Played On ...

As you get into the swing of things and get some experience working at home, use these tips to keep your communications open and direct:

- **Be clear and up-front.** Don't hide the fact that you enjoy being with your kids more. Tell your boss so. He'll pick up on it anyway—and if you try to hide it, you may give the impression you feel guilty about the time you spend with your kids.

- **Don't be afraid to tell the truth.** If you don't know the answer to a situation, say so. Then use your resources to find the answer. Being able to solve a problem is a more valuable asset than "knowing everything."

- **Do your best.** You are doing the same work at home that you did in the office. Be proud of it, and don't feel your best is compromised by the change in environment.

- **Welcome questions.** Make sure your boss knows you are accessible and open and will answer any questions or challenges she or your clients have. Keeping an open attitude with your employer is your best safeguard that your work-at-home situation will be seen as a success.

# It's Office Policy ...

This section lists practical how-tos for dealing with some of the peculiarities of working at home for someone else.

## Benefits

In most cases, full-time, work-at-home employees receive the same benefit packages they received in the office. Talk to your personnel manager to be sure. There are issues—such as workers' compensation and liability insurance (including coverage for clients who come to your home during the work hours)—that need to be ironed out by someone within your organization.

If you work for a large company where working at home is nothing new, the entire system probably is already worked out for you. Review the packet carefully, highlight things you don't understand, and schedule an appointment with the personnel manager before you make your final decision. Most companies that have begun allowing employees to work at home at least part-time have seen tremendous results, so don't expect to find anything sneaky in your work-at-home information.

## Sick Days

You probably already know your sick day policy in the office: how many days are paid, what time you need to call in by, and so on. How do they want you to handle sick days at home? For record-keeping purposes, they might want you to notify them as you would if you were an in-office employee.

On the flip side, one of the great things about working at home is that you can sit around in your robe, sipping chicken soup and hot tea while you work, if you have to. The number of days you can work—even if you're not feeling up to snuff—increases, which is better for the employer and better for you: Now you can reserve those sick days for the flat-on-your-back-in-bed days.

*Many employees take sick days when their children are sick, and people often feel guilty about that. It's not entirely true, after all. Some people claim that the system "forces" them to lie, but whatever rationalization they offer, it's still not true. If you're working at home, you can be there when Andrew has the flu—right there working beside him while he lays on the couch and watches cartoons all day. No lies, no sick days used. Much better.*

## Vacation Time

Can't you just hear your jealous coworkers now? "Vacation? Vacation! Your whole life is a vacation!" Maybe they'd like to come over and see the pictures of unicorns colored on the back of the annual report you just printed for the fourth time. Perhaps they'd change their tune if they saw you fitting 45 hours worth of work into life with three kids, two dogs, a hamster, and your visiting mother-in-law.

Work-at-home employees need vacations, too, and you shouldn't hesitate to ask for them. Will the same policies apply to you as a full-time, work-at-home employee? They should. What about traveling with your computer? If your family has a vacation scheduled and you can't get the time off, can you take your laptop and turn in your work from the road? You're already off-site, so the difference between turning in work from your Alameda home and your Des Moines cabin may be nil. Or your employer may want you to stay within earshot so she can call you in for emergency meetings as needed.

Whichever the case, asking about the vacation policy and scheduling your vacation early are good ideas.

## Expense Reimbursement

This is a question you'd probably like to take care of once and for all when you have the kick-off meeting with your boss. Who pays for what? It's a logical question.

The answer, however, probably will unfold over time. You'll find out right away who pays for things like the computer equipment, fax machine, disks, paper, labels, and so on. But what about these other items that might crop up over time?

- Long-distance phone charges for calls to clients

- Package shipping charges

- Internet access fees

- New software you need to be compatible with the office

- Packing materials for products you ship

- Overtime (even if you're on a salary)

- Storage boxes

- Shelves for office supplies

- Travel expenses and car mileage

Another issue is the home office deduction. If your office is in a room of your house, you can take a percentage (based on the square footage of your office) of your utility bills as a deduction. But you should check with your employer and your accountant on this one: If you are in the employ of another company, is the deduction yours to take? Or is that something the company will reimburse you for so they can take the deduction themselves?

*Take the straightest road possible through expense discussions. Some people get tied up in knots over money talk, but the simple approach is best: "Harvey, my Internet access bill is $19.95 a month. I only use it for work. Is that something you guys will reimburse me for?"*

## Goof-Ups

You worked until after midnight last night, doing data entry, getting more than 120 clients into the computer system so you could e-mail the file to your employer today.

When you turned on the computer this morning, the file was gone.

What happened? You didn't save the file before you shut down for the night, probably because you were so tired. Your boss is expecting that file so she can print out labels for the newsletter she mails to new clients. The newsletter is supposed to go out today.

What do you do? You call.

> *"Sheila?" you say, hesitantly.*

> *"Yes?" It's early. She's sleepy.*

> *"I finished all the data entry last night,"*

> *"Good!"*

> *" ... and then something happened to the file. It's not on my computer."*

You brace yourself.

She sighs.

*"Oh," she says.*

*"I'm really sorry. I must not have saved the file."*

*"Did you look on the backup disk?"*

*"Yes."*

*"Okay. Well, when can you get the file to me?"*

There, that wasn't so bad. The straight line through the issue is the best possible route. The fact that you goofed up doesn't have anything to do with working at home—so don't get that guilt mixed up in the situation. You could have done the same thing sitting in the office at work. Just admit that you made a mistake and set your sights on fixing the problem.

Some work-at-home employees feel guilty about their "cushy" position—and their coworkers sometimes want them to feel that way. Remember that people are people, and your coworkers are going to be working on their own agendas occasionally. So don't accept blame on your work-at-home situation simply because it's different from the way someone else is living his life. When your work-at-home status *does* cause a problem—if a client can't reach you, you can't make it in for a meeting because you don't have a sitter, or your computer crashes and the MIS person has to make a trip to your house—then simply recognize it and go on. Your working at home probably benefits your employer more than it costs him: You are doing valuable work, probably more effectively than you did in the office. The company is recouping the investment it made in your training. There's nothing to feel guilty about there.

**Profiles**
**Name:** *Sandra*
**Business:** *Human resources consulting*
**How long?** *$3\frac{1}{2}$ years*
**How many kids?** *Three, all under age 5*
**Biggest challenge:** *Helping the kids understand that Mom's home but she's working*
**Best answer to that challenge:** *I explain to them how lucky we all are to be able to spend more time together*

# What Do I Do About ... ?

If you work at home, you will have a unique set of challenges to face. This section offers practical how-tos for dealing with some of the most common ones.

## Scheduling

Scheduling is important, and so is flexibility. You need both a scheduled game plan and some built-in flexibility to keep your work and family running smoothly under one roof. Your employer should understand that you take your deadlines seriously and have every intention of keeping them. Your kids should know the same thing. But you know, deep inside, that if push comes to shove, you've got a little leeway when your family needs you.

If possible, schedule in a spare 30 to 60 minutes each day—maybe broken into several 5- to 10-minute breaks—to do things like play a game with the kids, fix a bike tire, walk to the mailbox, or play your guitar. If you were in the office, you'd have people stopping by your desk, chatting about the weather, or telling you what their kids did over the weekend. Now that you're home, you can turn those brief breaks into times to connect with your family.

### Been There, Done That

*"When I first worked at home, I made myself obey the clock. I sat down at 8:00. I got up for lunch at 12:00. I sat back down at 1:00 and worked until 5:00. After three or four days, I was miserable. A friend called and asked if I wanted to go to lunch. I told her I couldn't, I had to work. My son wanted to go see a movie in the middle of the afternoon. I wouldn't go. I felt chained to my desk. Then suddenly it hit me: I've got an opportunity that few people have—I can earn a living and enjoy the freedom to live the way I want to. So I went to the movie and now I take at least one afternoon each week to do things with my son. I love working at home."*

—work-at-home mother of one

## Isolation

When you first leave the office, you may be so glad to go you can't see straight. The office gossip has been driving you crazy. Your kids have been asking you every day for three weeks straight, "When will you be home? When does that start?" You've had your home office set up and waiting ... and now it's ready, set, go!

Two weeks later you find yourself standing at the door with a coffee cup in your hand. The bus stops at the end of the driveway and picks up your kids. You're alone, again. You turn around and walk down the hall to your office. Everything seems really, really quiet.

You work for a while at the computer, then stop and look around. No noise. You turn on a talk show, just to hear voices. People are yelling at each other. You feel better. Suddenly you realize what's wrong.

You feel isolated.

Not everyone goes through people withdrawal at the start of working at home. Some people are born for the work-at-home lifestyle; others must acquire the taste for long stretches of focused time. (Of course, if you've got infants, toddlers, or preschoolers at home, you're laughing right now!)

*If working at home is your choice, you're more likely to enjoy the time on your own, the freedom, and the opportunity. If you have been asked—or forced—to work at home, you might have more trouble adjusting to the new lifestyle. Getting used to a new work environment doesn't happen all of a sudden. It may take quite a while for your normal routine to feel normal.*

What should you do if you wake up one morning and feel isolated? Several things, for starters:

- Know that it's normal

- Call a coworker

- Make plans to have lunch with a friend

- Don't let yourself become a recluse—go to meetings, get out to the library

- Talk to other work-at-home employees

- Get online in a work-at-home forum

- Make sure you are involved in activities besides work after work hours

*What if a little isolation becomes the blues? Working at home isn't for everyone. Some people really miss the interaction with other adults. Give yourself time to acclimate, but don't force yourself to stick with something you're not happy with.*

## Staying Plugged In

Quick, take this quiz:

| | | | |
|---|---|---|---|
| 1. How's your grooming? | Poor | Fair | Terrific |
| 2. How was it when you went in to the office? | Poor | Fair | Terrific |
| 3. How good are you at computer games? | Poor | Fair | Terrific |
| 4. How good were you when you worked in the office? | Poor | Fair | Terrific |
| 5. How clean is your house? | Poor | Fair | Terrific |
| 6. How clean was it when you worked in the office? | Poor | Fair | Terrific |

If your grooming is suffering and your scores on computer games are vastly improving, you may be suffering the early stages of being unplugged from the real world. If you work all day in your bunny slippers and pajamas, you might want to think about getting dressed and going out to lunch with friends sometime this week. If you are having trouble remembering how to use your word processor but you've gotten really good at Solitaire, you might be spending too much time at your PC not producing anything profitable.

Mental health is a relative term, and the best way to keep it is to keep an eye on yourself and your emotions. The first few weeks of working at home may be heaven—or they may be tough. Allow yourself some emotional space to deal with the changes and expect some testing from the kids, as well. If stress turns into sickness or loneliness

becomes depression, talk to someone—your mother, a friend, a coworker, your boss, a counselor—but get an outside opinion and insight to help you through this transition time.

**Professional Parent Panic!**

*"One day, I had a client stop by unexpectedly. He came into the house and proceeded to the living room before I could direct him into the dining area, where I usually sit with clients. I yelled, "Aaahhh, don't go in there!" Too late. He saw my catastrophe. I was in the middle of folding laundry, the kids' toys were strewn all over, and the ironing board was in the middle of the room. Total embarrassment. My client just shrugged and came into the dining area with me."*
—work-at-home mother of two

## Interruptions

When you work at home, life *will* interfere. The dog will bark while you're on the phone with a client. The kids will answer the phone when

*Worst:*
"Stopping
when I'm
really
cooking on
something!"

they're not supposed to. The phone will ring during dinner.

In moments of high frustration, I've said to my kids, "If you interrupt me one more time, my head is going to explode." (Not a pretty picture, but it gets the point across.)

The easiest way to deal with interruptions is to expect them. Unless you are completely alone in the house, the phone is off the hook, the dog is muzzled, the doors are locked, and all the curtains are drawn, someone or something is going to interrupt you, probably every 20 minutes or so. If you expect interruptions to happen—and are thankful for the 19-minute intervals when you can work with relative focus—you keep those interruptions from turning into Huge Ordeals.

Another way of dealing with interruptions is to create an interruption board or an interruption time. The last 10 minutes of the hour could be interruption time: Ask Dad anything, no matter how silly, during the time from :50 to :00. Or let the kids use a big chalkboard to write or draw pictures of their questions, which you'll answer in that magical 10-minute slot.

Another interruption-buster is to parcel your work into bite-sized pieces. Do you have a number of quick tasks—things like copying files, formatting disks, filing documents, reading articles—that take less than 15 minutes and can be fit between interruptions? During the times you are most likely to be interrupted—like the hour between when the kids get off the school bus and when you start dinner—schedule those jobs. That way you never get so heavily into your project that surfacing to deal with an interruption is a monumental thing—you can simply move from task to task and wind up feeling that you got a lot done.

Many people feel guilty about letting the answering machine get the phone when they are in intense-work mode, but you shouldn't. You're entitled to some focused time. If it makes you feel better, put a message on the machine saying something like, "I'll be working nonstop this morning, but if you'll leave your name and number, I'll return your call early this afternoon."

The best way to handle interruptions is to work like crazy when you have got uninterrupted time. One mother does it this way:

### Been There, Done That

"When the kids were with Grandma or at preschool, I told myself I needed to use that time to do the things I couldn't do with them home, like make phone calls I needed to make or get work done at the computer."

## Neighbors and Friends

Not only will you need to help your employer and your family understand your priorities, your work schedule, and your availability, you'll also have to tell your neighbors and friends.

The head of the PTO may hear that you're home and ask you to volunteer for the bake sale. Your minister might learn about your change in work situations and invite you to be part of a Bible study. You sister might ask you to teach her kids to play the piano, now that you're home all day.

They just don't understand.

The best way to handle the shift from work-to-home and circumvent misunderstandings later is to be clear from the start. When you first tell someone you're working at home, explain, "Yes, I'm working full-time from an office in my home. I'm still working normal work hours—so I don't get to play all day—but it is nice to be home for the kids, and for myself, too!"

And just because you've got to be close to home and working during traditional work hours doesn't mean your friends can't bring lunch over and visit for a while. (No, I don't think your employer will spring for it.)

> **Been There, Done That**
> *"Set up clear boundaries, both time and space; make sure everybody knows them, and don't break them yourself."*
> —work-at-home mother of three

## Summing Up

Working at home for an employer can be a great opportunity. You've got security, you've got space, you've got work to do, and you've got the freedom to be with the people you love most in the world. If you keep communication lines open between you and your employer and you and your family, you really can have the best of both worlds—and get paid for it, too!

## Notes

1. Paul and Sara Edwards, *Working From Home* (New York: Tarcher Books, 1994), p. 77.

# The Parents' Guide to Business Management

*"Even if you're on the right track you'll get run over if you just sit there."*
—Will Rogers

Never thought of yourself as a manager? You will now! When you stop to think about all the things you manage in a day's time—managing children, a house, and a business is no small feat—you'll be amazed at the management skills you already have.

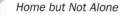

What is management? It's handling things so they work well for you. The more experience you gain running your business from home, keeping your kids busy, dealing with clients, answering questions, and communing with your spouse, the better you'll get at it. You'll learn to identify places where you could manage better. You'll discover opportunities for creative problem solving. And—little by little—you'll master the tricks of managing your work-at-home situation.

## What Do You Manage?

As a parent, you manage meals, schedules, bedtimes, homework, conferences, sibling squabbles, in-laws and grandparents, doctor's appointments, soccer practice, injuries, and demands for attention.

As an adult, you manage your household, bills, repairs, expenses, improvements, cars, machinery, appliances, groceries, financial planning, friends, relatives, and (perhaps most difficult, assuming you have the time) yourself.

As a businessperson, you manage projects, planning, schedules, bills, people, clients, long-range plans, short-range plans, bank accounts, meetings, tax information, payroll, your business plan, marketing, sales, distribution, files, purchases, and more.

**BEST** &
WORST

*Best:*
"Being here when the kids get home from school."

# Get Your Act Together!

Do you know what happens when you're standing in a group of people and you start talking about getting organized? Suddenly you're a "neat freak." People roll their eyes. They grumble about not being able to find anything, about having bell bottoms from the '70s (hey, my daughter would love those!), and about drowning in a sea of papers they never use but are afraid to throw away. But when you make a few suggestions about how they might organize things better, they laugh and declare the situation hopeless.

Unless they own a business. Then they listen.

As a business owner, you soon learn that disorganization costs money. The notes you made on that new project were right here a minute ago; now you've got the client on the phone, long-distance, and you can't find the notes. Your phone bill is climbing while you dig furiously through the papers on your desk. And moment by moment, you're losing credibility with your client, which in the long run could cost you a lot more than your phone bill.

Organization not only saves you money, it makes you money. You start to see trends in your business you didn't see before. You begin thinking about new ways to branch out, new marketing ideas to try, and new ways to use your time effectively. And you've got more time to work with productively because you spend less time in frantic searches for lost files.

Being organized also helps you look good as a business. When you're just starting out, you may be on a financial shoestring, but paying bills on time is important for the startup business. If you organize your bills and your payment schedule, and you pay when you plan to, you'll build up good credit for your business. And organizing your office, so you know what goes where, and taking pains to keep it that way not only makes it easier on you but sets clear guidelines for the kids—so they know Mom *will* notice when they get into the laser printer paper or play Frisbee with the CD-ROMs.

You really do yourself a favor when you organize yourself. Put yourself on a schedule. Know when you pay bills, when you make phone calls, and when you're free for lunches out. It simplifies your business and your life. It takes the "What?

Where? When?" out of your day so you have more time to plan your work and work your plan. (Okay, so it's a business cliché. I couldn't avoid it.)

When you are thinking about organizing your business at home, you can approach it using these three steps:

 Tame your inbox

 Increase your storage space

 Put your work systems in place

## Tame Your Inbox

Left unchecked, your inbox soon becomes your entire office. You put yesterday's mail there on the credenza—you'll get to it as soon as you have time. Then, two weeks down the road when you have the time, you've got little piles of papers all over the place: bills that need to be paid, flyers that can be thrown out, maybe even important contact cards on clients you should have called by now.

The best way to handle your inbox is to stay on top of it. When you put something in there—you need to type up that report, enter those customer names, balance your checkbook—make an agreement with yourself to complete it by the end of the day. *Then do it.* If it's something too big and you can't finish it in one day—such as writing the annual report for a client's company—put a yellow sticky note on the front of the document with today's date and what you *will* accomplish today. When you finish one task, cross off the item but leave the sticky note on the front. It will encourage you tomorrow, when you've got yet another part of the same project to master.

If you never let your inbox build up, it won't take over. But if you take the *fire fighting approach* to business management—putting out "fires" that need your immediate attention instead of planning what you will work on that day—you may wind up neglecting the important but quiet things that can make or break your business: things like bookkeeping, taxes, marketing, and networking. Such things don't sit up and scream your name, but they will cause a downslide in your business—and may get you into real trouble—if they're neglected.

The best way to take care of those important-but-quiet-things is to schedule them on your monthly write-in calendar or your DayTimer so they don't get overlooked. Then you must remember to *use* your calendar or DayTimer, of course, but that (almost) goes without saying.

*The trick of the Inbox is to train yourself. Deal with whatever's in it today, today. If you do, tomorrow will look a lot brighter. Even if you can't get the entire project done in one day, resolve to make some progress on that project so it never just sits there dormant, taking up space.*

## Inbox Management Tips

- **If you put it in there today, do it today.**

- **Break large projects into small tasks and work on them every day.**

- **If your inbox starts piling up, block out a morning for "inbox cleaning time."** If this won't fit in your regularly scheduled week, spend a Saturday morning in the office.

- **Never put something that's already done in the inbox.** Use a separate box for things waiting to be filed. (*There's* a job for the kids!)

- **Don't put your bills in the inbox.** Have a separate place for bills that you pay on a regular basis. (More about that later in this chapter.)

## Store Up Storage Space

Hey, you can never have too much space. Sooner or later, your stuff expands to fill whatever space you've got. So take some time now, as you're starting out, to think about how you want your office to be organized, where you need space, and how you can rearrange things to get the space you need.

What are the things you'll need quickly? What will you need only occasionally? Items like envelopes, reference books, paper supplies, and program documentation that you need *right now* should be stored where you can get to them easily—preferably on a shelf close enough to your desk that you can simply turn around and grab them when you need them. Things like last year's checkbook registers, insurance policies, past income reports, and old marketing directories you may need to refer to now and again—which means you should keep them. But you can clear them out of your "right now" area and put them in the closet or even in another room or the basement.

### Pocket, Pocket ... Who's Got the Pocket?

The cliché "Out with the old and in with the new" doesn't mean you should throw out all of last year's receipts and check stubs on January 1. You and your accountant might need them someday. A few years ago, I started a new tracking system: I use an accordion folder and label each pocket with a bill I pay month-to-month: Accounting, American Express, Federal Express, Insurance, and so on. In the front pocket, I keep my monthly bill sheets; then I file the bill stubs from each paid bill in its appropriate pocket. At the end of the year, I take that accordion folder out of the filing cabinet, label the new folder, and put the old folder in the basement with all the other past years' bills. It's an easy system that doesn't take up much room, and it gives me the reassurance of knowing that I can easily get back into 1993 if I really need to.

In an ideal situation, you've got your own office, your own shelves, and your own closet. Enough storage space, right? Wrong! You'll fill it up quickly, if you're not watching how you use it. Many work-at-home parents don't have the benefit of their "own" office: They may share the computer room, out of necessity or by choice, with their wonderful offspring and all the toys, blocks, and video games in their entourage.

If that is your situation, consider organizing your office into territories: my stuff, your stuff. It's not exactly like drawing battle lines, but it does help you stay clear on responsibilities. If Lucas wants to use your laser printer paper to draw on, he needs to ask first, because it's on your office side of the room. (And here's a tree-saving tip: Save all your rough drafts and old printouts for your kids to draw on.)

You also may need to preserve your space on your PC. Launch Pad (from Berkeley Systems) is a program that enables you, your spouse, and your kids to have all your favorite programs on the PC—all in different places. This keeps the kids out of your financial files and keeps you from accidentally starting Super Mario Brothers.

So how do you get more storage space? Here are a few ideas:

**Clean out your storage space regularly.** Keep only what you need right now. Remove things for occasional use to areas you visit only occasionally. How often you do this will depend on how quickly you accumulate things. Once a month is great. Once a quarter is still on the right road. Once a year, and you've got a major cleaning job on your hands.

**Add shelves.** Shelves turn a one-surface area (a floor or desktop) into a four-surface area. That's a 300 percent increase in storage space. You don't have to be elaborate with your shelving, either: A $19.95 wire shelf or even a $9.95 plastic one will give you more space than you've got now. Depending on the environment you work in, however, you may need to think about your shelving's ability to stand up against two wrestling 3-year-olds.

 **Reduce paperwork.** This is a suggestion I'm only half comfortable with, so I'm only going to half recommend it. Some PC enthusiasts claim we are moving toward the paperless office—that one day *everything* will be stored on disks, tapes, and other electronic whatnot. You can significantly reduce clutter and increase the amount of storage space you have by not keeping every printed document you've ever received. *However*, I'm still an advocate of keeping a paper backup of all important things—legal documents, proposals, financial statements, and the like—stored safely in the good old filing cabinet. PCs can be funny creatures, and I wouldn't want to gamble all my business data on my computer's willingness to do its tricks.

 **Beef up your PC.** And, on the flip side of the paperwork storage issue, we have PC storage. Your computer needs plenty of storage space to hold all the programs you install, the documents you create, and the graphics you download. Your PC's storage space is its hard drive. Keep an eye on how much storage space you have left, so your PC doesn't find itself full one afternoon and unable to save that important file you've been working on. You can add storage space to your computer in much the same way you get more storage space in your office: by cleaning off programs and files you don't need anymore, moving items you use occasionally to an occasional place (like a floppy disk or tape backup), or compressing files into a smaller space using a file compression program like *PKZIP* or *WinZIP*.

## Set Up Work Systems

The word *systems* doesn't evoke exciting pictures of adventure and success. Yet you will find that if you think through how you want your week to proceed, write it down (there's the system), and then follow it, your life becomes much easier.

You don't have to design the perfect system. Some of us wait to try anything because we're hoping for a divine revelation to hit—some message from beyond that shows us how to organize our work weeks. Some of us just fix whatever's broken, which may keep us in business but won't grow our businesses into anything successful over the long term.

Starting, establishing, then growing a business— right in the comfort of your home, with your happy family involved—means having a plan in place. You need to think about where you want to be, so you'll know how to get there, one step at a time. That's what systems are all about.

In this section we'll look at a few of the major tasks—things you're going to have to do anyway, whether you plan them or not—and how you can design a system for dealing with them.

No matter what, you need some method of planning what you're going to accomplish this week. You also need clarity on how to get those little things done, things like running to the printer to pick up the brochures or sending the forms off to the accountant. You also need some way to organize how you contact your clients, which helps you stay on top of an important aspect of your business and keep it growing in the right direction.

Yet another necessary task is paying bills. You can do it haphazardly, but you may wind up paying consequences—and late fees—you won't like. Finally, you need to focus on your invoicing system: When do you charge? How do you expect payment? When do you follow up? Not staying on top of this one may cause you unexpected trouble when an invoice or two falls through the cracks and nobody notices until your checks start bouncing.

### Been There, Done That

*"Depending on the type of business you do, remember that rejection does not mean that your business does not have the potential to be successful. With every rejection, there's something you can learn. Keep focused and keep your confidence up, and keep plugging away."*

—work-at-home mother of two

## A Plan-Your-Week System

Every Monday morning, first thing, sit down with a cup of coffee and plan out the major goals you have for the week. What do you want to have accomplished by Friday afternoon? Break those goals into steps and assign them days. Write them on your calendar. Then simply follow the schedule: That's your "big picture" for the week!

*Fight the temptation to start worrying about or planning work on Sunday night. Tell yourself, "No, that's work—I'll think about it when I'm in the office tomorrow." I've found that that helps me enjoy my Sundays and leaves me refreshed and ready to tackle work on the workdays.*

| What do I need to accomplish by Friday? | What day will I do this? |
| --- | --- |
| 1. _____ | _____ |
| 2. _____ | _____ |
| 3. _____ | _____ |
| 4. _____ | _____ |
| 5. _____ | _____ |

At the end of the week, review your list. What did you get done? What didn't you get done? Evaluate how realistic your goals were and focus on how much you *did* accomplish during the week.

## A To-Do or Not To-Do System

Now you know how you're going to spend your week. Great! But invariably little things will pop up. How will you handle all the little to-dos that force their way into your days? The to-do list is a great tool, as long as you don't let it control your life. Things that go on the to-do list are those you need to get done as soon as possible but that generally won't make or break your business if they go on until tomorrow. Your to-do list might look like this:

- Print the checkbook register report for my accountant

- Mail bills

- Send out contracts

- Call Cindy about cards

- Follow up on three client contacts

- Sketch out the new logo

It's easy to spend out entire day working on the to-do list and never get around to the big picture items we've already defined. Here are a few ways to keep to-dos under control:

**Have a to-do list cutoff time.** For example, any to-do you add to your list after lunch, don't even think about doing until tomorrow. That enables you to do whatever you'd planned on your Weekly Schedule, plus any to-dos on your list from this morning, in one workday. If Paul calls and wants you to read through his report at 3:00 this afternoon, tell him you'll do it first thing in the morning. If he calls you at 8:30 in the morning and you've got time to fit it in, put in on your to-do list for today.

**Prioritize and arrange your to-dos.** For a long time I didn't prioritize to-do items. I'd make myself follow the list, one by one. It wasn't much fun and, with hindsight, I see it wasn't very efficient either. Some to-do items might take just a moment, like calling Cindy and telling her the business cards are in. Others might take an hour, like driving to town to deliver the newsletters to your client. Arrange your to-dos from most important to least important, and be willing to pull one from the middle of the list if it fits the time you have available.

**Delegate to-dos whenever possible.** Being in business for yourself doesn't mean being in business *by* yourself. There are other people at home—enlist their help! The kids can make copies, older kids can file things, younger kids can staple and stack. Ask them what they'd like to do. And best of all, from their perspective anyway, you can pay them! Many home businesses rely on child labor to fill in the to-do gaps. Talk to your accountant about how to arrange it so your kids are on the payroll if they'd like to be involved.

*Involving your kids in your business is a great idea, and one I didn't think of on my own. One night quite a while ago, my kids were grumbling because I was working late. I was feeling guilty, and tired, and stressed from a deadline looming in my not-so-distant future. A friend had a suggestion. "Sit down and explain exactly what you're trying to do and tell them how they can help," she said. "If they learn more about your business, they'll feel a part of it and won't resent it when it demands more of your time than they want to give." Smart words from a smart lady.*

## A System for Staying in Contact

It's sounds funny, but it's true: Other people are the lifeblood of our businesses. Oh, we may do the work of providing the service or making the product, but it's our customers' desire for what we do or make that enables us to earn a living. How do you keep track of potential customers? What do you do when someone has a question about your business? Do you actively pursue new clients, or do you think you have all the work you need?

**BEST &
WORST**

*Worst:
"Trying to find
time alone
with my wife."*

The way you answer those questions will affect how quickly your business grows and, perhaps, how steady your work will be. The way you work with contacts will depend largely on the type of business you have. Your product or service may apply to the masses or be targeted at a select few. In either case, organizing, maintaining, and responding to contacts is an important part of running a successful business.

As you think about setting up a system to organize your contacts, ask yourself these questions:

How do you get new business?

 What do you do with the names of potential customers?

 How do you keep customers once you've got them?

 How often do you contact your customers?

You might get names of potential customers from client lists, from the phone book, from friends and neighbors, from networking luncheons, or by personal contact. Once you have a new customer's name, what do you do with it? Do you file it away in your "someday" file, in case he or she ever calls you? Do you take action with the information by sending a flyer or following up with a phone call?

Once you have a new customer, do you do anything special to keep her happy? Of course, quality services or products are the best customer-service item you can offer, but there are other things you can do, too. Send out postcard mailings every so often. Get your name in front of your customers again, and let them know you remember them. Announce specials, sales, or new promotions. Let your customers know you're still around, doing what you do, and that you hope you get the opportunity to serve them again ... soon.

*Give yourself a deadline for acting on your contacts. When you get a new name or business card, for example, resolve to contact the person—by phone or mail— within three business days. Then follow your resolution. Make it a standard in your business. You'll soon find that you're acting on more leads, following up on more business, and finding more doors open to you.*

There are several software programs that can help you keep up with your contacts. One of these is *Contact Manager*, a program available for both Macs and IBM-compatibles that enables you to track, plan, and schedule the contacts you need to make. If you call a client on Monday, for example, and he asks you to touch base in two weeks when he's ready to reorder, you can enter that information directly in the program and then be reminded when it's time to call him back. The *Contact Manager* lists all the contacts you need to make and provides a history of past information related to that client.

Another kind of program that's invaluable for organizing customer data is the database. There are several good database programs available, for all kinds of computers. Some of the most popular are *Microsoft Access, Paradox for Windows,* and *FileMaker Pro.* Some database programs are included in a collection (or suite) of different applications: That's the case with *Microsoft Works for Windows*, which has an easy-to-use database as well as a word processor, spreadsheet, and communications program. A database program lets you to enter all the necessary information—name, address, city, state, ZIP, phone, fax, order number, comments, interests, profession, and so on—about your contacts. From the information you enter, you can create mailing labels and reports and sort your data according to specific items. ("Let's see how many clients I've got living in Seymour.")

One parent I interviewed was having trouble with his partner, who worked from home but without kids.

## Money out the Door: A Bill-Paying System

Perhaps I was naive, but for the longest time I didn't have any kind of bill-paying system. I was just too busy. I was writing, writing, writing. Once in a while I'd look up and notice that some of the bills on the top of Bill Mountain said "past due." Then I'd pay those bills and go back to writing, writing, writing.

> ### Professional Parent Panic!
> *"I have explained to my partner in as many ways as I know how about the fact that I am the primary caregiver and therefore not as flexible as he is. He continues to suggest that we could hire people to do this for me, completely missing the point that I don't want someone else taking care of my daughter. I believe that the primary caregiver for my child should be one or both of her parents. I don't want to hire a nanny. That's part of the reason I work at home."*
>
> —work-at-home father of one

Finally, I began realizing that probably wasn't a good thing, and if I wanted to be more responsible, I'd have to start bulldozing Bill Mountain and taking charge of my payables.

If you have a household method of paying bills, you can extend that to your home-based business. I've found that choosing a different day to pay business bills has helped me keep business and personal expenses straight. If your bills are such that, either for cash-flow reasons or for scheduling reasons, you need to choose more than one day a month, by all means do it. The idea is simply to choose the day you *will* pay the bills, and then do it on the day you said you would.

One item that can help you keep your bills organized is a monthly bill sheet. This little beauty not only reminds you of what's due but helps you see when something's missing. ("Hey, I don't remember getting a long-distance bill this month!") It also reminds you of the repeating costs you can expect for the months to come. A monthly bill sheet might look something like this:

## My-at-Home-Business, Inc.
Monthly Bill Sheet: May 1999

| Date Due | Bill | Amount | Date Paid | Balance |
|---|---|---|---|---|
| 3 | Dell Computer | 125.00 | 5-1-99 | 279.00 |
| 5 | Accountant | 75.00 | 5-1-99 | 115.00 |
| 7 | Internet Services | 19.95 | 5-1-99 | on-going |
| | | | | |
| | | | | |
| | | | | |
| | | | | |
| | | | | |
| | | | | |
| | | | | |
| | | | | |
| | | | | |
| | | | | |
| | | | | |
| | | | | |
| | | | | |

**Total Monthly Business Debt:**_____

**Total Balance Debt:** _____

## Money in the Door: An Invoicing System

You won't be in business very long if you don't
have some kind of invoicing system. How do you
charge for what you do? Do you rely on your
clients to pay you whenever they get around to it?
Probably not. You need a method of billing them,
letting them know that your work is complete and
it's time to pay the provider.

Depending on your personality and your business,
you may feel strange invoicing at first. Don't.
Invoicing is nothing to be sheepish about. You've
provided a service or a product the client is
willing—and expected—to pay for. When a client is
late on a payment, contact him. Don't be
embarrassed—it's his failure to pay, not yours. You
don't need to be antagonistic, either: Just call to let
him know *you* know his check has been in the
mail a long, long time.

But let's concentrate on the pleasant end first.
Once you've got an invoice you can use (you can
design your own based on the example later in
this chapter or buy a pad of invoices at your local
office supply store), decide how soon after you
complete your work you will send it out. Within
one day? Two days? A week? A good rule of thumb
is, the sooner the better. If you resolve to send out
the invoice the day you complete the work or ship
the product, you are more likely to stay on top of
the billing, and the customer is more likely to pay
while the service is fresh in his mind.

What terms do you expect? Do you expect the
client to pay in full? Will you accept partial
payments? Do you want to offer a discount for
customers who pay within a 30-day time frame?
There are several options you can consider: After
all, it's your invoicing system.

Once you receive a payment, how do you track it?
Years ago many small businesses relied on a
bookkeeping system called a One-Write system to
track their income and expenses. The good old-

fashioned Dome book was another way to record the receivables and payables of business. Today there computer programs that do the same kinds of things faster, better, and (if you add like I do) more accurately. Talk to your accountant about programs like *Quicken* and *QuickBooks for Windows* to see if his system is set up to receive electronic files. If so, using a program to record invoices when they come in and your expenses when they go out takes a lot of hassle out of your business bookkeeping.

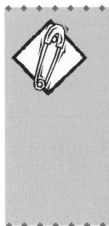

*And don't forget the sprinkler system. What? Yes, that's what it says. While we're talking about systems, don't forget the most important part of working at home: sprinkles of real life throughout the day. Enjoy those pieces of your life, let your kids make you laugh, take a moment to share a cookie and a cup of cocoa. We should allow ourselves those little moments with our families during the day—or we might as well be back in the office.*

# Getting the Word Out

Your reputation is an important part of your business success. When you have a service or product to offer, the world needs to know what you've got and why they should choose your business over the competition.

### How Do People Get the Word Out?

Here are a few traditional ways of marketing your home-based business:

   Direct mail

   Brochures

- Faxes
- Telemarketing
- Online networking
- Referrals
- Friends and relatives
- Newsletters
- The *Yellow Pages*
- Trade shows
- Demonstrations
- Print and radio advertising

When you first start your business, you may not have money to invest in "real" advertising—that is, print, radio, or television advertisements; mailings; billboards; Web site ads; and such. There are a number of ways you can increase visibility for your business, however, and start building your reputation in the meantime.

## Low-Cost Marketing

Think about raising awareness of your business with these ideas:

**Put a blurb in the paper.** Most newspapers have a kind of "Who's News?" column in which they announce business promotions, new hires, whatever local businesses send them. You can send in a short paragraph (under 200 words) and even a picture of yourself, announcing your business, what you'll be doing, and how long you've been a resident in the community. Papers won't do this more than once (although you can send in a "new hire" paragraph if you hire

someone), but you may be able to get a
reporter interested in a feature story if your
idea or your business is unique or tied to a
community activity or a seasonal theme.

**Create a presence at community events.**
Depending on the service or product you're
offering, you might get a booth for your
products at a home show, display your crafts
in the local mall, or volunteer your party-
planning service for a local school event.

**Send out letters.** Well-thought-out letters to
the right people can do a lot toward
spreading the word about your new business.
Which people in your community would
benefit from your service? If you sell a line
of holistic pet care items, you don't need to
send a blanket letter to the entire city; just
target the veterinarians in your area who
might be interested in holistic animal care
items. And remember, it's always better to
send a letter to a specific person, and not just
"to whom it may concern" or "office
manager."

*Don't underestimate the value of
volunteering. If you've got a service to
offer—perhaps you have a window-
cleaning business—donate your services
to a humanitarian organization once in a
while. You might clean the windows of a
local youth home, offer to remove the
Christmas paint from your church's
windows, help elderly folk in your
community caulk and seal their windows
for winter—you get the idea. This is not
only good for your business, increasing
good will and spreading a positive feeling
about your company, it's good for you,
too. You might be surprised when you
see the return on your investment.*

**Get listed in directories.** Your local phone company lists businesses with business lines in the *Yellow Pages*. There are other business directories published in your area, as well. Talk to the Chamber of Commerce to find out what kind of business directories are produced in your city and find out how to become part of them.

 **Teach at your local community college.** With the exploding popularity of community colleges and continuing education classes, you may have a marketable, teachable skill. Perhaps you could do a seminar introducing pet lovers to your holistic pet care products. Or you could teach a Saturday class on planning and giving parties (and raise awareness of your party-planning service). Each time you face a class, you are introducing your business to a room full of people, who will then go out and talk to even more people, who will talk to still more people. Pretty good awareness-raising for an afternoon's work.

 **Think cable.** No, don't laugh—cable is the airwave for the rest of us. You don't have to be Martha Stewart to have a show on cable; in fact, your local public access channel is required by law to give the public the airwaves. Contact your local cable station director with an idea related to your business: *Party Planning with Pamela* or *Holistic Pet Handling*. Be aware that you'll have to do it all yourself, from writing to taping to editing to producing. And there will be costs involved. Still, it's a creative way to get potentially massive business exposure.

 **Be aware of personal contacts.** Remember that each time you speak to another person about your business, you are a living advertisement. The way you speak, dress, move, and laugh all tell the other person something about you, your motivation, and the kind of work you could do for them. Don't be afraid to mention that you are working at home and tell other people what you do. That contact could grow into a customer. If you are caring and attentive to other people, you are telling them that you will listen to their needs as customers. If you are brash and dominate the conversation, they'll think you're more interested in hearing yourself talk than in tending to their needs, which doesn't make for a good business partnership.

**Use the phone.** You might be surprised to see how many potential clients you can find in the *Yellow Pages* or a local business directory. Don't be afraid to call a company that could use your service and talk about what you're offering. If doesn't cost a cent to make a local call, and the next call after that "No, thanks" might be a "Yes."

*Dedicate a set number of hours per week to marketing your business. Maybe every Wednesday afternoon you can spend an hour thinking about how you'll market your business. And make sure your thinking doesn't go to waste: End the hour with a list of specific to-do items to add to your list (and when you plan to do them), so that you are gradually implementing your marketing ideas.*

## Testing Your Ideas

One of the potential hazards of working at home by yourself (and this I know from experience) is the danger of thinking you're right all the time. There's only one way to do something, and you've thought of it! Great, but before you act, take your idea to two or three trusted friends, peers, or mentors. (This is where a business advisor really comes in handy.) What is your marketing plan? Write it down and take it to your advisor and ask, "Okay, what's wrong with this?"

If your plan involves spending $1,000 to market a $5 item, you may need someone to point out that it might be too early in your business process for that kind of expense. If there's something you haven't thought of, someone with an objective opinion may be able to spot it. If there's a better way, you want to know, right?

Be prepared to be shot out of the water a few times. When you ask for other peoples' opinions, you're usually going to get them. The opinions may be right or they may not. But at least you'll be able to take all the data you accumulate and make your decision from a broader vantage point. And you'll have an idea of how the masses will react, even if they are wrong and don't know it.

Marketing ideas I'd like to try:

1. _____

2. _____

3. _____

4. _____

5. _____

Friends or advisors who can review these ideas:

_____

_____

_____

_____

## Software Supports for Marketing

A number of different programs can help you learn about marketing techniques and then apply them to your specific business. Here are a few of the most popular:

- *Advertise Your Business* is a CD-ROM published by NEBS Software that teaches you the basics of marketing your business. You'll learn the value and differences of various marketing campaigns and find out how to get the most from your marketing dollar.

- Another CD-ROM that helps you master the basics of marketing is *Guerrilla Marketing*, from Houghton Mifflin Interactive. This is actually a tutorial program that helps you create a marketing program, complete with 25 marketing tools unique for your needs.

A program popular with work-at-home telemarketers is *PhoneDisc Powerfinder Plus*, a CD-ROM that includes a national telephone directory.

You'll also find places on the World Wide Web that can give you new angles and help you evaluate old ones on marketing your business:

 Want to trade horror stories or get advice from the pros? Visit the Idea Cafe, a cyberspace coffee house where business owners gather to toss around good, original, or tried-and-true ideas. You'll find the Idea Cafe at http://www.IdeaCafe.com/.

 It's no secret that the phone line doesn't just take us to another phone anymore: It can move us across the world, through cyberspace, and into new realities. AT&T offers the AT&T Home Business Resource Center to help you learn to use your computer to create a communications center for your home-based business. Visit their Web page at http://www.att.com/bhr/.

 *Talk to your kids about your business and ask their ideas for getting the word out. If you've got the kind of service or product they go for—such as Internet publishing, children's book writing, party planning, or mobile DJ services—they might have some new, creative ideas for you. If your service or product is related to kids, you can even enlist their help in drawing your logo, designing a flyer, or proposing a slogan for your business cards. And even if you don't use their ideas, they'll appreciate being asked. It puts the "family" feeling in family business.*

> **Profiles**
> **Name:** Susan
> **Business:** Writing and editing
> **How long?** Nine years
> **How many kids?** One, age 8
> **Biggest challenge:** Not letting work take over the rest of my life.
> **Best answer to that challenge:** Set up work hours and stick to them. I try not to work evenings and weekends.

## The Check Is in the Mail

For many of us, billing isn't the easiest part of running a home-based business. We're not sure what our invoices should look like, how long we should give our customers to pay, and how often we should follow up, among other things.

First and foremost, you should strive to look professional. Create an invoice that lists your company name (and logo, if you've got one), address, phone, fax, and e-mail. Include a space for your customer's name, the contact person, the address, and the type of work performed. Include a space for comments, a column for hours worked, a total line, and a place for the total amount due. If your business is incorporated, you need to include your Federal ID number. If you are a sole proprietor, list your Social Security number.

Make sure your invoice is easy for your customer to read. Clearly marked in a Remit to: area of the Invoice, you should include the name and address you want the payment sent to. On page 250, you'll find a sample invoice:

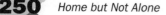

# My-at-Home-Business, Inc.
Federal ID: 35-19999999
2323 West Hill Blvd.
South Bend, IN 47401
Phone: 219-333-3333
Fax: 219-333-3334

Date: _____

Invoice #:_____

## Customer Information
Customer: _____

Contact name: _____

Address: _____

City/St: _____

ZIP code: _____

Phone: _____

## Project Description
Work performed: _____

Date begun: _____

Date completed:_____

Total number of hours: _____

## Project Cost
Charge per hour _____

Total amount due this invoice: _____

*Please remit to the address shown above.*
*Thank you for your business!*

*If you want to encourage your customers to pay promptly, offer a small percentage off for accounts paid within 30 days of the billing date.*

A number of software programs can help you with billing. *Microsoft Works for Windows* includes several templates (that is, predesigned files) you can use for a variety of business documents. You can use a Wizard (an automated program feature) to create your own invoice just the way you want it. Other programs, like *QuickBooks for Windows* or *Simply Business,* help you create and use the invoices you need, calculating and displaying the amounts you enter and printing invoices from within the program.

## Staying on Top of Time

In this chapter, you've learned about different ways to organize the different aspects of your business. What does all this organization give you? More time. More time to work productively. More time to be creative. More time with your family. More time to relax. Less clutter in your brain, which causes you to work more slowly, eating up more time.

You already know about scheduling, and how important it is to create a plan for your week and then follow it. You also learned what to do about the to-dos that creep into your day. You decided when and how to deal with billing and invoicing, and set aside a certain amount of time each week to work on marketing ideas. This section spotlights a few more ideas on how to use your time during the week:

> **Think about how much delay is costing you.** When you begin to realize how much more money and time you spend when you don't act on something immediately, it will

motivate you to take care of it quickly. When you don't make the computer payment on time and must pay a $20 late fee, it costs you money. When you don't return that client's call and she goes to your competitor, it costs you money. When you don't keep track of your income and expenses and your accountant has to sort through it all at the end of the year, believe me, it's going to cost you money.

**If you're stuck, you'll only get stuck-er.** When you find yourself slowing down in your business, feeling either listless or confused, and you're not sure what to do next, get yourself moving again by working on whatever's nearest. That feeling of being overwhelmed by work—20 phone calls to return, e-mail to answer, a report to finish, and dogs to bathe (oh, wait, scratch that last one)—can make you want to just go back to bed and stay there. But don't give up! Look at your weekly schedule and use your to-do list to get moving again, even if you don't feel like it. Once you start accomplishing things, you'll feel better, and soon you'll find yourself ripping full-speed through the rest of your day.

**Use deadlines to your advantage.** Many people cringe when they hear the word *deadline*. But deadlines can be useful if you use them as end-points. Where do I want to be by Friday afternoon? That's a kind of deadline, but it's really a goal. It's what you're shooting for. And having goals— especially specific, targeted goals—is an important part of starting your home business. Plan the small steps and reach them, and before you know it you'll be a lot further down the path than you had expected to be. Each goal you reach gives you added momentum to the reach the next. So set deadlines for yourself—or call them goals, if that's better—and then reward yourself when you make them.

**Break a huge job into small steps.** When you've got a major project under way, keep yourself moving forward by dividing into small steps what you need to accomplish. Each step you take—like the goals we just talked about—gives you something you've accomplished, which adds to your confidence and strengthens you as you continue working on the job. Celebrate the small successes along the way while you work toward the big picture.

**Leave yourself a clean office to come back to in the morning.** Late in the afternoon, or at the end of your workday, straighten up your office. Put away files you got out. Put the books back on the shelf. Put the pens back in the holder. Throw away the scraps of paper you doodled on while you were talking to your supplier on the phone. When you come in to the office in the morning, you'll be ready to work in a clean, neat space, and you won't have yesterday's mess to clear away first.

**At the end of the day, do a review.** Use the last five minutes of your workday to look back over what you've accomplished. Allow yourself to feel some satisfaction. Another day spent building your home business. There will be things that didn't get done, but don't let them overshadow the things you *did* get done. Add them to tomorrow's list, if you need to, but end the day on a positive note.

Now take a deep breath, let the workday go, and go play with your family.

# On the Home Front

*Did you think, now that you're working at home, your house would always be clean? Did you hope your kids would be so glad to have you home they would stop fighting forever? Soon after we make the initial decision, life begins to fall short of our expectations. This part of the book starts with a reality check. Adjustments aren't fun, but they are easier if you see them coming.*

*Can't do all the household tasks you used to? Delegate them! (This part tells you how.)*

*The book winds up with two important chapters on finding time for yourself and living happily ever after. Finding time for yourself starts with small things—like taking a deep breath when you need it—and living happily ever after happens almost by accident. One day you look back and realize the kids are happy, the house is passably clean, your business is thriving, and life is good. I can't wait! Can you?*

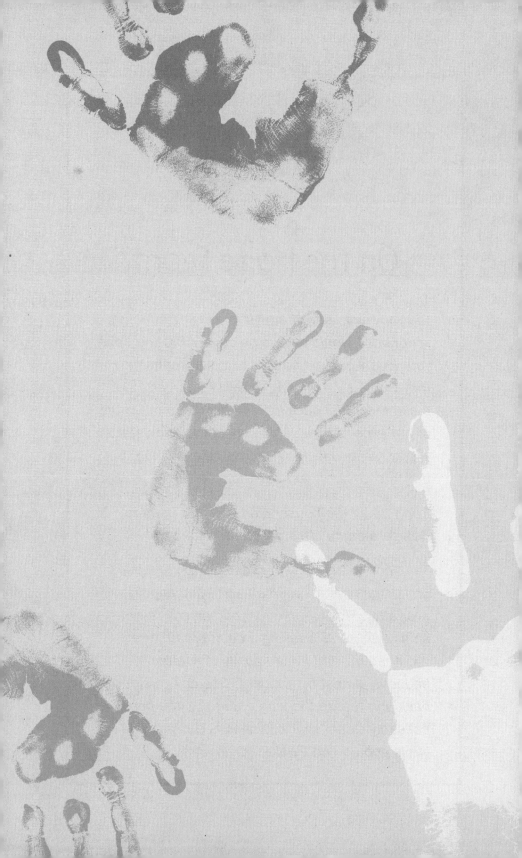

# Adjustments, Adjustments

> *"If life is a bowl of cherries, what am I doing in the pits?"*
> —Erma Bombeck[1]

You may think you've taken the easy road. Working at home cuts out many of the "have tos." You know,

> *"I have to get to work on time."*

> *"I have to get my suit back from the cleaner so I can wear it to work tomorrow."*

*"I have to take Stephanie to the daycare center early so I'll have time to stop and get gas."*

Trading in your leisure suit for a jogging suit seems like a good trade, after all. Getting the kids busy with the modeling clay in the family room while you look over your list of morning calls is less stressful than getting them dressed, ready, in the car on time, and delivered to the daycare center, sleepy-eyed, thumbs in mouths, with their blankies still tucked under their little arms.

**BEST** & WORST

*Best:* "Being able to go on school field trips."

But the move from work to home, albeit a good one, also brings a number of adjustments. Boundaries you used to count on are gone. The way you knew yourself—as both a professional and a parent—is in the process of changing. And change brings stress.

This chapter helps you think about some of the issues you face as you begin adjusting to life as a work-at-home parent. And remember, you're not doing this in a vacuum: Your whole family is feeling the change. With some anticipation and some communication, however, you can make sure your family pulls together to keep stress from pulling you apart.

## Take a Reality Check

Sometimes we get going so fast we don't stop to consider how far we've come. Take a little mental trip with me back to a point in time six months ago.

For the full effect, flip back in your DayTimer to the date six months ago today. What did you have planned? What was your life like? What was your morning routine?

Perhaps you were working in an office eight hours a day. It was a mad dash in the morning: gobbling down breakfast as fast as you could (or skipping it completely) and getting the kids to the bus stop and yourself to the on-ramp on time. After school, Michael and Mindy stayed home alone until you arrived back as close to 5:30 as you could manage. Life was short, fast, and exhausting. Looking back, you might feel a sense of awe that you were able to keep up with the pace. And you might catch a glimpse of how far toward your goals you've come in half a year.

Maybe you were working happily for a company that, unknown to you, was about to close. You were comfortable with your child-care arrangements and settled in your situation. Looking back, you might feel a mix of emotions, both happy and sad. Even though the event that closed your company was an unhappy one, many good things have resulted from it. If you focus on the amount of ground you've covered since then, you'll be able to see how many doors have begun to open to you since the old one closed.

You might have been preparing to leave work for the birth of your first child. (If that's the case, what an amazing six months you've been through!) After the birth, you began working at home for your employer. The months that have passed have brought many changes for your family, for you, and in your professional situation. Looking back, you might feel amazed at the number of things you had to learn; you might also feel some pride in having learned so much.

Perhaps six months ago you were right where you are now: at home. You may have been thinking about starting your own business or talking to your employer about working at home. Maybe you're thinking the same thing today. Or maybe you've taken steps toward that goal. In any case, feel good about where you are and recognize that nobody leapfrogs through life—we all learn what we need a day at a time. Any progress you've made is progress to celebrate.

When you look at your life in terms of what's changed for you, you can easily see where the adjustments come in. What's changed in the last six months?

_____

_____

_____

_____

# Welcome to Fantasy Island

In his book *Jobshift*, William Bridges writes about "islands of order," places where you go to find yourself again, to stop the flow of constant information you process in your mind.[2] Your island might be a place, such as the kitchen table, the laundry room, the swing in the backyard, or the corner coffee shop. It might be a time, like sunrise, sunset, nap time, or some other sacred moment. Or it might be an activity, such as gardening, walking the dog, folding laundry (*really?*), or cooking.

Whatever the case for you, it's important to realize that as you move from the workforce to the homeforce, you might be losing one or more of your islands of order. Not going to lunch with coworkers may not seem like such a big price, but there are days when you'll miss it. Those few quiet moments after the sales meeting when you could review life issues with your boss—that may seem like a silly thing compared to the freedom and excitement of running your own business, but there will be times when you feel the loss of the relationship, the time, and the deep shared thought.

Keep an eye on yourself as you make the shift. And remember that those islands need replacing. Give yourself time to relax, to dream, to get away. Not only does all work make Jack a dull boy; it also makes him ineffective, unproductive, and unpleasant.

| Here's what I do to not think: | (Here are some ideas) |
|---|---|
| _____ | work in the garden |
| _____ | watch sports |
| _____ | jog |
| _____ | read |
| _____ | sew |
| _____ | play the guitar |

# The Times, They Are a'Changin'

Who said it? "The only thing you can count on around here is that things will change." Change is a permanent part of our lives. Keisha won't be wearing braces in two years, and Tony will be walking by Christmas. Your business won't be in the same place, with the same clients, and the same projects next week, next month, or next year. Each day you live, you'll do things just a little differently than you did the day before.

It's part of the human condition.

Since we know we can bank on change (although not what change will bring), it's in our best interests to learn how to work with it. You can use change to your advantage, but you've got to be quick on your feet, riding your business like a surfboard on a tricky wave.

◆ ◆ ◆ ◆ ◆ ◆ ◆ ◆ ◆ ◆ ◆ ◆ ◆ ◆ ◆ ◆ ◆ ◆ ◆ ◆ ◆ ◆ ◆ ◆ ◆ ◆

*"When you make peace with changes in your life, adjusting to them is as simple as accepting what's going on."*

◆ ◆ ◆ ◆ ◆ ◆ ◆ ◆ ◆ ◆ ◆ ◆ ◆ ◆ ◆ ◆ ◆ ◆ ◆ ◆ ◆ ◆ ◆ ◆ ◆

Mastering change means being able to ride out tumultuous waters in both your professional and personal life, and (let me be the first to admit it) it's not always easy. But working on your ability to handle change—and even learning to welcome and thrive on it—means being ahead of the game in accepting things as they are, which gives you a decided advantage. You won't be afraid to try new things. You'll have an open mind about your family, about business, about life. Your chances of succeeding—*really* succeeding, beyond your current dreams—are dramatically increased when you open yourself up to change, because you won't just stick with a proven path for solving your problems. You'll be creative and discover your own unique ways to achieve the goals you've set for yourself and your family.

## Hold Those Expectations Loosely

Part of what keeps us from accepting change is that the situations we're presented with don't match the ones we've created in our minds. For example, suppose you thought your mornings would go like this when you started working at home:

 Up at 6:00

 Shower and dressed by 7:00

 Kids fed and dressed by 7:30

 Kids ready for the school bus at 7:45

## What's Your Change Factor?

Circle the number in the following columns that best fits your attitude for each listed item.

|  | Not! | So-So |  | That's Me! |  |
|---|---|---|---|---|---|
| I like trying new things. | 1 | 2 | 3 | 4 | 5 |
| I like adventures. | 1 | 2 | 3 | 4 | 5 |
| I like trying new restaurants. | 1 | 2 | 3 | 4 | 5 |
| I enjoy learning a new skill. | 1 | 2 | 3 | 4 | 5 |
| I like meeting new people. | 1 | 2 | 3 | 4 | 5 |
| Change is easy for me. | 1 | 2 | 3 | 4 | 5 |

Now add up all the points you circled and read on:

**30 points:** What?! Perfect score. You should be writing this chapter.

**20 to 29:** Consider yourself well-versed in change management. You probably are already seeing more fun, freedom, and creativity—and less stress—in your life

**10 to 19:** There's an opportunity for some stretching here. Try one of these items—a new restaurant, a new skill, meeting new people, having an adventure—once a week for six weeks. You'll see yourself getting more comfortable with change, and you'll like the results.

**1 to 9:** Okay, so taking a quiz like this is a change for you, isn't it? Don't be disheartened: A low score is really a great opportunity waiting to be seized. Stretch your horizons; try something new. Or, if that feels too far out for you right now, read a book or article about someone you admire. Notice the places in the person's life that brought about the changes that made him or her great.

Work from 8:00 to 3:00

 Housework from 3:00 to 4:00

 Fun with the kids from 4:00 to 5:30

 Start supper at 5:30

 Evening with family

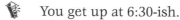

*"Hold on to your expectations loosely, because what really happens during your day may be more wonderful than what you expected to happen."*

Sounds pretty nice, pretty relaxed. You may have even had one or two days that worked out that way. But days can also go something like this:

 You get up at 6:30-ish.

 The kids take forever getting ready.

 Keith can't find his homework.

 Sandy forgets to brush her teeth until the bus is coming down the road.

 The dog tears up the morning newspaper.

 You don't get your shower until everybody leaves at 7:45.

 Just as you step out of the shower, Keith calls from school to say he left his homework on the kitchen table.

 From 9:00 to 9:30, you're out taking Keith's homework to school.

 You decide to stop by the printer to check on a project.

 You get home and turn on the computer, ready to work, at 11:00.

The phone rings; it's your mother-in-law.

   You begin working at 11:25 and can't find the
file you need. You spend the next 30 minutes
searching through your disk boxes for the
right file.

And we haven't even gotten to lunch yet. Reality
and expectations rarely match; that's where the
ability to accept change, to ride the waves, comes
in really handy. If you can hold on loosely to what
you hope to accomplish this week—not moment
by moment or even day by day—and do your best
to get there, knowing that life will throw curve
balls at you along the way, you'll be doing a great
job of adjusting as you go. Which helps your
spouse adjust, and your kids adjust, and your pets
adjust. (Even my plants were happier when I
started letting go of some of my unrealistic
expectations.)

## An Important Difference

There's a difference between looking at your expectations
realistically and just lowering your expectations. I wouldn't want
to tell anyone to settle for less than they hope for. Don't lower
your expectations of having a happy family, a successful home
business, a great work-at-home arrangement, health,
prosperity, togetherness, and more. Those are great
expectations and worth working for.

The difficulty comes when we lock ourselves into those
expectations right now, thinking if we aren't a happy family
*today*, if we don't reach the deadline we set for ourselves *this
afternoon*, or our kids aren't pitching in *right now*, we are failing
somehow. This sets us up for major stress, which ripples into
every facet of our lives. Holding on to those expectations
loosely means that you know they are your ideal, and you'll get
there sooner or later (probably later). You can learn to be okay
with that, and relax a little even in the midst of imperfections,
without lowering your standards.

## Making Peace with the Process

Even though many of the significant events in our lives—getting married, becoming parents, changing jobs—happen all of a sudden, we continue processing those events for a lifetime. For example, one minute you weren't married. The next—after you put the ring on her finger, flipped back the veil, and kissed her—you were. One minute you weren't a parent. The next, someone is handing you a squalling red infant and calling you "Mommy." Two months ago, you didn't work at home. One day between then and now, perhaps, you closed the door to that office, turned in your key, and started working at home.

Although each of those events represents a turning point, we spend each day of our lives walking on the paths those events opened for us. Most of us aren't terrific at being married as soon as we leave the church. It takes years (and *years and years*, my ex-husband would say) to get good at being married. And you've heard the old cliché that kids don't come with instruction books? Well, it's worse than that: They actually are programmed to do just the opposite of what you want them to, right from the start. You've got to overcome your own stuff before you can even begin to deal with their stuff. How long does it take to be a good parent? I don't know if anyone has ever lived long enough to figure that one out.

Similarly, working at home is going to be a daily walk. Each day you'll learn something that will help you tomorrow. You'll look back after a month and see that your family is adjusting better, that you're drawing better boundaries, that more work is getting done, and that you're happier with your schedule. And you'll look back from a point even farther down the road and see even greater improvements. And then will come that terrific revelation, sometime after the kids are all in school all day and you've actually got a moment when you don't have anything at all to do, when the thought will bubble up: "Gosh, I'm glad I work at home!"

# Are You Resisting Change?

For a long time I was a work-at-home soldier. I regimented myself with a particular schedule and I stuck with it, no matter what. I was very productive. I was highly efficient. But I wasn't enjoying myself very much.

One rainy, self-analyzing afternoon, I realized I was resisting the idea that anything could change. The way I'd been running my business had been successful for me. I was scared that if I changed things I wouldn't be as successful as I had been. If I let go of my process, I might not be motivated the way I needed to be. If I gave myself permission to play, I ran the danger of not ever wanting to work.

When you first begin working at home, enjoying yourself may not be foremost in your mind. In fact, it probably shouldn't be your primary goal, although it should have a part in the work you choose to do and where and how you do it. But as you continue your business or your work-at-home arrangement, you'll realize that you do need to be happy in what you're doing. Contentment, happiness, and joy are all emotions that make you more productive, more creative, and more fun to be around. (Just ask your kids!)

Are you resisting change? Is there an easier way to do what you do? Are there changes you could make that would give you more freedom, more time, more play opportunities, while still enabling you to get your work done?

## Hearing the Voice of Change

How do you know things need to change? There are two very real (and very similar) symptoms:

   Points of pressure

   Points of pain

A point of pressure is something—or some area—in your life that makes you cringe inside. There's something on your mind, or on your heart, that is worrying you. It might not be a big thing; in fact, in might be an imaginary thing that will never even happen. But a point of pressure feels very real, and it usually is a symptom of something that could be looked at in a different light.

For example, this morning, at 6:00 A.M., I shuffled down to my kitchen, gave my dogs breakfast, and noticed ... silence. Worry shot through me. Was the refrigerator working? I opened the door and looked in. Everything seemed okay, but there was no sound. No humming. I worried.

This morning, that was a point of pressure for me. Would it cost a lot to fix? How could I store the food that was in there until the repairman came? It's Friday, so that means I'd better call him today unless I want to pay double-time on the weekend.

Around 10:00, I went to the kitchen to get some tea. Much to the surprise of my wondering ears, the refrigerator was humming. All that worry—thankfully—came to nothing.

Points of pain are similar, but different. What jabs you every time you think about it? Do you feel guilty for not calling your mother? Should you have told that client you'd be unavailable for a week? Do you feel bad every time you have to tell your daughter you can't take her to a friend's house in the middle of the day? Do you sigh when you see the school bus coming because that means you won't get any more work done for the rest of the day?

For me, points of pain usually have nothing to do with my professional life: When there's something to be dealt with work-wise, it hits me as pressure. When there's pain, something has caused trouble in one of my most important relationships.

A recent example was a situation with my almost 16-year-old daughter, Kelly. She and I usually have an easy, lighthearted relationship. There's very little squaring off between us. But over a period of days, our time together had begun feeling strained. Pretty soon, every time I thought of her during the day, I felt this stab of pain. I knew the pain was a symptom. Something was wrong. I went to her and asked if there was something between us that needed to be addressed. It turned out I had said something in jest to a friend of mine and had hurt Kelly's feelings—she had felt I was making fun of her in front of my friends. The point of pain turned out to be right, and we were able to resolve it: I apologized, resolved to be more careful with my joking, and she promised to bring those kinds of things to my attention sooner so we don't go through three or four days of misunderstandings.

Your points of pressure might be deadlines in your work, people you dread dealing with, driving on the interstate, giving presentations to clients, or talking with your spouse about finances.

Points of pain might include that twinge you feel when you miss your friends at work; thinking of a project you lost to another business; the ache when you drop your daughter off at daycare for the third time in a week; or the guilt you feel when you realize your family had to skip the vacation to Florida this year because your business didn't take off as quickly as you'd hoped.

Give yourself 60 seconds and jot down in the space below a list of things in your life that are causing you either pressure or pain.

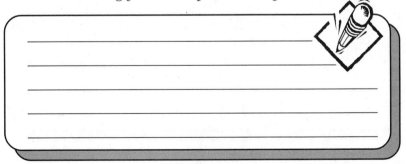

Everything that pops up in our lives as either a pressure point or a painful spot is something that requires creative thinking, problem solving—change. Otherwise, the pressure or pain wouldn't be there.

In my own case, I began to see the problem I'd created for myself. I started feeling bored and lonely while I was working. I'd look out the window on a sunny day and wish to be anywhere but inside those four office walls. My mind was leaving, even if I was forcing my body to stay at the desk.

## What Needs to Change?

You may need to make a change in your professional life, your emotional life, your marriage or relationship, your family, your communications with others, your profession, or on any number of other levels. Here are a few examples of points of pressure or pain and the possible changes they represent:

Now take another look at your own pressures list from a different perspective. Each pressure or pain you're experiencing is a call for attention to the trouble spot. What can you do to change it?

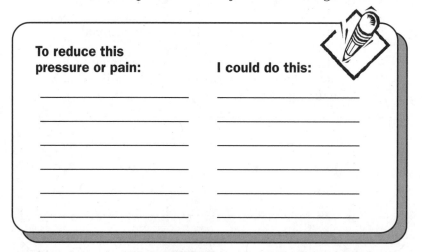

**To reduce this pressure or pain:**

**I could do this:**

| **Pressure/Pain** | **Change** |
|---|---|
| Meetings stress me out. | I can change the way I think about meetings. What stresses me most? If I make sure I'm prepared and go into the meeting with the idea that I can contribute something worth while and will benefit from the ideas others have, it will be a better experience. |
| I dread Sundays. | Why do I dread Sundays? I can change what I do on Sundays; what I do on Mondays (if that's what's stressing me out); what I think about; where I go; and, ultimately, my own attitude about Sundays. |
| The kids won't help me. | I can change the way I communicate with my kids so they understand that helping out is something we do as part of our family, not something that is a token "chore" they have to do to get an allowance. |
| I miss my friends at work. | Maybe I need to throw the window open and let some fresh air in, to change the way I look at my job and be more flexible with myself: Go to lunch once in a while. Play in the garden one morning. Visit friends in person or by phone once a week or so. |
| My daughter has green hair. | Here's one from my list—and it was a real perspective changer for me. Yes, my daughter had green hair for a while. And blue. And purple. I had to change my expectations of my daughter—what she should look like and who she was. She was getting older and looking for ways to be her own colorful personality. |

# Things Are Gonna Change Around Here!

So now you've identified a few areas presenting you with opportunities for change. Those thorns in your side—the neighbor who won't return your hedge clippers, the dog that keeps ... well, you know ... in your yard, the business partner who keeps scheduling meetings for the one time during the week you volunteer at your daughter's school, the 4-year-old who fingerpaints on your proposals—they are all there to test you.

How are you going to respond?

 You could run out to the end of your driveway and scream obscenities at your neighbor until he remembers that he borrowed the clippers last July and forgot to bring them back.

You could buy a bigger dog to attack the wandering canine that's leaving presents on your lawn.

You could bring your daughter's entire third-grade class to your meeting the next time your partner schedules a conflict.

  You could have your 4-year-old retype the entire proposal, even though he doesn't know how to read yet and you need to use the typewriter today.

None of those responses would be constructive, of course, although when we're hopping mad (and a few of us *do* get mad enough to hop about it), it feels good to fantasize about the look on your partner's face when he sees 23 9-year-olds filing into the conference room.

If each point of pressure or pain is simply a wake-up call to a change we need to make, what's the best way to make that change?

The first and most important answer is this: *Think.* Give yourself time to breathe a little, and think about what the best response would be. Think long enough that the emotion dies down and you can see, from a business perspective, what action is called for.

In the last section, you identified the problem and suggested a way to change it so you could resolve the issue. Once you've seen the problem clearly and considered a general solution, you can take a few steps to help make sure everyone affected understands (1) the need for the change; (2) what exactly is going to change; and (3) what to do if they don't like the change.

## Clueing Everybody In

**The scenario:** Dylan is 8 years old and he's messing up mornings. His mother, father, and sister are all morning people. Dylan wakes up grumpy. He doesn't want anyone to talk to him until after breakfast. He doesn't like cheery faces peering at him over his orange juice. It's summer and his mother runs a sales business from home.

**The problem:** Three mornings this week, Mom has had to cut business calls short because of Dylan's grumpiness. Once he fought with his sister; once he spilled his juice on the living room carpet and sat there yelling "Mom! Mom!" until she got off the phone; and once he answered the business phone (which he's not supposed to do) with a curt, "Waddya' want?"

**What needs to change?** It's easy to say "Dylan," isn't it? But Mom really needs to change the way mornings are set up. If she wants to work on Dylan's attitude, that's up to her, but the point of pressure is really where Dylan's early-morning grumpiness is impeding her business. With some thought, she can come up with a clear plan for early mornings that her kids can follow while she works: who does what, where, and when.

**Some solutions:** Perhaps Dylan will be allowed to sleep in or have his breakfast by himself in the family room. Maybe Mom will have Dylan stay right there with her, in a quiet space, until he's ready to interact with humans. In any case, Mom—and Dad—should communicate the need for change, explain what will change, and let the kids know that they will all reevaluate in a few weeks to assess the changes.

**Let's take another one.** Melissa is 13 and at the beginning of the mall-hopping stage of life. Over the summer, Mom and Dad have been giving her more responsibility and more freedom, and she's been doing a fine job with it. They hope she'll want to help out in their family home-based business, although in the few months since Dad started working full-time at home, she hasn't shown much interest.

**The problem:** Increasingly, Melissa has been asking Dad to take her here and there during normal business hours. She wants rides to the pool, to the store, and to her friends' houses. She asks Dad to pick up friends and bring them over. She has library plans, picnics, and church outings—all kinds of things during the day. At first, Dad was glad to help; he was pleased to be home and able to encourage her to make the most of her summer. But now he's beginning to feel like a taxi service, and Melissa is getting more and more demanding and increasingly petulant about the issue.

**What needs to change?** This situation gives both Dad and Mom the opportunity to explain their vision of the business to Melissa—what it means for them as a family, what they hope to achieve, how much work it requires, why they need to be accessible during work hours. They need to show Melissa where the boundaries are. How many times a week is Dad willing to take Melissa somewhere during work hours? Only during lunch time? After work?

**Some solutions:** Explaining what they are willing to do, why they are setting that boundary, and that, in special circumstances, they would consider exceptions, will help Melissa understand there's a reason behind the rule. And this resolution puts a clear system in place so Dad doesn't have to feel guilty or put-upon. He just follows the system.

There's one other opportunity here: the opportunity to help Melissa feel more a part of the business. After explaining what they need and why, Mom and Dad could enlist Melissa's help and concern—and perhaps encourage her to work with them—and take a step toward achieving that "family feeling" they hope for in their home-based business.

## Five Steps Toward a Kinder, Gentler Change

So you've established what the problem is, and you've given yourself time to think about a possible plan of action. Now you are ready to introduce the plan to the people it affects. You could go rip-roaring through the house in full battle gear like General Patton ... but there is an easier way. You can introduce the change—which really is the solution to some problem you're experiencing—very gently, by following these steps:

1.  **Think and plan first.** Take time to identify the problem and plan out your response. If you're still seeing red, you haven't waited long enough. If you can't remember what was bothering you, you've waited too long.

2.  **Get counsel.** Once you get an idea for how to solve the problem, ask a trusted friend, co-worker, or advisor what they think. "This is the situation," you might say. "And here's what I'm thinking about doing. What do you think?" Whether you agree with the other person's take or not, getting the insight is important, especially when the changes you want to make affect other people too.

3.  **Explain the change to the people it affects.** If this change will happen at home, call a family meeting. If the change affects your work relationships, schedule a meeting at the office. Speak from your own perspective ("This has been giving me fits lately" or "I've been having trouble with this project because of this") and *avoid blaming anybody for anything.* After you state the point of pressure or pain, explain your proposed change. Ask for input. Be prepared for other insights. Remember that the idea is to welcome change—to be open-minded and creative in solving the problem.

4. **Put the change in action.** Once you've decided on the change, do it. Let the kids know the change is effective immediately and stick with it for a period you've all agreed to.

5. **Review the change and, if necessary, revise it.** After a specified period of time, call another meeting and ask everyone how the change is working. Is anyone having trouble with the new rule about phone messages? Did anyone miss out on anything important now that you're willing to drive only one way (*to* the mall or home *from* the mall, but not *to* and *from* in the same day). Now that you're returning business calls only from 3:00 to 5:00 in the afternoon, has your boss been having trouble reaching you? You might not like the answers you get, but it's important that you ask the questions. If there is still a problem lurking, remember: It's just an opportunity for another creative change.

---

### Change in Action

You can use this worksheet to get a handle on the adjustments you want to make, whether you want to revise your work schedule, get your household organized, find more time for yourself, or change the world.

**Step 1: Think and plan.**

Here's the problem:

_____

_____

Here's the change I think will solve the problem:

_____

_____

Here are the specific steps I will take to make the change:

_____

_____

**Step 2: Get counsel.**

These are people I can talk to about the situation:

_____

_____

This is the result of the discussion:

_____

_____

**Step 3: Explain the change to the people it affects.**

These are the people I need to speak to about the situation:

_____

_____

Here's when we will discuss it:

_____

_____

These are the key points I need to explain:

_____

_____

**Step 4: Put the plan in action.**

This is when the change will begin:

_____

_____

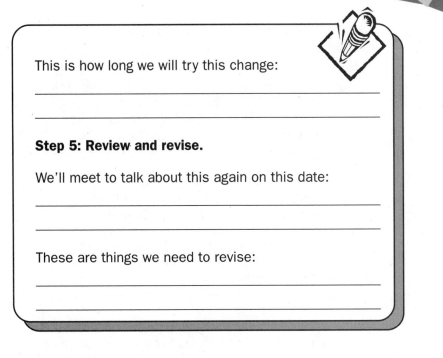

This is how long we will try this change:

_____

_____

**Step 5: Review and revise.**

We'll meet to talk about this again on this date:

_____

_____

These are things we need to revise:

_____

_____

# Home Adjustments

One of the reasons we humans dislike change so much is that we don't know what to do when we're in the midst of it. When things plod along on their normal course, we feel relatively secure. We know what's going on. When things change, we don't know what to expect—or worse, what's expected of us.

This is particularly true with kids. Boundaries are important not just as guidelines to keep bad behaviors in check but as a kind of bumper within which the kids learn to stay in-bounds. When you switch from working at the office—with its demanding schedule, frantic "I'll-pick-you-up-at-the-front-door-don't-be-a-minute-late!" phone calls, and carefully planned and enforced mealtimes, bath times, and bed times—your kids may react in some funny ways.

All those carefully scheduled activities gave a certain rhyme and reason to your life that will now be replaced, to a certain degree, by choice. You'll still say, "I can't! I've got to work this afternoon," but the kids will see that you're home, they know that you're home, and they'll wonder just how much you have to work—and is it *really* more important than going to the movies this afternoon?

So expect the boundaries to be tested. In order to pass the test, you'll need to be dead-eye sure what those boundaries are. Because if you waffle just a little, pretty soon your kids will have you waffling a lot. (Funny how that happens!) To help everyone make the adjustment more smoothly—and to let them know there *are* systems in place even if you're not getting in the car and driving to work every day—write out a plan for each of the following issues:

- **Mom's or Dad's work-at-home hours.** This is your work schedule, which you need to design and stick to. Post it at the beginning of each week on your Family Bulletin Board. (For a schedule worksheet, see Chapter 6.)

- **Your family rules.** Can your kids have friends over while you're working? Can Brandy go to the mall without a parent? Can Brian use your business phone, or does he have to wait until his sister is finished?

Setting up rules helps you define the way life at home will work in the midst of a growing business.

**Your family chore list and calendar.** These two items go a long way toward getting the family pulling together in the same direction and organizing everybody's "want tos" and "have tos" into a doable list. (Chapter 9 shows you how to create both the chore list and the calendar for your Family Bulletin Board.)

## What? You Don't *Have* a Family Bulletin Board?

Whether we realize it or not, most of us have a central area in the house where we stick notes, put up prized artwork, tag coupons, or pin Christmas lists. It may be the front of the fridge in your house, or it might be a write-on, pin-up bulletin board. Maybe it's just a countertop or drawer where everybody throws things they want to find again later.

By creating a visible place for your family stuff—notes about who called whom when, a calendar for trips to friends' houses, planned overnights, meetings for Mom and Dad, nights out, and so on—you give your family a communication center where they can find out what's going on and let others know the same about upcoming events in their lives.

What should you put on your Family Bulletin Board? Your work schedule, your family rules, the chore list, a sheet of emergency phone numbers, the ongoing grocery list, questions, phone messages, and more.

The only trick to using the Family Bulletin Board is to use it religiously. When your kids ask you if they can go to a movie next Friday night, tell them to write it on the calendar. When someone calls, put a note on the board. When your daughter asks you to pick up more bubble bath, ask her to add it to the grocery list on the board. Once your family gets used to using the bulletin board, it will become second nature—and they will always have a sense of who's doing what when and how (or if) it affects them.

# What Are Your Family Rules?

What are the rules in your house? You may not have them written down, but they're there. In my house, they go like this: no Sega before breakfast; no pushing, prodding, or punching; no language you wouldn't say in front of Grandma; and so on. We have other rules, too, about things like phone time, homework, bedtimes, chores, curfews, and on and on and on.

I didn't realize for a long time the value of writing these things down. Once they are written and posted on the bulletin board, they are *The Rules of the House*. It's not just Mom being difficult. When Kelly talks too long on the phone, I simply point at the list. She gets the message. Cameron doesn't even ask to play Sega before he finishes his cereal anymore. My life has gotten easier.

So what are your family rules? Use the following space to jot them down. And try to catch those sneaky ones that you are always having to enforce. (Here's a hint: They begin with the words "How many times have I *told* you ... ?")

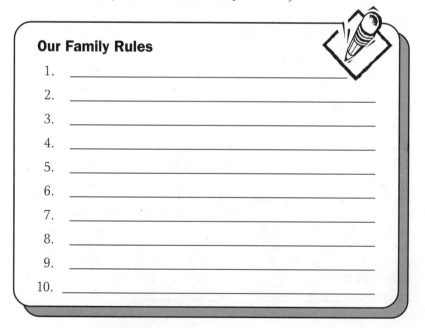

**Our Family Rules**

1. _____
2. _____
3. _____
4. _____
5. _____
6. _____
7. _____
8. _____
9. _____
10. _____

*This is a good time to have a nice quiet dinner with your spouse, someplace the kids aren't. Make sure you two are in agreement about what's a rule and what's not a rule. That way you can present a united front when you formally introduce the rules to the kids.*

Now that you've got the idea, you may want to revise the rules into the list you post for your family public to see. Here are a few ideas that will help make the rules more palatable for the kids:

- **Avoid naming a child in the rules.** "Brandy's got to finish her homework before she uses the phone" becomes "Finish all homework before you use the phone."

- **Don't use the rules to criticize.** "Don't ask for new clothes when your room is a pig pen" isn't really a rule—it's more of a jab. "New clothes will be purchased only when they are needed or earned" is a rule. (But it will be difficult to enforce if you've got anyone over 10 in your house!)

- **Say it positively.** Avoid the "Don'ts": "Don't pig out before dinner" becomes "Help yourself to one snack right after school, and then wait for dinner."

## A Rule Reality Check

What family issues cause you the most grief? These are opportunities for rules, and they are the ones you need to be clearest about. A well-written rule can end all the "But, Mom ... " hassles you've been wrestling with.

Expect your rules to be tested and broken. Remember the boundary idea? Your kids will bump up against them—and perhaps through them—a few times before they get the idea.

When your kids do go beyond the bounds, be ready with consequences that fit the crime. Write the consequences on the rule sheet so your kids know what they are bargaining for when they break the rule.

Don't be swayed by grumbling. Especially if you haven't had formal family rules posted before, your kids may make some noise about it. The noise is to be expected, but so is obedience. (Hey, if I could get out of a speeding ticket by whining about it, I'd try, too!)

## Setting Rules and Consequences

Earlier, we talked about using change to address a pressure or problem. A good rule is based on the same philosophy. In the last section, you listed the rules you've already got going in your house. Now you can think about using rules as they were meant to be used: to correct or solve issues that need addressing. That's a positive change. And that's really what rules are all about.

You can think through the rules you've got and come up with logical consequences by asking yourself these four questions:

**What's the problem?**

**What's the answer?**

**What's the rule?**

**What's the consequence?**

For example, suppose Dad is working for a long-distance phone company from home. He does a considerable amount of business in the early evenings and on weekends.

**What's the problem?** Daughter Sara's friends keep calling on Dad's business line while he is talking to customers.

**What's the answer?** Make it clear to Sara that she is not to give out Dad's work number to her friends.

**What's the rule?** The business phone is to be used only for Dad's business.

**What's the consequence?** Sara will have to call all the friends she's given the number to and tell them not to use it anymore. And she will lose her phone time, one hour per friend she gave the number to. In the future, if the rule is broken, Sara will lose her phone privileges for an entire day.

Of course, the situation, the rule, and the consequence will depend on your unique work-at-home situation, the job you perform, and the ages of your children. Here's another idea:

 **What's the problem?** Alyssa is refusing to take naps at the baby-sitter's house.

**What's the answer?** Make it clear to Alyssa that you expect her to take naps.

 **What's the rule?** You must take a nap at the sitter's house.

 **What's the consequence?** If she doesn't take a nap at the sitter's, Alyssa will have an earlier bedtime.

Be prepared to give plenty of thought to the consequences you assign. The reaction should fit the action. If Sara violates the phone rule, it's logical to curb her phone time. If Alyssa refuses to take a nap, it makes sense to add a rest time or to make her bedtime earlier.

But be willing to look at the bigger picture too. Maybe Alyssa really doesn't need the nap. Perhaps the room where she's resting is too noisy and she can't sleep. Maybe a rest time during which she looks at a picture book or listens to music would be enough. Know the whole story before you choose your consequences, and they will be easier to enforce—and be more effective—in the long run.

## Rules and Consequences

Now you can use the rules you came up with earlier to make a list of actions and reactions for your refrigerator door (or your bulletin board):

If you break this rule: _____

    Expect this: _____

If you break this rule: _____

    Expect this: _____

If you break this rule: _____

    Expect this: _____

If you break this rule: _____

    Expect this: _____

If you break this rule: _____

    Expect this: _____

### Been There, Done That

*"One of the hardest things about running a business from home, when it's your own business, is that there's no place to escape when you have a couple of bad days. The kids are there, the business is there, and there's no place to go to get rid of the stress. I've learned that when I start feeling stressed, I've got to do something fun with my kids and get my mind totally off work. Otherwise, I start feeling overwhelmed, and both my business and my family suffer."*

## Changing the Rules

As long as you have a family, you'll need some kind of rule system in place. If you are using rules to answer challenges, to help everyone adjust and know where their boundaries are, the rules on your sheet will appear and disappear as they are needed and outgrow their usefulness.

You'll soon discover you have two different kinds of rules: Foundational rules and situational rules. **Foundational rules** are basic, no-kidding rules that your family lives by no matter what. These will not change, and you want to be sure your children know they are important to you. **Situational rules** are those you develop in answer to specific problems. Things like Alyssa's refusing to nap or Sara's marathon phone conversations can be solved with situational rules. When the problem goes away, the rule can go, too. Of course, if the problem returns, the rule can be put back into effect.

Remember to delete rules you no longer need. Otherwise, you'll have a rule list the length of your refrigerator! Seeing the rules go away makes your kids feel good, too—they are accomplishing things, they are learning, and you no longer need the rules you once did. This teaches them something positive about the world at large, and helps them to work within and respect authority without feeling controlled, oppressed, or judged.

**Profiles**
**Name:** Julie
**Type of business:** Word processing services and bookkeeping
**How long?** $3\frac{1}{2}$ years
**How many kids?** Two, ages 7 and 5
**Biggest challenge:** Finding time for business without taking it away from the boys.
**Best response to that challenge:** Creative scheduling.

## A Final Word on Adjustments

Throughout this chapter, we've talked about adjustments. As you become accustomed to working at home, you may deal with the deflation of your own expectations, the realities of life after the honeymoon, and the testing and trying of your kids—and maybe even your spouse.

These things can be hard to handle if you're not expecting them. The best way to navigate through this trying period is to:

1. expect challenges,

2. prepare solutions,

3. remember that this too shall pass, and

4. keep your sense of humor.

Focusing on the positive things your family is doing to help you get your work-at-home venture off the ground—even if you need to go on a treasure hunt to find them—will encourage your family to help more. Let the rules take care of the things they *aren't* doing: no more nagging, no more exasperation; if they broke the rule, they pay the consequence. This leaves you free to focus on the things they *are* doing: how well they are doing in school, how straight they are keeping their rooms, how promptly they got off the phone after their phone time, how pleasant they were at dinner.

Being a positive parent is a lot more fun than being a negative parent. Designing and implementing a good set of family rules—and seeing the adjustment phrase as a time when you have the chance to make things even better—helps you be more productive and centered in your work and lets you remove yourself from law enforcement and concentrate on the nurturing, teaching, and loving parts of the job.

# Notes

1.  Erma Bombeck, *If Life Is a Bowl of Cherries, What Am I Doing in the Pits?* (New York: McGraw-Hill, 1978).

2.  William Bridges, *Jobshift: How to Prosper in a Workplace Without Jobs* (New York: Addison-Wesley, 1994).

# Housework? What Housework?

*"You start at the beginning, go on until you get to the end, then stop."*
—Lewis Carroll

Life is messy, with or without kids. We've all got spills and splatters, normal wear-and-tear dirt, and routine household maintenance tasks to deal with. We've got to fit in our cleaning sprees between trips to the dentist, grocery shopping, bus schedules, and now work-at-home sessions.

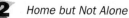

It's one of the most common misconceptions about working at home: "*Now* I'll be able to keep up with the housework!" If this is your expectation, go for it—but don't be surprised when you look around a few weeks from now and find laundry piled three feet high in your basement, fingerprints all over the walls, and handwritten messages in the dust on your end tables.

**BEST** &
WORST

*Best:*
"Being in
control of
my time."

In this chapter, you'll take a look at the housework issue and determine where it fits in your work-at-home priority bank. And don't forget about scheduling: You can make a date with yourself to clear away the clutter and save the Big Dig-In for those spare hours on the weekend. However you decide to arrange it, knowing *when* you're going to take care of the house, *who* is going to help you (that's important), and *what* you're going to do when you've got the time will help you stay on top of things and clear your mind for the work in front of you.

# Solving Problems <u>Before</u> They Happen

When's the best time to solve a problem? Before it happens. Best fix for financial trouble? Don't get into debt. Best cure for illness? Make your health a priority. Best solution to the housework blues? Don't let the mess accumulate.

Some people clean house the way they face a problem. They wait until they can't avoid it anymore, when the trouble is So Big and So Ugly they can't do anything else but deal with it. Then, in a fit of self-disgust, they face the thing that was so much smaller when it first appeared. One pair of socks is much easier to pick up off the floor than an entire drawerful. One meal's worth of dishes is much easier to wash than four days' worth of dishes that completely fill one side of the sink.

It's the same with organizing at home. If you begin organizing *after* everything explodes and you can't find something you really need, you're going to be organizing in fire-fighting mode. ("Things are really a mess! I've got to do something about this!") But if you look around calmly one afternoon and say "Hmmm. I'll bet there's an easier way to do this," you can begin calmly and organize your life a little bit at a time. This second approach—fire prevention as opposed to fire fighting—is much gentler and easier to follow through with in the long run.

# A New Twist to an Old Problem

Now that you're home, you may think you should be able to keep a perfect house. Or, worse, your spouse may think so. Yes, you're right there in the house, not far from the washer and dryer. Not too far removed from the dust cloth, the mop, and the bucket. You even go into the bathroom a few times a day—not like when you were working in the office—so what's so hard about picking up a sponge and cleaning the tub?

The problem with the mix-and-match approach to housecleaning—doing the bathrooms, the windows, the woodwork whenever it occurs to you to do them—is that sooner or later it becomes counterproductive for your work. You'll spend less time focused on your work and more time scurrying around doing this and that and fitting work in-between. Unless you do the kind of work that fits well to that type of harried schedule, it's going to prove difficult over the long term.

## What's Your Comfort Zone?

Even though working at home affords more flexibility than any office job ever could, you still need guidelines. Only you and your family know what kind of housekeeping expectations you've got set up. Are you happy with the level of clutter in your house? Should it be more or less? If you keep your house pinpoint straight and can't think of a good reason why, you may be able to relax your standards a little. If you walk around feeling guilty that you don't keep things as straight as you should, you need to do something to get rid of that guilt, which means putting a system into place to deal with the housework more effectively. (It *doesn't* mean, by the way, doing it all yourself.)

And don't think I'm just talking to moms, here— because I'm not. Work-at-home dads have opportunities too, and should be just as actively involved in house upkeep as their mates and their children. When you first start talking about putting a housecleaning system in place, have a family meeting about it. Ask this question:

> *"Do you think we keep the house clean enough?" (Notice the "we!")*

What will they say? Maybe yes, maybe no. Roger may complain about Renee's room. Renee may complain about Roger's room. Kristen will tell you how embarrassed she was when she and her friend went to raid the refrigerator last Friday night and found moldy, three-week-old spaghetti.

*If you've got to give the illusion of "clean" quickly but you don't have time to do a full cleaning, hit the obvious points—dust major pieces of furniture and run the sweeper—then burn a candle or two or use potpourri to lighten the cleaning smell. The house seems fresher, even if it isn't sparkling clean, and most likely no one will notice the items you have to leave till the weekend.*

If you get a widespread "Yes" to your "Clean enough?" question, you can relax. Your family is basically happy with things the way they are, and if you are too, you don't have to worry about upping your standards. If you get a family "No," you'll need to follow with a "Why not?" and make a list of items your family members mention. Then, before the end of the meeting, assign those items to family members—preferably the ones who noticed in the first place.

**Do We Keep the House Clean Enough?**

Jobs to Do                    Who Will Do Them?

_____            _____

_____            _____

_____            _____

_____            _____

_____            _____

## Get Yourself a Merry Little Schedule

How often do you clean house? How often do you *need* to clean house? Can you do it all in one swoop, or do you need to break it up?

One of the easiest ways to make sure things get done regularly is to create a housework schedule. When do you do what you need to do around the house? You can look at what you've got and decide when you really *want* to do all those things. Once you get a basic idea of when you mop the floor, dust the furniture, run the sweeper, and so on, you can see how much time you need to plan for and decide when you want to spend that time on the house.

First, make a list of all the jobs you have to do, inside and outside your home. (And note by "you"

I don't mean just you personally, I mean you collectively, as a family, as in "you guys.") Then determine how often the jobs need to be done. Finally, think of the best time to tackle the jobs— all at once or scheduled on different days— however it fits your cleaning personality best. Your housework schedule might look something like this:

## Housework Schedule

| To Do | How Often? | When? |
|---|---|---|
| Clean bathrooms | Once a week | Saturday mornings |
| Run the sweeper | Twice a week | Tues. & Fri. evenings |
| Dust the furniture | Once a week | Saturday mornings |
| Mop the kitchen | Every two weeks | Saturday afternoons |
| Wipe fingerprints | Once a month | Saturday afternoons |
| Empty trash cans | Twice a week | Tues. & Fri. evenings |

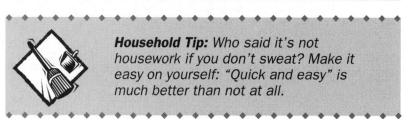

**Household Tip:** *Who said it's not housework if you don't sweat? Make it easy on yourself: "Quick and easy" is much better than not at all.*

Remember not to schedule yourself to do all the work. If there are some jobs you want to reserve for yourself, take a look at your weekly work schedule (we created one in Chapter 6) to see when you're free to do those tasks. Otherwise, have a family meeting and divvy up the chores.

Now it's your turn. Take a few moments and write in the important tasks you've got to do in order to keep up with the housework in your home. Make a list of how often they need to be done and write a tentative plan for when they will be completed— either by you or by another member of your family.

### Housework Myth #1

**Fiction**: A good housekeeper is one who keeps a spotless home.

**Fact**: A good housekeeping system is created by a family that works together to keep their house in whatever shape they feel most comfortable with.

**Housework Schedule**

| To Do | How Often? | When? |
|-------|-----------|-------|
|       |           |       |
|       |           |       |
|       |           |       |
|       |           |       |
|       |           |       |
|       |           |       |
|       |           |       |

# Basic Housework 101

You've already got some kind of system in place for keeping your house straight. Working at home will both help and hinder the way you've been doing things. Here are the benefits:

   You're closer, so you can catch those juice spills immediately.

   When things *really* must be done, you're there.

You can do small things around the house while you're working (on the phone, waiting for a client, etc.).

Now the downsides:

 You're there all day, so you make more of a mess.

 You may become blind to things that need to be done, things you see every day.

 You may feel guilty every time you walk by the clothes hamper, the dirty dishes in the sink, or the less-than-clean bathroom.

**Household Tip:**
*Don't sweat the small stuff.*

In the last section, you learned to identify just how clean you and your family want your house to be and to make a list of things you want to improve on. You also set up a schedule for the big tasks you have to do every week as a routine part of housekeeping. There are other things you can do to lighten the load of to-dos that can accumulate during the week.

First, you can be prepared to make the most of your time by using every spare moment to the fullest. Second, you can tackle big jobs in sections, to help you feel you're accomplishing things even when you haven't hit the big goal. And a third component, which is perhaps the most important, is to make sure you get the help you need in order to organize and maintain the house. It's not just *your* house—you don't live there alone. Each member of your family under your roof should share in the joys and responsibilities of home ownership. That means you need to put on a grin, get your pen and paper, call a family meeting, and create a family chore list. All these ideas, and more, are covered in the rest of this chapter.

# 10-Minute Tasks Make a Big Difference

It's hard to keep up with the house when you just don't have the time. If you wait for a big block of time to do the work you need to do, you may wait a long time. But if you grab free moments—like when Patsy is running in for her ice skates, you're waiting for the bus to come, or dinner is almost-but-not-quite-ready—you can fit in quick tasks you've been meaning to get to but haven't had the time for.

What kinds of things can you do in a spare moment or two? Pick up toys, open mail, read teachers' notes, put away dried dishes, plan dinner, fold socks, wipe a countertop, start a load of laundry, make a bed, open curtains, sweep a floor, or straighten a cabinet. If you have trouble thinking of things you can do quickly, make a list as they occur to you; then, when you find yourself waiting for the bus to turn down your street, you can read through the list and choose something you can do quickly.

What quick jobs can be done around your house to lighten your "cleaning detail" later? You might want to give some serious thought to the things that drive you crazy because you never seem to get to them. In my house, that includes fingerprints (*lots* of them) on the doorframes, catalogs that need to be sorted and thrown away, a toy box that needs to be gone through, a bag of clothes that needs to be carried to the car so I'll remember to take it to Goodwill, and at least 20 other things.

Make a list of the simple tasks you can do in a "while-you-wait" 10-minute period. Then put the list somewhere easy to find—on the fridge, on the bulletin board—and refer to it when you have a moment to spare. Wherever you put it, show your spouse and the kids, too, so they can knock out a couple of items (and initial them, so you'll know they're done) and help you cut down the to-dos dramatically.

---

**While-You-Wait 10-Minute Jobs**

_____

_____

_____

_____

_____

_____

_____

_____

---

## Housework Myth #2

**Fiction:** People will think less of you if your house is cluttered.

**Fact:** People probably won't notice if your house is cluttered. And if they do, they'll be glad you can't see *their* house.

---

# Do a Little at a Time

Some things are never done. Things like dishes. And laundry. And bed making. You do it today, but there will be more to do tomorrow. The tasks that continue—and that accumulate if you don't stay on top of them—are the ones you need to do a little at a time. For example, do one load of laundry a day, rather than waiting to do five loads on Saturday. (Really makes you look forward to the weekend, doesn't it?) If you do one load completely, every day, it will never accumulate. The same goes for dishes. And bills. And clutter.

What kinds of things can you manage a little at a time? Think of the things you spend a lot of time on, things that you will be doing over and over, no matter what. Not one-time projects, like building a minibarn or caulking the tub. Tasks you do repeatedly will seem considerably shorter and more manageable if you tackle them frequently.

Here are the jobs we could tackle a little at a time:

_____

_____

_____

_____

_____

## Break Big Jobs into Doable Chunks

Another problem with working at home is that we see how many things need to be done. Those boxes that have been stacked in the den since you moved in—you know they need to be unpacked, but you haven't been able to get to it. When you worked in the office, you could simply go to work and forget about them. Now, at home, you see those boxes every time you go in the den for a book. And nagging in the back of your head is the idea that if you cleaned out that room, you'd have much more space for your work-at-home office.

BEST &
**WORST**

*Worst:*
"Dealing with clients who don't understand family priorities."

First things first. Know what big jobs need to be done in your house. Then make a tentative plan for getting them done. Here are a few ideas:

| Winterizing the back porch | *November (before winter really hits)* |
| Cleaning the cabinets | *Right before the holidays, when Mom comes to visit* |
| Organizing the attic | *By March (before the garage sale)* |

What big jobs
need to be done?               By when?

_____   _____

_____   _____

_____   _____

_____   _____

Because your time is limited and controlled by your weekly work schedule, you've only got so much space for Big Time Cleaning. You can knock out the big projects more easily by coming at them from two angles:

 **Divide the job into tasks.** You probably know this one from the times your mom made you clean your room when you were small. "Is this enough?" you'd ask after putting the clothes in the laundry hamper. "Is this enough?" you'd ask after straightening the papers on your desk. "Is *this* enough?" you'd ask after shoving all the toys under the bed. Dividing a job into tasks makes it seem much more doable. For example, if you want the attic organized by March, what steps can you take this week, next weekend, by the end of the month? One corner at a time? Steamer trunks first? Making stacks of like items?

**Delegate what you can.** Once they are divided into smaller tasks, some jobs turn out to be just the right size for small helpers. Take the attic again. As you sort through the clothes in the steamer trunks, Johnny can carry the bags of Goodwill-bound items to the garage. Laura can fold the items that are going back into the trunks. Sam can take empty boxes to the basement. Crystal can sweep when you're finished.

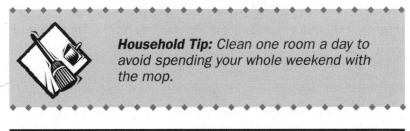

**Household Tip:** *Clean one room a day to avoid spending your whole weekend with the mop.*

## Housework Myth #3

**Fiction:** A cluttered house is a sign of a cluttered mind.
**Fact:** A cluttered house is a clean house with a busy family.

## Get the Help You Need

We all have a lot to do, there's no doubt about it. You, your spouse, your kids, even your pets have their own agendas. But sometimes it's a necessary part of family life to be willing to drop your own agenda for a while in favor of the family system. And part of that family system means joining in and helping each other—support-wise, listening-wise, and cleaning-wise.

I made it into my 30s before I realized that I wasn't the housekeeper because I was a woman: I was the housekeeper because I was willing. I had never really asked my family to help me. I had never explained the hows, whys, and wherefores of digging in together and getting things done as a family. It was one of the many wonderful lessons I learned after becoming a single parent: I don't have to do everything alone. In fact, my kids and I gain more by helping each other (even when we grumble about it) than we do when we each live our own isolated, you-do-your-thing-and-I'll-do-mine lives. We are learning to depend on each other in a real way, and to ask for help as well as give it. Pretty important lessons you can learn from 15 minutes folding laundry with your kids.

 **Dos and Don'ts of Asking for Help**

Do ...

🥾 **Be specific.** "I've only got 10 minutes to finish this, and I need to get dinner started. Will you start it for me?"

🥾 **Be respectful.** "Could you please take these boxes out to the trash while I put the files away?"

🥾 **Be appreciative.** "Thanks for taking the dogs out twice this afternoon. I had to finish that phone call, and you really helped me."

**Be willing to reciprocate.** "Sure, I'll help you with the trash. It's extra heavy this week, isn't it?"

Don't ...

**Be exasperated.** "Why am I the only one who works around here? Would *someone* please help me with this?"

**Be sarcastic.** "Oh, sure, *now* you want to help me, when I'm doing something you *like* to do."

**Be critical.** "Why can't you do it the way I asked you to? I'll just have to redo what you've done."

**Be ungracious.** "It's about time you did *something* around here!"

**Household Tip:** *Be willing to let things look less than perfect.*

## 10 Ways to Get the Help You Need

Though it may appear at first glance to be an "easier" lifestyle, working at home is fraught with its own challenges and hidden pressures. With a few clear discussions, you can help your family understand that "home" does not mean "not working," and that you still need their help to keep things running smoothly—perhaps more than ever. Here's a list of 10 ways you can get help for tackling the household and organizing and controlling the chaos:

1. **Have a clear picture of what you need help with.**

2. **Ask.**

3. **Be realistic about "when."** If you have a situation that needs to be resolved now, do your best to take care of it quickly. But don't put unnecessary time pressure on yourself—or on anyone else—when it's unwarranted.

4. **Focus on one task and finish it before moving on to the next.**

5. **Be willing to be less than perfect.** Don't feel bad that you can't finish everything. Reverse your thinking and celebrate when you do finish something.

6. **Use your resources.** If friends or relatives offer help, accept it.

7. **Let the people who offer help do it their way.** Don't insist that the T-shirts be folded the way you've always done them. If they're folded, they're folded.

8. **Focus on the most important stuff first.** Take time to prioritize what you need to spend your time working on. The less important things can be dealt with later.

9. **Don't rule out paid help.** Ask yourself if you need a housekeeper, a professional organizer, a lawn service, or a handyman—even if it's just a one-shot deal. If it makes your life easier and it's worth the investment, go for it.

10. **When you tackle a problem, think creatively about a solution—don't just pick the first thing that comes to mind.**

## Creating a Chore List

If you want to get the whole family involved in doing things around the house, you need a system to let them know what they are responsible for and when it needs to be done. That's where a chore list comes in.

### Been There, Done That

*"My first few weeks at home, I did everything but work. I felt so free— I didn't want to go sit down at the computer. If you can, give yourself a vacation before you start working at home. After a week or two, you'll feel refreshed and eager to start. Otherwise, you might have trouble getting disciplined at the start."*

Like anything else, you should present the chore list in a family meeting with a "let's-make-this-family-work" attitude. Everyone helps; everyone is important. The only time a chore list doesn't work is when it's uneven or unfair, with one or more of the kids getting more work than the others, or when you assign all the jobs and don't do anything yourself (and how likely is *that?*)

A chore list should include the name of each person in your family and the jobs he or she needs to do, along with the day the jobs need to be done. At our house, that looks something like this:

| Who? | What? | When? |
|---|---|---|
| Kelly, age 15 | Put away dishes | Every weeknight |
| | Clean sinks | Saturday mornings |
| | Run the sweeper in the family room | Tuesday and Friday after school |
| Christopher, age 9 | Walk the dogs | Every weeknight |
| | Bring in the trash cans | Tuesday after school |
| | Straighten the video shelves | As needed |
| Cameron, age $3\frac{1}{2}$ | Clear the table (his dishes only) | Every weeknight |
| | Help Mom make his bed | Every morning |
| | Straighten the couch pillows | As needed |

> Teach your toddler to put away as part of the game you're playing. Getting-out and putting-away are the beginning and ending points of playing with blocks, puzzles, crayons, trucks, whatever. The earlier you start, the easier it will be to enlist your child's help.

Here are a few suggestions for creating a chore list:

- **Let the kids choose what chores they want to do.** If they select things that are too easy, give them a list of chores and ask them to pick two or three.

- **Set a time limit.** Try the chores for a month and then reevaluate or let the kids trade chores.

- **Make sure the chores are useful.** Don't have the kids doing chores for chores' sakes. Kelly doesn't need to run the sweeper on Friday if we've been away on vacation all week.

- **Give all the kids chores.** Everyone can do something; except for infants, age does not matter.

## Chore Possibilities

Pick up toys     Set the table

Fold laundry     Make the bed

Run the sweeper     Bring in the newspaper

Take out the trash     Bring in the trash cans

Clear the table     Wind the clock

Dust furniture     Get the mail

Let the dog out     Feed the pets

🧦 Water plants         🧦 Clip coupons

🧦 Throw out old        🧦 Wash mirrors
   magazines

🧦 Make snacks          🧦 Weed the garden

🧦 Mow the lawn         🧦 Sweep tile floors

🧦 Wash the car         🧦 Start dinner

**Household Tip:** *Don't answer the phone while you're on a cleaning marathon.*

## Seven Good Reasons to Have a Chore List

Okay, Dad, so you're trying to make sure the housework gets done while Mom is away at her office job and you are working at home. You ask the kids to help when they get home from school. Instead of enlistment, you get excuses:

> *"Mom will just redo it anyway."*
>
> *"I don't know what she wants me to do."*
>
> *"I don't know where the mop is."*
>
> *"I don't know how she wants it."*
>
> *"Mom would tell me to do my homework first."*
>
> *"Can't I get a snack first? I'm starving!"*
>
> *"Let Justin do it. I did it last time."*

A chore list says "Do this, now!" when *you* can't. It says who does what and when it gets done. The kids know their jobs, they know the expectations, and they know the score (and the penalty, if necessary). There. Now you can work in peace.

Okay, so are you ready to tackle the chore list? First gather the family and discuss jobs. Then decide when each job needs to be done and how long you will keep the plan in place.

Consider also the rewards of doing chores faithfully. Your kids may do their chores simply because you've asked—and, indeed, they should—but it will be a more pleasant experience for them, and they will be more willing to help, if you build in some kind of reward system. You might try these ideas:

   **A competition:** Whoever does their chores for the greatest number of days in a certain period without being asked wins.

   **A family goal:** When we get all our chores done for the week, we'll go ice skating.

   **An individual goal:** "Laurel, if you get all your chores done this week on time, we'll give you an extra three hours of phone time next week."

Some parents choose to give an allowance for chores done, which is a good way for kids to learn the work ethic early. You do a job, you get paid for a job. You don't work, you don't get paid. Seems pretty clear. Other parents feel that chores should simply be a part of the child's contribution to the home and the family and don't want their children doing their jobs with their hands out. Whichever philosophy works for you, just make it part of your system and then stick with it for a specified period of time. If it works, great. If it doesn't, revise. At least things will be getting done around the house, and you won't be doing it all yourself.

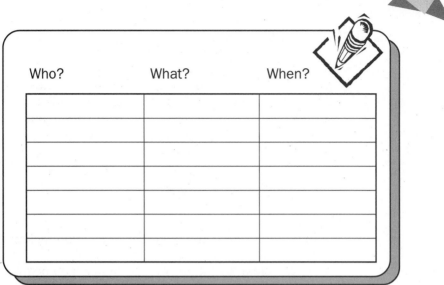

| Who? | What? | When? |
|------|-------|-------|
|      |       |       |
|      |       |       |
|      |       |       |
|      |       |       |
|      |       |       |
|      |       |       |
|      |       |       |

## Basic House Rules

- If you got it out, put it back.
- If you're finished with it, put it away.
- If you wore it, hang it up.
- If you spilled it, clean it up.
- If you broke it, admit it.
- If you'll help me, I'll help you.

**Household Tip:** *When the family helps, let them do it their way—and be appreciative.*

# Getting Organized

By now, you've explored the different ways you can handle some of the household jobs that are piling up around you. You can deal with quick things in spare moments. You can spread big jobs out and do a little at a time. You can delegate chores, so everybody is helping.

## Housecleaning Kits

Another way to simplify housekeeping duty is to plan what you're going to tackle before you tackle it. Make sure you've got the tools you need—a mop, the cleaner, a bucket, etc.—before you begin. In fact, you could make up cleaning kits, so each job has its own supplies ready and handy. That way whoever is assigned to the job has everything he or she needs to complete it. Here are a few kit ideas:

-  **A mopping kit:** mop, bucket, and floor cleaner

- **A dusting kit:** spray or oil, duster or cloths

- **A spills kit:** a roll of paper towels, sponge, small container for water

- **A carpet care kit:** carpet spot cleaner, a scrub brush, sponge, small container

- **A bathroom cleaning kit:** sink and tub cleaner, toilet cleaner, gloves, a sponge, toilet brush

Be sure to take the kids on a tour and show them where everything is and what everything's for. Especially if you have little ones, make sure the dangerous chemicals are someplace else—so someone young doesn't grab the wrong green bottle when she's looking for the plant food.

## Housecleaning Calendars

Another way to organize the housecleaning events in your house is to take the schedule you made earlier and apply it to a monthly calendar. Then you can see at a glance when you're going to do what: mop downstairs every two weeks, vacuum on Tuesdays and Fridays, and so on.

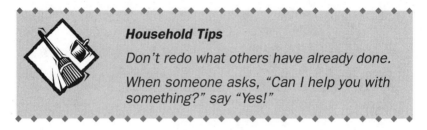

**Household Tips**

*Don't redo what others have already done.*

*When someone asks, "Can I help you with something?" say "Yes!"*

### Housework Calendar

| SUNDAY | MONDAY | TUESDAY | WEDNESDAY | THURSDAY | FRIDAY | SATURDAY |
|---|---|---|---|---|---|---|
| **1** | **2** Wash sheets | **3** Dust | **4** | **5** Vacuum | **6** | **7** Bathrooms Fingerprint |
| **8** | **9** | **10** Dust | **11** | **12** Vacuum | **13** | **14** Bathrooms Mop floors |
| **15** | **16** Wash sheets | **17** Dust | **18** | **19** Vacuum | **20** | **21** Bathrooms Windows Carpet spots |
| **22** | **23** | **24** Dust | **25** | **26** Vacuum | **27** | **28** Bathrooms Mop floors Closets |
| **29** | **30** Wash sheets Check fire alarms | **31** Dust | | | | |

When you're writing those important jobs on the calendar, choose a Fix-It day when you check for burned-out light bulbs; test your fire alarms; and check the heater vent, the furnace filter, and more.

**Profiles**
  **Name:** Chris
    **Type of business:** Writing
    **How long?** Two years
    **How many kids?** One teenager
   **Biggest challenge:** The feast-or-famine flow of work.
**Best response to that challenge:** Keep a contact schedule and follow up religiously.

## Keeping Things Straight

Positive reinforcement is your best insurance that good things will keep happening. Even if there aren't many good things to focus on, find what you can: "Sam! You remembered the forks tonight! That's great!" Focusing on the positive, even if you need a magnifying glass to see it, will encourage your family to keep trying and show you that they really are learning to help out around the house.

Once a week, perhaps on Friday evenings, sit down with your spouse and review the week. What got done and what didn't? Did you wind up meeting more goals than you missed? Have a discussion about what worked well and what you might want to change for next week.

Once a month—or sooner if something isn't working properly and you think a change is needed—sit down in a family meeting and talk about how things are going. How does the family feel about the system in place? Make sure the discussion is open and honest; even if you hear lots of grumbling and griping, try to hear what's really being said. Be open to alternatives; if a suggestion sounds as if it might work, try it. (You might want to vote on it first.) The great thing about establishing a family system is that, once it's established, you can change it easily. Developing a system that works is a process that will grow and change as long as your family does.

## Handling Housework

- **H**ave a schedule for important household tasks.

- **O**rganize the what, where, when, and who for big and little jobs.

- **U**se your resources wisely. Accept all offers of help.

- **S**hare the work. Everyone in the family should help.

- **E**xpect grumbling. But don't let it stop you from assigning chores.

- **W**ork on the stuff that bugs you most.

- **O**rganize your supplies. Have what you need ready to be used.

- **R**eward the kids for chores well done. Praise works wonders in grumbling hearts.

- **K**now that working together will strengthen your family.

# Kids at Work

*"Pretty much all of the honest truth telling there is in the world is done by children."*
—Oliver Wendell Holmes, Sr.[1]

No matter what your reason for initially working at home—whether by choice or by necessity—sooner or later you'll marvel at the idea that you can actually earn a living right there in one of your favorite spots on earth. There are challenges, to be sure, but the benefits are many. You can set your priorities the way you want to; you can be close to your children and have more contact with them during the day; you can work independently and get a sense of your own inventiveness, resourcefulness, and self-discipline.

Those are just a few of the perks, adult-style. But kids have ideas of their own. How is your work-at-home experience affecting your kids? You might be surprised to find out. I had a great time interviewing both parents and kids for this book. And I learned some interesting things:

 Kids are proud of their parents.

Kids give credit for work done, not money earned.

Kids admire what their parents do and, especially when they're young, plan to do the same thing.

Kids absorb information, tasks, goals, and projects when they hear their parents talk about work, whether they are actively involved or not.

Kids see how their parents handle stress, and they learn how they will handle their own.

Kids who see their parents deal with others professionally figure out how people treat one another in business.

Kids see how hard their parents work, and they understand the value of earning a living.

Kids who see their parents treating customers fairly understand the importance of ethics in the workplace.

 Kids who hear their parents talk about the family business feel a part of it.

🔔 Kids who watch their parents start a business—struggles and all—learn how they can do it one day, too.

🔔 Kids see their parents make choices that are in line with their priorities for the family, and they will one day make choices in line with their own priorities, too.

🔔 Kids who see their parents doing something off the beaten path will be less apt to follow the crowd when choosing their own careers.

## What the Kids Say

**BEST** &
WORST

*Best:*
"Building a snowman when I should be working."

It's a safe bet that your kids won't rate your business success or failure on how much money you make, how comfortable life is, or how many clients you've got. They see the work you do, and that's all they need to know. The kids I interviewed in Mrs. Garber's third-grade class at Southside Elementary School in Columbus, Indiana, knew that the true value of work goes beyond a price tag.[2] When I asked who among them had parents working at home, almost every hand went up. Surprised at the percentage (the number of us working at home is still relatively low compared to the general population), I asked what type of jobs their parents had. I got answers like these:

*"She watches my baby brother all day and then takes care of my cousin at night."*

*"Dad fixes everybody's cars. He's good at it, too."*

*"Mom cleans the whole house."*

*"She baby-sits."*

*"Dad works on the computer."*

Whether or not their parents did these things for money, in their kids eyes they were working at home. So if you think your kids don't notice what you do, think again. They'll gladly tell the visiting writer who comes into their classroom what their parents do to make life better at home. And they'll have a proud gleam in their eye as they do.

I got lots of nods when we talked about computers and how they were making things easier for people to work wherever they needed to work. What do people do with computers? "Write stuff" and "Talk to each other." That's about the size of it.

When I asked whether they would like to work at home someday, several faces lit up. Brock wants to be an astronomer and work from the skylab on top of his house; then he'll travel around the world to do his research and come back to his home office to put together his reports. Christopher thinks he'd be a good oceanographer, but when he isn't out at sea, he'll be home in his office so he can be close to his wife and kids. One budding teacher said she will work on many of her projects and lesson plans at home so she can be prepared for her students during the day. A someday artist plans a home studio, and a mechanic-in-training thinks it will be neat to have a home-run body shop in his own garage.

"If your parents had their own business at home, would you want to help?" Every hand in the place shot up. What kinds of things would they be willing to do? Running the copy machine was the favorite task. But things like stapling, paper clipping, filing, dumping trash, and even walking to the store for groceries came up. The enthusiasm was evident. The possibilities are endless. These kids—these bright, creative kids—will grow up quite comfortable in the technological world you and I are just beginning to explore. By the time they reach adulthood, working at the office may be the exception rather than the norm.

# What Do <u>Your</u> Kids Think?

You may have been so busy getting your work-at-home situation up and running that you haven't had time to consider what your kids are thinking. Oh, sure, you can tell when they are stressed and when they are irritated that you're not spending more time with them. (How could you miss that *look*?) But have you had a conversation about the changes that are happening, whether they are neat, and what reactions your kids are having?

You may want to consider interviewing your child: Find out what he likes and doesn't like about the new arrangement, and why. What's cool about it? What's a real drag? You can be sure there will be some of both.

And don't expect to get gushy "Oh-I'm-so-glad-you're-home-with-me, Mommy!" answers. Most of the kids I talked to were much more practical. "Now I can play with my best friend next door. When I was in daycare, I only saw him on the weekends." Or "I'm tired of being home all the time." And you can expect a fair smattering of the ever-popular, "I dunno."

Just because the kids don't talk about the security they feel, the comfort of being at home, the feeling they experience of being loved and cared for when they come home from school doesn't mean they don't feel it. They do. Most of the language for those deep feelings comes later. It's a lot easier, when you're 9, to talk about being able to play Nintendo after school and visit with your best friend. But the big issues aren't slipping by unnoticed.

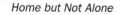

### Interview Your Kids

One great way to find out what your kids think about *their* side of the work-at-home experience is to ask them. They'll probably be more than glad to offer their opinions. If not, negotiate; maybe you can pay them for their time and effort with ice cream later.

1. If your teacher asks you, "What do your parents do at work?" what would you say?

2. Do you like it that I work at home?

3. What do you like about it?

4. What *don't* you like about it?

5. Do you think you might want to work at home someday?

6. What kind of work would you want to do at home?

7. Would you like to help me with my work here at home?

Although you could do the interview in a group meeting, you'll get better, more individual answers if you talk with your kids one-on-one. That way you'll get more original thought and fewer "Me toos!"

## The Upside

We already know we don't always see the world in the same way our kids do. In fact, "rarely" might be closer to the mark. We know that working at home benefits the kids; that's one of the main reasons many of us do it. But the benefits parents think they are giving their kids and the benefits the kids see are often two different things.

Here are a few of the answers parents gave to the question, "How do you think working at home benefits your kids?"

◆ ◆ ◆ ◆ ◆ ◆ ◆ ◆ ◆ ◆ ◆ ◆ ◆ ◆ ◆ ◆ ◆ ◆ ◆ ◆ ◆ ◆ ◆

*"My son sees that I'm determined to do what I believe I'm best at."*

*"Hopefully I'm creating something my kids can inherit."*

*"My business is 98 percent brainpower—I have to use my own creativity for the stuff I do. Hopefully my son will see how important it is to use his own ideas."*

*"I hope my kids learn that when you do what you're best at, you can get ahead in the world."*

*"I'm always available for my kids and they know that. They come first, no matter what. I think that's important for them to know."*

◆ ◆ ◆ ◆ ◆ ◆ ◆ ◆ ◆ ◆ ◆ ◆ ◆ ◆ ◆ ◆ ◆ ◆ ◆ ◆ ◆ ◆ ◆

Kids give slightly different answers when you ask them to list the benefits of having a work-at-home parent. They tend to see the right now and not the long-term. One third-grader responded that it meant his big sister didn't have to watch him after school anymore (with a huge sigh of relief). Another boy said the biggest benefit was that his mom picked him up from school and he didn't have to ride the bus. One young lady said having her mom work at home meant she could always reach her, no matter what, which was a good feeling. And I have to add what my 3-year-old Cameron said when I asked him this question (bear with me—it's verbatim):

◆ ◆ ◆ ◆ ◆ ◆ ◆ ◆ ◆ ◆ ◆ ◆ ◆ ◆ ◆ ◆ ◆ ◆ ◆ ◆ ◆ ◆ ◆

*"Yes. I like it when you work home. Because it ... when you go to meetings, it would be like a long time and when you work here it doesn't take very long and you, you know, work here at home. That's why I like about it. Now, would you gimme some water?"*

◆ ◆ ◆ ◆ ◆ ◆ ◆ ◆ ◆ ◆ ◆ ◆ ◆ ◆ ◆ ◆ ◆ ◆ ◆ ◆ ◆ ◆ ◆

## The Downside

As a work-at-home parent, I hope there are not many downsides of the situation for my kids. I must admit I don't see many. Sure, they grumble from time to time. They get bored. They want to go places when I've got a strict deadline, and there are many times I'm typing away while they are having Galaga contests and enjoying life.

But overall, the downsides are few and temporary. In fact, almost all the parents I interviewed who said their kids were having problems with the arrangement mentioned the same thing: To kids, home means fun; home means freedom; home means out-of-school-do-what-you-want. Home doesn't mean work; and when you're home and working, they want you to stop and play.

Here are some of the responses parents shared about the downsides their kids see in the work-at-home situation:

*"My daughter doesn't like it when I work. In some ways I think it's harder on her when she knows I'm home but that I can't play with her because I'm in my office working. Because she sees me working, she thinks I 'work all the time!' Since she doesn't see her mother working, she doesn't think about the time she's gone during the day."*
—work-at-home father of one

*"The biggest challenge for me as a mother of a preschool-aged child is finding the time to perform my business functions while not ignoring my 5-year-old son because I've got a deadline to complete. He has told me he doesn't want me to get new clients because then I don't spend enough time with him. This really tugs at my heart and I think I'm not succeeding at my dual role."*
—work-at-home mother of two

When you ask the kids themselves, their responses pretty much echo what their parents are saying: "Dad works too much," or "Mom is right there in the office, but she can't play." Playing quietly while the parent is on the phone, always thinking about Mom's deadlines, and inflexibility ("You never take me anywhere anymore!") are three major complaints.

BEST &
**WORST**

*Worst:*
"Contact
with other
professional
adults."

My almost-driving daughter (egad!) Kelly had an interesting comment on the downside: "Sometimes I wish you worked in an office. I'm envious of the other kids who get to go home to an empty (quiet) house, unlock the door, go in and get a snack, and have some time to themselves before everyone gets home and all the craziness begins." At her age, she's ready for more autonomy—and more peace—than my work-at-home status affords her. Her brothers, however, are still in the "Louder is better!" phase of life.

## Talk About It

What can you do about the problems that crop up for your kids? First, encourage your children to share them with you. Especially at first, kids know how hard we're trying and how much we've got to do to get the work-at-home venture rolling. If you've had your family meetings and set up schedules and chore lists, they know how important it is that they do their part to help things run smoothly. They may be hesitant to voice any negative issues, but those unresolved items may pop up in some disruptive behaviors if they go unchecked.

The trick to talking about the bad stuff is to make sure you talk about the good stuff first. Then, when the difficult issues surface, you and your kids already have communication channels established. Routinely discuss what's happening in your business—from a bird's-eye view; they don't need to know all the details—and ask them what they think of this work-at-home thing. Get a feel for where they are. Check in once a month, or more or less, whatever feels right for your family. But when the complaints start rolling in—and at least a few will, at some point—your kids will be more likely to let you know because you've been talking about the good things all along.

## Resolving Problems

Shelby tells you, during one of these discussions, that she saw more of you—the "real" you, who gave her your complete attention—when you were working in the office. Now you are always thinking about the business and never seem to "see" her anymore. What can you do about it?

 **First, identify the problem.** Shelby misses close time with you.

 **Second, brainstorm solutions.** What can you do to resolve this? Set aside a special time for Shelby—on a regular basis—so you get quiet time together. Include Shelby in your work so she feels a part of things. Explain why you've been so busy and show her that this hectic time will pass.

 **Third, fit the problem with a solution.** Review the solutions you came up with and choose the one that feels like the best fit. In this scenario, the first solution is the best, but the other two should be used, too. Shelby should feel more a part of your business, and you should be explaining what's going on to help her do so.

"If you have a partner, make sure he or she really understands what you're doing. This caused a problem in my relationship at first—you can drift apart so easily. Talk about everything, especially what's going on in your business. Watch for signs that he doesn't feel part of it and make sure your family feels included."

## Working with Your Kids

What kinds of things can your kids do for you in
the office? Just about anything you take the time
to teach them. Older children can learn your filing
system and take care of filing things from the To-
Be-Filed box. Younger children can bring in the
mail, fill the paper clip container, sharpen pencils,
dust, bring you envelopes, straighten magazines,
and maybe even run the copier.

If you think of your business as a teaching arena
for your kids, you'll see all kinds of opportunities:

- Have your teenager search for something
  you need on the Internet.

- Show your 9-year-old how to fold and tab
  three-fold brochures.

- Have your 6-year-old design your logo (okay,
  maybe not), water plants (but not around the
  computer), or sort client cards according to
  the first letter of the business name.

## Kid-Potential Tasks

Here are some things your kids can do to help out in your work-at-home venture:

- Address envelopes
- Put mailing labels on envelopes
- Seal envelopes
- Put stamps on envelopes
- Stuff envelopes
- Fold brochures
- Stamp brochures
- Count and bundle mailing items
- Assemble multipage documents
- Fill supply containers
- Make copies
- Send faxes
- Enter client information (older kids)
- Do an Internet search
- Take phone messages
- Help with general straightening
- File documents
- Help with simple research
- Review competing products

What opportunities did I miss today to teach my kids something? When I looked up the word *vicarious*, I could have asked Christopher to do it for me. When I went to get my interview clipboard on which I keep all my interview notes, I could have asked Cameron to do it. When I let the answering machine get those calls while I was putting Cameron down for his nap, I could have had Kelly answer the phone in a professional manner.

**Profiles**
**Name**: Sharon
**Type of business:** Sales
**How long?** Two years
**How many kids?** Two, ages 5 and 2
**Biggest challenge:** Keeping the kids busy while I work.
**Best response to that challenge:** Scheduling activities for them when I need quiet time.

## How Can Your Kids Help You Work at Home?

The kinds of things you can have your kids do on a regular basis will depend on the kinds of things you do on a regular basis. Your work will determine their work. What kinds of tasks can you delegate to your potential helpers?

_____

_____

_____

_____

_____

_____

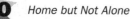

## Paying Your Kids

Besides the fact that having your entire family involved in your work-at-home business is a great experience for all of you, there are practical benefits, as well. You can pay your children (and your spouse, for that matter) for work done in your business. Because your kids are taxed at a lower rate than you are—and if they are under 21, they are not subject to Social Security tax—you save money by paying them for their contribution. And you can claim their pay as a business expense.

The guidelines for paying your kids involve the following:

- Make sure the wages are reasonable.

- They need to be doing real work.

- You must keep records of when they worked, what they did, and how much you paid, as you would for any other employee.

Before you put your kids on the payroll, talk to your accountant or tax advisor for any regulations that apply to your circumstance or business.

## The Happy Worker

Above all, don't let your kids get bogged down in your business worries. Work should be a fun for your kids—a light learning experience. You want them to like what they are doing, feel like they are contributing, and want to do more. You *don't* want them worried about whether or not you lost a client, how much someone paid for that last project, and whether your new customers paid their bills on time.

How can you make sure the work-at-home experience is a happy one for your child? Here are a few ideas:

**Think carefully about the tasks you assign them;** begin with simple tasks they can accomplish easily.

**Praise, praise, praise!**

**Say thank you,** even when the job isn't done exactly the way you wanted it.

**Be careful with criticism.** If Tim spent two hours organizing files by first names instead of last, thank him for his effort; maybe later you can explain that, in a traditional office, files are organized by last names. If you can get by with them the way Tim set them up, do so for a while.

**Give very clear instructions.** Don't assume Tim knows how to organize files. Don't expect Samantha to know that you are used to having documents stapled in the upper left corner. State explicitly what you expect, in small doses, and then reward with praise (and paychecks!).

**Always have them stop working *before* they want to.** You don't want working in your business to be like cleaning their rooms. ("How much more do I have to do? Mom! I've been in here for an hour already!") If you have them knock off an hour before they want to, they'll be eager to come back and work the next time.

## Summing Up

Your kids are learning from you—more than from any other person on the face of the earth—on a daily basis. Now that you're working at home, they have even more opportunity to see you in action and observe how you handle the circumstances in your life. Remember, as you start working with your kids, that you don't need to hide bad days or trouble with clients from them. Instead, approach problems with a positive attitude. Let your kids see how you handle the stresses of your own business. In the short-term, they'll be proud of you. In the long-term, they'll learn to handle the tight spots with courage, which is one of the best lessons you can give them for life.

## Notes

1. *21st Century Dictionary of Quotations,* by the Princeton Language Institute (New York: Dell Publishing, 1993).

2. A special thank you to Mrs. Garber and her kids for welcoming me into their classroom and helping me with this chapter!

# Time for You

*"Know the true value of time; snatch, seize, and enjoy every moment of it."*
—Lord Chesterfield

When you first step out of the fast-paced corporate world and move into what looks like the slower pace of the home-worker, you may think you're going to have all kinds of time to get things done. After all, you used to keep the house relatively clean, care for your kids, fix meals, mend broken things, and generally maintain when you were away at the office 40 hours or more each week. Now that you're home, shouldn't life be easier?

**BEST** &
WORST

*Best:*
"Being able
to live my
dream."

You quickly learn that working at home isn't Mayberry, either. (Unless you have an Aunt Bea to do your cooking and cleaning for you!) You may have pulled off the corporate interstate for the home byroads, but working at home is like driving on the German Autobahn—you set your own speed. You can go as fast as you want or as slow as you want. And if you've got the pressure of carrying your family's financial security, or the desire to please your in-the-office employer, you will probably push yourself quickly instead of risking a slower pace.

What all this means is that the change—and life at home—will take a toll on you if you don't pay attention to what's happening. Humans are complex creatures, and when we experience a change in our lives (and changing jobs ranks right up there with the loss of a loved one or divorce), we feel that change on all levels. And our families feel it, too. Tuning in to yourself during these transitional times is important. It will help you stay well; be more positive; feel balanced; and, ultimately, be on the road to a successful work-at-home experience.

# Tuning In

The change to a work-at-home situation has affected all areas of your life, and you are adjusting emotionally, physically, and mentally. These areas are interrelated, which means that the more you worry, the more tired you are. The more you add to your daily schedule, the more worn down you become. The more you use your brain, the more you need time to rest it.

Being run down—temporarily or continually—has a dramatic effect on you as a complete package: Your emotions are more volatile and less consistent, your physical stamina is noticeably lessened, and your mental sharpness fogs into a fuzziness that may really alarm you.

The answer? Realize how much you've changed and commit to taking good care of yourself. Rest more, eat right, and sleep whenever you can—at least $7\frac{1}{2}$ hours a night.

When you take better care of you, you have more emotional wherewithal to deal with the everyday stresses of running a business from home. You have the clarity to respond to your children's challenges and the mental acuity to communicate professionally with your clients. When you allow yourself to run on empty—with not enough rest, not enough nourishment, and not enough joy— everyone else's emotions stick to you like ping pong balls on Velcro, and sooner or later you can't see your way out.

### Are You Tuned In or Tuned Out?

It's easy to overlook your own needs without knowing you're doing it. Take this quick quiz to see whether you've been caring for yourself:

How many times this week have you …

\_\_\_\_ told yourself you did a good job?

\_\_\_\_ done something you really wanted to do?

\_\_\_\_ felt proud of an accomplishment?

\_\_\_\_ made it a point to eat well-balanced meals?

\_\_\_\_ rested in the afternoon?

\_\_\_\_ gone to bed early, just because you felt like it?

\_\_\_\_ accepted a well-deserved compliment?

\_\_\_\_ let someone help you when they offered?

\_\_\_\_ done something just for fun?

# Tuning Out the World

Most of us don't give ourselves enough credit for the thoughts we think. Thousands and thousands of creative, emotional, inspirational, and destructive thoughts flow through our brains each day.

But thinking can be both a blessing and a curse. It you're one of those people who lies awake at 3:00 A.M. worrying about tomorrow's meeting, your thoughts have hold of you; you don't have hold of your thoughts. If you replay a look, or a conversation, or a fear over and over in your mind, you are letting your mind dictate what you're going to think about, rather than vice versa.

In order to get rest, to get time away from our home-working environment, to let our spirits relax and play awhile, we've got to be able to turn thoughts off when we need to.

## Leaving the Office—Really

When your office is in your home, it's hard to "go home" for the day. The project is in there, on your desk, calling your name. The kids are playing a game, and you've got a few quiet minutes. You think, "I could just run back in there and finish up," but when you do, the minutes stretch into hours, the kids put themselves to bed (again), and you're up until 2:00 A.M. finishing up the last little bit of that project.

Once in a while, it's great to be able to do that—especially when you're finishing a project and are eager to get it off your desk. But if you make it a habit, you're going to be burning your candle from both ends and the middle too.

Back in Chapter 6, you created a weekly work schedule. Stick to it. When you review the week on Friday, if you feel like you didn't get enough done, consider how you might revise the schedule, but try to avoid working all hours of the day and night.

I learned this lesson fairly recently, and it was a sudden paradigm shift, as Stephen Covey would say.[1] I was driving Christopher to trumpet lessons. The boys were in the back seat, haggling over something. I was driving fast—which was my habit back then—in a hurry to get him to lessons so we could get home and I could get back to work. I was thinking about the outline for the next chapter of the book I was writing and paying almost no attention to either my driving or my kids. Suddenly it occurred to me that I wasn't really "there." I wasn't in the car; I wasn't with my kids; I wasn't on the way to trumpet lessons. I was still back in my office, planning out my next business step. I realized I was spending almost every waking hour working; and when the situation was such that I couldn't work, I flew through it so I could get back to work.

My entire life was working or waiting to work again. I decided things had to change.

Now I'm very stern with my thoughts. When I'm downstairs fixing supper, I'm cooking. When I'm playing games with the kids, I'm really there. (I'm getting much better at the games, too!). When I start to think about this book or that book while I'm doing something else, I say to myself, "No, I'm not going to think about that now. I'm doing such-and-such." And it works! The work thought scampers away, leaving me free to do whatever I'm doing.

If you try to get control of your thoughts and they stubbornly come back to harass you, carry a small notebook to write them down and get them out of your head. Then make it a point to review your notebook as soon as you start work the next day so those important thoughts don't slip through the cracks. After a short time of doing this consistently, you'll find that work thoughts don't

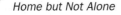

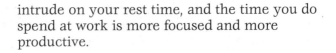

intrude on your rest time, and the time you do spend at work is more focused and more productive.

## Focusing Is Half the Battle

You've heard the old saying, "You can't think two things at once." It's true. Try it. Imagine that pile of papers sitting on your desk, waiting to be read. Now imagine yourself on a white sand beach in Cancun. Feel the sun on your shoulders. See the little pink umbrella in your drink.

BEST & **WORST**

Now, what about those papers on your desk?

*Worst:* The house looks too "lived in."

Whatever you focus on grows. If you want more time with your family, more quality fun time with your kids, more peace of mind, more joy, more laughter, or simply more sleep, put your focus on that idea. When you leave work, *leave work* and put your focus on what is really important to you, what you'd like to grow in your real, "I'm-not-working-right-now" life.

*One of the best gifts you can give another person is the gift of your full attention. As you begin to focus on the things most important to you, don't forget how much it means to your 8-year-old to be able to tell you every subtle nuance of the playground skirmish today.*

## Simplify Things

Your move from the office to home was a big step in the direction of simplicity. You cut out a number of details: the trip to the office, perhaps stopping at daycare or school on the way, lunch arrangements, the trip home, and on and on. Now you're home, and life seems somewhat simplified.

But now that you are home, you are a target for every volunteer effort in your community. The school needs you. The church needs you. Civic organizations need you. Humanitarian organizations need you.

Volunteering is an important part of life; helping others is part of the key to a successful, healthy life. But when you are struggling to make adjustments in your lifestyle for yourself and your family, you must be careful not to overcommit. Choose the involvements that are most important to you; then weed the others out. And this doesn't apply only to personal commitments but to anything you make an investment in: time obligations, material possessions, and more.

### Been There, Done That

*"I sometimes have to make a special effort to say, 'Okay, that work can wait. I'm going to go out and enjoy this time with my kids.' I really have to focus on what's important and the reason I'm staying home. I want to enjoy their childhood experience, not from someone telling me what they did on such-and-such a day."*

## Simplify ... Priorities

What are the priorities in your life? If you list five or six different things, you're not thinking "priority." A priority is what's *most* important. If you *do* have a list of most important things, prioritize them. There should be only one priority at the top of your list and your life. Everything else falls beneath that.

When you know what your priorities are, you can say "no" more easily to things that are further down the list. If the garden club wants you to host a meeting and it means you've got to be away from your kids at a time you don't way to be away, you can weigh the priorities to make your decision. If you are asked to help with a retreat on a weekend when you have planned a work-related trip, you have other priorities to weigh.

You may be surprised to find out how many things you "think" are important and how many things are actually priorities for you and your family. Make a list of these "priorities" that pressure you; then scan through the list. Only one or two will emerge as truly important. The great thing about this exercise is that, when you see what really *is* important, you also see what's really *not* important. So when those issues begin to loom on your horizon, you can dismiss them or deal with them with the importance-level they deserve.

### What's Are My Priorities?

_____

_____

_____

_____

_____

## Simplify ... Time Investments

Some things you just don't have to do. Do you have to be the one to take Carlos to hockey every other day? Is there some kind of trade-off you can make with another parent or with your spouse? Do you really need to make four trips to the grocery in a week; or, with a little time management and planning, could you consolidate it into one trip? Do you spend more time on the phone than you want to? Would organizing a phone time when you return calls to friends and relatives save some time for you in the long run?

When you think about your priorities and recognize the two or three things you really want to spend your time on, you're free to consider how much time you're spending on those things. The time investment you spend on unimportant things becomes less and less; you begin looking for people to delegate those tasks to. You begin spending more time on the things that really matter to you, the things you need to see through to completion yourself.

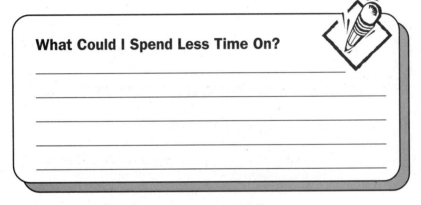

**What Could I Spend Less Time On?**

_____

_____

_____

_____

_____

## Simplify ... Material Possessions

In many ways, we don't really own our possessions—they own us. The more things we've got, the more we've got to take care of. Dusting and polishing. Washing and waxing. Servicing, repairing, insuring, improving. Don't wait for a garage sale: Go through your possessions and ask yourself what you use and what you don't, what you want and what you're ready to let go. Think of your things in terms of how much time, trouble, and money they cost you; then compare that reality with the pleasure they bring you, the convenience they offer, and so on. The bottom line? If you want it, keep it. But remember, the investment you make in your possessions is more than a monetary one.

Start by making a list of the possessions that take up a lot of your time. If you're spending two hours every Saturday fixing the lawn mower, for example, maybe it's time to get a new lawn mower. Once you determine which of your possessions, if any, are possessing you, you can decide what you want to do about it.

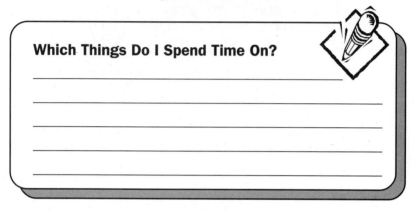

**Which Things Do I Spend Time On?**

## Simplify ... Commitments

Sometimes it's other people—and our reaction to their expectations—that keeps us spinning our wheels on things that aren't priorities. Do you say "yes" to everything? If you're not sure, watch yourself through the course of the day and see how many times you volunteer for something no one else wants to do, suggest a solution that involves some work on your part, or say yes when inside you wish you could say no. When they ask you to serve as the Historical Society's newsletter editor, you might be honored—but you might also be pressed for time. A clear "No, thank you," gets you free of the responsibility and lets the society look for someone who has the time and inclination to do the job.

How can you evaluate which commitments are important and which ones you should pass by? A commitment you accept should meet these criteria:

 It should fit within your time constraints; you shouldn't have to rearrange your life to fulfill it.

It should be worth—emotionally, physically, and spiritually—what it costs you in terms of effort, investment, and family time.

 It should be fun, challenging, or stretch your creative spirit.

You may not need to relinquish any of the commitments you have now. Or you may decide, after some careful thought, to keep a few and release those that are taking up time you don't want to invest.

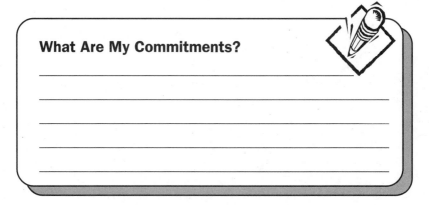

**What Are My Commitments?**

_____

_____

_____

_____

_____

Saying no isn't easy, especially when you're not accustomed to it. But you should sidestep the commitment early if you get any of these warnings:

 You know you don't want to do it.

 You feel coerced or guilty.

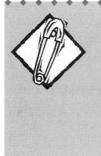

*The clearer you are about your priorities, the easier it is to say no to commitments you don't want. When someone asks you to head the neighborhood task force, check it against your priority list. If it doesn't fit—and especially if it will take away from one of your top priorities—just say no.*

People are appealing to you with a "But-no-one-else-can-take-care-of-this" attitude. (If no one else is willing to help, there must be a reason why.)

# Are We Saving Time Yet?

You can see that you can get more time for yourself and your family by following three simple guidelines:

1.  Stick to your weekly work schedule.

2.  Focus on what you're doing and get control of your thoughts.

3.  Simplify your priorities, possessions, and commitments.

Once you find more time for yourself, what you do with it makes all the difference. If you carry your work stress around with you for those extra few hours, they aren't going to do you or your family any good. If you can find ways to release that stress—and to live a little—the hours will be full, joyful, and refreshing for you and the other people under your roof. That, in turn, helps you stay happier, healthier, and ready to put your best into your work the next time you walk into your office.

## Stressbusting

Some of us are so busy we don't even notice the stress we're under. Statistics show that 30 percent of working Americans experience what they consider "high stress" nearly every day. That percentage is even higher for people who say they feel acute stress once or twice a week.

What does "high stress" feel like?

The moment of panic when you realize your client is expecting a fax from you and you're not finished.

 The knot of anxiety you feel when you're facing a new computer program for the first time.

The sick-to-your-stomach upset that hangs on after your daughter throws a temper tantrum.

The tightness in your neck and shoulders when your spouse comes home stressed and asks, "So, what did you do here at home all day?"

## What Are Your Stress Signs?

What symptoms tell you that you are stressed? Headaches? A racing pulse? Take a few minutes to think about how you react, physically and emotionally, when you are under stress. Then write down your stress signs here:

_____

_____

_____

_____

_____

Your reaction to stress may be to play it down. After all, everyone lives with a certain amount of stress. But in recent years, research has shown that stress definitely affects our systems in a negative way.

When you are under stress—whether it's acute stress or prolonged stress—your body overproduces adrenaline and other powerful hormones. This, in turn, suppresses the production of T-cells, which are an important part of your immune system.

The result? More colds. More flu. Lower resistance.

There are a number of things you can do to reduce your stress level and set up a self-care system so you don't wind up going down for the count. Here are a few ideas that can help when you're experiencing a stressful situation that you can't change:

 **Turn your thoughts to something pleasant.**

 **Take three or four deep breaths.**

**If you can, get outside and go for a walk.**

**Change your focus.** If you're preparing for a meeting, stop and make a few phone calls

or make those copies you were putting off. If you're trying to get the laundry done, put everything down and read your 2-year-old the story she's been wanting to hear.

   **Meditate or pray.**

   **Look at the pictures your kids made for your office.**

   **Listen to music that calms and soothes you.**

*In order for stressbusters to work, you've got to be tuned in to yourself. What are your signs of stress? Do you start snapping at the kids? Do you get sick? Does your neck get tight? Know what your signs are so you can start taking positive action when you feel your stress level climbing. In the long run, you'll be doing yourself a big favor. And your family will not only benefit by having a happier work-at-home parent; they'll also learn new ways of dealing with the stress they experience in their own lives.*

## A Healthier You

One of the perks of tuning into yourself and getting a handle on stress is that you start paying more attention to your physical and emotional condition. That ultimately leads to a healthier you. There are several ways you can start to work on your health; and, since you're working at home, you're in just the right place to do it. You can control what you eat by focusing on healthier foods; you can go for a walk when you need to; you can use the stair-stepper or the treadmill; you can do hand exercises while you talk on the phone, neck rolls while you work at the computer, and stretches on the carpet with your kids.

## Doing the Gym Thing

Who has time to go to a gym? Not that many of us—unless it's a priority. If going to the gym is your quiet time, the time that gets you out of the house and away from the business, it's a great outlet. You get stronger, healthier, and more fit—and you get to carry on non-work-related conversations with people over the age of 6. For a work-at-home parent, that can be a real plus. Another option is enrolling in a class that interests you and gets you moving. Most communities offer classes in tennis, racquetball, golf, yoga, aerobics, tai chi, and more.

But many of us are buying workout equipment and setting up our own home gyms. In 1995, Americans spent more than $2.5 billion dollars on home gym equipment. The most popular pieces of equipment were (in this order) stair climbers, aerobic steps, stationery bikes, ski machines, and treadmills.[2]

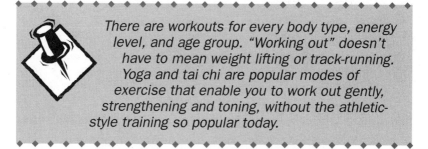

There are workouts for every body type, energy level, and age group. "Working out" doesn't have to mean weight lifting or track-running. Yoga and tai chi are popular modes of exercise that enable you to work out gently, strengthening and toning, without the athletic-style training so popular today.

If you participate in a sports activity, either on a team or for recreation, you have a good start. Softball, football, hockey, tennis, bicycling, and swimming all use a variety of muscles and muscle groups and provide a good workout. Remember, you don't have to have a set routine in order to improve your physical stamina, although it helps. If you make sure you're active, and that your mental exercises are balanced with some physical ones, you'll see a positive change in your overall health, your strength, and your ability to withstand both the illnesses and stresses of everyday life.

## How Much Do You Exercise?

|  | Never | Rarely | Regularly |
|---|:---:|:---:|:---:|
| 1. How often do you go for a walk? | ❏ | ❏ | ❏ |
| 2. How often do you participate in a sport? | ❏ | ❏ | ❏ |
| 3. How frequently do you play a game with the kids? (Not including board games!) | ❏ | ❏ | ❏ |
| 4. How often do you do heavy lifting? | ❏ | ❏ | ❏ |
| 5. How often do you go up and down stairs? | ❏ | ❏ | ❏ |
| 6. How often do you ride a bike? | ❏ | ❏ | ❏ |
| 7. How frequently do you do stretches? | ❏ | ❏ | ❏ |
| 8. How often do you do common exercises? | ❏ | ❏ | ❏ |

## Ready, Set, Move!

Experts say that exercising 20 minutes—less time than you spend watching one news show—five times a week will make a difference, especially if your routine is focused and intensive. Or, if you can stand the extra wear and tear, three 45-minute sessions a week—which may be easier to keep up with—will give you the same results.

What kind of exercising should you do? Before you start any new kind of physical regimen, consult your doctor. He or she may have some suggestions about the types of exercise that will best meet your physical requirements.

As you think about putting together an exercise program for yourself, consider these basic guidelines:

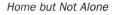 **Start and end with stretching.** Every exercise routine needs a warm-up and a cool-down. Slow stretches—doing different stretches for your back, legs, and arms—prepares your muscles for the coming increase in activity and raises your heart rate gradually. At the end of your workout, stretching helps your now-quick heart rate return gradually to normal. Experts agree that maintaining the longest stretch you can for a moment or two is more helpful and better for you than "bobbing" to a stretch that's hard and then immediately releasing it. It's not how far you get; it's how well you get there that counts.

## The Wake-Up Stretch

One great wake-up stretch is a yoga position that stretches and lengthens the spine. You'll feel lighter and clearer as you stretch all the sleep out of your system:

1. Sit on the floor, in a kneeling position. (If this hurts either your ankles or your knees, put a rolled-up towel across your ankles before you sit back on them.)

2. Lean forward until your forehead touches the floor.

3. Stretch first your right arm, then your left, straight over your head and place your palms down on the floor.

4. Walk your fingers up as far as you can reach. Hold to a count of 10. Remember to breathe slowly and evenly as you stretch.

5. Push up from your kneeling position to straighten your legs. You should now be in a triangle position, with your hands and feet evenly spaced and flat on the floor.

6. Push your hip bones up toward the ceiling and hold to a count of 5. This stretches your spine and releases all the little knots and tight places that accumulated while you slept.

7. Slowly return to the kneeling position; then walk yourself up to sitting using your hands as supports.

8. Take several deep breaths and exhale slowly before standing.

---

**Do what you like.** When you're planning your workout, make sure you include activities you like. If running isn't your thing, consider any of the hundreds of other activities you could try. Popular and beneficial exercises you can do at home include knee bends, toe touches, side bends, leg lifts, and jumping jacks.

**Listen to your body.** We're all different, and our bodies react to activities differently. Be sure to get advice from your doctor on things you should consider when you are designing an exercise program. Aches and pains are not unusual, especially at first, when your body is not used to the exercise. But if you're having chronic pain or feel something sharp and stabbing, like a pulled muscle or some other kind of injury, back off your program until you get professional advice.

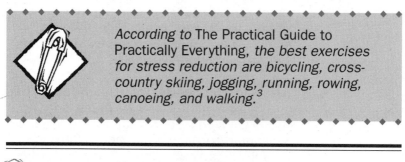

## Pain in the Back?

A great exercise for relieving simple back pain—caused by being on your feet too long, lifting something you shouldn't, or carrying too much stress without a break—takes just a minute and enough room to lie down:

1. Lie down on your back on a bed, couch, or floor.

2. Take a deep breath and exhale slowly.

3. As you exhale, push the small of your back toward the floor.

4. Inhale and allow your back to return to normal.

5. Exhale, and press your back to the floor once again.

*A simple variation:* If your back is feeling tight in addition to being sore, put one hand on the floor at the small of your back; then, when you exhale, press your back against your hand. This modified intensity releases tension, and the counterpressure of your hand helps the muscles relax.

*According to* The Practical Guide to Practically Everything, *the best exercises for stress reduction are bicycling, cross-country skiing, jogging, running, rowing, canoeing, and walking.*[3]

## An Afternoon Wake-Me-Up

Do you get the 2:00 lags? If you're feeling fuzzy by mid-afternoon and need to get the blood circulating back to your brain, you can try this one right at your desk:

1. Take a deep breath; exhale slowly.

2. Nod your head forward as far as you can; repeat three times.

3. Lean your head back as far as you can; repeat three times.

4. Nod toward your left shoulder; repeat three times.

5. Nod your head to your right shoulder three times.

6. Allow your head to roll forward and then rotate around left, back, right, and straighten.

7. Repeat entire exercise two more times.

Your neck will feel more relaxed (your headache may be gone!), and you'll feel more awake and invigorated. Your thoughts will appear more easily, too, so get ready to work.

---

Here are a few more suggestions for a good exercise plan:

 **Stop if anything hurts.**

 **Especially at first, don't push too hard.** Stop as soon as you feel tired or if you become short of breath.

 **Concentrate more on doing the exercise right than on doing it quickly.** Form is more important than speed. When you're stretching, stretch full out and hold the stretch. It's much better for you than stretching-releasing, stretching-releasing a number of times.

 **Increase weight, resistance, and pressure gradually.** Build up a little at a time, over many days (or weeks). Improving your physical health is a process, not something you can achieve in a few afternoons.

> **Be realistic.** If you follow a simple exercise plan, you'll see some changes—tightening, toning, strengthening—in 6 to 12 weeks.

*If you're a work-at-home parent, you have two things work-in-the-office parents do not: the flexibility to do your exercising whenever you want to, and kids right there. Enlist your kids in your exercise routine: Schedule a 20-minute break mid-morning or mid-afternoon and have the kids join in. It breaks up their playtime (or movie time) and refreshes you for work. And it teaches them some good habits for taking care of themselves and handling stress.*

## Touch: A Terrific Stress-Reducer

Have you ever been stressed to the max when one of your kids, or your spouse, walked up and gave you a hug? It's an amazing phenomenon: Your chest lightens, the clenching releases, you sigh a great sigh, and allow yourself to be embraced.

The power of touch is something that medical science is exploring more and more, and we have only to see our own effects on each other to know that there's something healing about touching and being touched by someone you care about.

As part of your stress-reducing plans, consider these ideas:

- Hug your kids more.

- Ask for more hugs.

- Touch people you care about when you talk to them.

- Hold hands with your spouse.

Rub your neck when you begin feeling stressed (or ask your spouse to do it for you).

 Cuddle up with your kids when you read to them.

 Learn to give and receive back rubs.

 Read a book on foot reflexology and experiment on yourself or your family.

 When your kids are grumpy or unruly, touch them gently. I learned when Cameron was 2 that if I smoothed his hair off his forehead when he was on the verge of a tantrum, he would invariably calm down enough that we could avoid the tirade.

# Live a Little!

Up to this point, we've talked about getting in touch with yourself, judging your stress level, and taking better care of yourself physically to avoid wearing down or wearing out. But there's another something that will help you reduce the stress level in your life, find more time for you, and enjoy what you're doing more: Joy.

Not too long ago, as I was rushing through my days trying to find more ways to work for longer periods, all of a sudden I saw before my eyes a phrase that looked as though it had come off someone's bumper sticker:

 **Joy. If not now, when?**

When I finish the book, I said, *then* I'll do something fun. When I finish the article, *then* I'll find the time to laugh more. When I get this paid off, or that handled, *then* I'll be able to relax and enjoy life.

 **Joy. If not now, when?**

Okay, I thought. If I learn to enjoy life, even in the midst of this craziness, it will be a piece of cake when life gets easier. So I set about the task of discovering what it means to have joy in my life in spite of difficult circumstances.

## What Gives You Joy?

The change for me didn't happen overnight. I had to allow myself to let some stress go. I had to stop and laugh once in a while, when the dog raided the trash can and Cameron let the little star fighter man get sucked down the bathroom drain. I had to stand back and shake my head sometimes when my kids started fighting. I had to be willing to let go of some of the control I had on things.

Joy, for me, comes in small parcels of time, usually when I'm not expecting it. Something Christopher says that really cracks me up. A moment when all three kids are doing something together—without realizing it, of course. Driving on a really beautiful evening. Sitting outside on the step and watching stars. Singing harmonies with other choir members. Playing my guitar. Unplanned hugs and candy-coated kisses.

Take some time and think about what gives you joy. You're probably working at home for part of that reason. What's the rest?

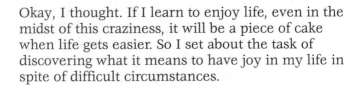

**What Gives Me Joy?**

_____

_____

_____

_____

_____

Perhaps the single best thing you can do for yourself is to decide that you will enjoy life— whatever that means for you. Take classes. Expand your horizons. Meet new friends. Take wonderful trips with your kids. Be creative, and let yourself experience life like a child again. All these things translate into a better you—more creative, more fun, more relaxed, more open to experiences.

# What Will You Do with Your Free Time?

Some people don't think about their free time because they don't have any. And if they did, they wouldn't know what to do with it. If you're one of these people, a little daydreaming is in order.

Perhaps we should define "free time." While taking a month-long sabbatical certainly is free time, it's probably not practical for most of us. Free time, in the context of the working parent, is a spare hour at the end of the day, a few hours on the weekend, perhaps a long weekend getaway.

For best results, especially if you're not used to having any free time at all, start small. Think about where your time goes. Then think about where you *want* your time to go.

## What About a Hobby?

Unless you had a hobby before your kids were born, it's unlikely that you'll have the time or energy to devote to acquiring a new one while they are small. A hobby is simply something you're interested in, something you do for fun, something that isn't you (1) earning a living, (2) being a parent, (3) being a business owner, or (4) being a spouse. A hobby is something you like to do just because you like to do it.

People have all kinds of hobbies—from sports to crafts to cooking to music to any number of other worldwide interests. The word "hobby" tends to put an unimportant-sounding front on the concept, but it's something you should consider. When you're not being Mom or Dad, Wife or Husband, Daughter or Son, Employee or Employer, what do you like to do? There might be a clue there that could lead you into an enjoyable way to spend your free time.

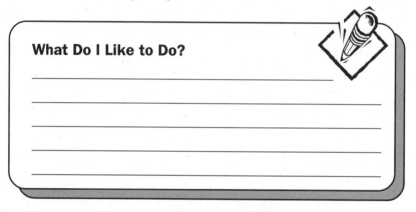

**What Do I Like to Do?**

_____

_____

_____

_____

_____

**Profiles**
**Name:** Kathy
**Type of business:** Writing and editing
**How long?** 8 years
**How many kids?** Three, ages $15\frac{1}{2}$, 9, and $3\frac{1}{2}$
**Biggest challenge:** Stopping and listening to my kids while I'm working.
**Best response to that challenge:** Helping them learn when it's okay to interrupt, and training myself to really listen during that time.

## Expand Your Horizons

When you're thinking about what you'd like to do in your downtime, you might consider taking a class or learning more about a subject that's always interested you. There doesn't even need to be any practical application; just learn it because you want to.

How can you expand your horizons? Here are a few ideas:

- Take a cooking class.

- Go see a movie that's different from the kind you usually see.

- Go online and chat with other computer users across town or across the world.

- Read about an upcoming holiday and find out how other cultures celebrate it.

- Try camping.

- Look through *The New Yorker* and *MAD Magazine* in the same afternoon.

- Watch cartoons with your kids.

- Audition for a part in a community theater production.

- Listen to music outside your usual tastes.

- Spend a rainy afternoon at the library.

**Horizon Expanders**

What would I like to try during my free time?

_____

_____

_____

_____

_____

There's really only one answer to the question, "What will you do with your free time?" The answer is, "Anything you want to." Contrary to popular opinion, free time is not free at all. It comes at a cost. The time and effort you invest balancing work and family earns you whatever time you can find for yourself. And chances are, it's less than you deserve.

## Summing Up

The bottom line, when it comes to working with your kids, is to trust your instincts. If Randy is excited about what you do and wants to help, try it out. If Amanda has absolutely no interest in what you do at that computer eight hours a day, don't feel bad. You don't need to push your family into a family business. Worry about getting yourself set up and functioning in your new home-based enterprise first. When—and if—the kids want to join you, they'll let you know. For now, relax, enjoy being where you are and doing what you do, and the rest will unfold in time.

## Notes

1. Stephen Covey, *The 7 Habits of Highly Effective People* (New York: Simon & Schuster, 1989).

2. Peter Bernstein and Christopher Ma, *The Practical Guide to Practically Everything* (New York: Random House, 1995).

3. Bernstein and Ma.

# Living and Working Happily Ever After

*"Life is like a bicycle. You don't fall off unless you stop peddling."*
—Claude Pepper

Is there a happily ever after for the work-at-home parent? Yes—definitely, yes! In fact, many of the work-at-home parents I interviewed said they were living the "happily ever after" right now. They had found the utopian work arrangement they'd always longed for. Sure, there are trials. Yes, there are headaches and worries. But if faced with the same decision all over again, would they choose the same road? Absolutely!

# What Is a Balanced Life?

The key most people seem to be searching for is balance. How to balance work and family; job and home; responsibility and fun; single goals and family goals? It seems whichever way we turn, we've got priorities to weigh, decisions to make, and courses to navigate.

The most important perspective I've found along the way is the one that recognizes that *balance* is a verb, not a destination. You're not done balancing at some point: You are always balancing. Like the tightrope walker 100 feet above the circus ring, if you stop moving, you'll fall off. If you quit trying new things; learning from your experiences; revising your schedules, task lists, and priorities; and loving, growing, and teaching your kids, you'll fall off the wire. And it won't be pretty. The only choice is to keep moving—which is both reassuring (there are always things to learn and change) and somewhat overwhelming (there are always things to learn and change).

When you look at balance as a verb, you don't beat yourself up when nothing seems to go right. When the kids are mad at you, and your clients aren't happy, and you're not too fond of yourself, come to think of it, you can shrug your shoulders and resolve to learn from the situation. When you feel those points of pressure and pain, you know they are simply signals that something in that situation needs your attention. Balance is a verb, and you're doing the best you can right now with the knowledge and experience you've got.

# Will You Know Happily Ever After When You See It?

Your idea of a balanced life depends on your priorities. What are you balancing? That will be different for different people. Achieving a sense of balance in your life means feeling fairly comfortable about how much time, energy, enjoyment, and investment you experience in several areas: work, kids, home, marriage, personal time, and so on. When things feel balanced, no area is crying louder than another. Life is—almost—peaceful. You experience those sudden pangs, "Hey! I can *do* this!" more often than you did before.

Here are a few signs of a balanced life:

  You feel less guilt than you did before.

  You can smile (even weakly) at the end of the day.

  You find more time for you.

  You walk into your office on Monday morning feeling refreshed.

  You participate in your kids' lives more than ever.

  Thinking about the house doesn't make you cringe.

  Your business is on the up-swing.

  You feel more and more creative.

Not there yet? That's okay. It's a journey, not a destination. There will be first days, then weeks, and then maybe even months where everything feels balanced. And then something shifts—like the kids getting out of school for the summer—and the balance is thrown off for a while.

# Sara at Work; Sara at Home

Sara wasn't always a work-at-home mom. For almost two years she took now-5-year-old Steven to the baby-sitter's house and made the 30-minute commute into town to her job as an acquisitions editor for a book publishing company. She remembers life being a big, difficult blur: Steven was continually catching colds and flu from the other kids; and she was forever asking for time off or time to work at home so she could take care of her son and still get work done.

It occurred to her during this time that there was a career in that pattern: doing acquisitions from home. Her job required computer work, phone work, and contact with authors, but in order for her to complete her most important tasks, she didn't need to be on-site. She proposed the idea to her employers; they raised a collective eyebrow and said it was an interesting idea, but not one they were ready for.

When Sara and her husband were preparing for the birth of their daughter, Sara began thinking through the work-at-home idea more practically. How would she do it? What would make her employers seriously entertain the idea? She put together a list of ideas and scheduled another meeting with her employers. This time, they were more receptive and agreed to a trial period of several months following the birth of her baby.

Sara loves working at home. Steven had some transitions to make, both to the new baby and to his loss of socialization at preschool. "The first few months were hard," Sara said. "I don't know what I would have done without my mother helping a couple mornings a week." Now Steven goes to a nearby preschool several afternoons a week, and baby Emily spends time playing in Mom's office while she works. Sara does the contact part of her business—the phone calls to authors—while Steven is at school and Emily is napping.

Would she do it again?

◆ ◆ ◆ ◆ ◆ ◆ ◆ ◆ ◆ ◆ ◆ ◆ ◆ ◆ ◆ ◆ ◆ ◆ ◆ ◆ ◆ ◆ ◆

*"I can't see myself ever doing anything else."*

◆ ◆ ◆ ◆ ◆ ◆ ◆ ◆ ◆ ◆ ◆ ◆ ◆ ◆ ◆ ◆ ◆ ◆ ◆ ◆ ◆ ◆ ◆

## An Entrepreneurial Kevin

Kevin is a partner in a software and computer consulting firm. He left his salaried status with an employer in April of 1993. He works on all kinds of cool projects, ranging from Intranet and Internet systems to digital audio/visual work to tracking sports data for ESPN.

Kevin works at home and cares for his 5-year-old daughter while his wife teaches outside the home. He balances life, he says, by accepting it as it is: "When you are at home, there are always things that come up that invade that 'work time.' That's part of the advantage of working at home ... you can respond to those things." He has learned to stop fighting the differences and make the most of the available time he has, instead of fretting about interruptions during his day.

Working at home is still a challenge, even after a few years. One of the hardest parts for him is leaving work at work: He's tempted to go back into his office after dinner, or after his daughter goes to bed, or on free weekends. He tries to temper the impulse and make sure he has plenty of focused family time—with frequent breaks when he's working on a project that seems to be overtaking his free time.

And although he says some clients initially don't take him as seriously as they might if he were working in an office environment, they change their tune when they see the quality of his work. Working at home is better for him, better for his wife and daughter, better for his business, and better for his clients.

Would he make the same decision again?

◆ ◆ ◆ ◆ ◆ ◆ ◆ ◆ ◆ ◆ ◆ ◆ ◆ ◆ ◆ ◆ ◆ ◆ ◆ ◆ ◆ ◆ ◆ ◆

*"In a second!!! In fact I do. I make that decision every morning when I get up."*

◆ ◆ ◆ ◆ ◆ ◆ ◆ ◆ ◆ ◆ ◆ ◆ ◆ ◆ ◆ ◆ ◆ ◆ ◆ ◆ ◆ ◆ ◆ ◆

# Happily Yours, Julie

Julie is effervescent, fun, and a delight to talk to. She has a great sense of humor about the whole work-at-home phenomenon, as well. She needs to, raising two young boys and running a word processing business from her home. Unlike many work-at-home moms, Julie didn't leave the workforce to start her home-run business. She was already home, raising her sons, when she began taking on work. She comes at the situation from a unique perspective: She sees the joys and benefits of working at home, but at times she struggles with the loss of individualized attention—the 100 percent mom she used to be to her two young boys.

Balance for Julie includes planning her day carefully so she can spend good time with her youngest son and still make headway in her business. She breaks up her schedule with activities and field trips (which might be as simple as a trip to the grocery) so her young son isn't stuck in her office for long stretches at a time.

One of the greatest things working at home offers Julie is the opportunity to be actively involved in her older son's school. She can go to holiday parties, participate in school events, and help out in the classroom. The best thing about it? How much it means to her son: "He gives me the biggest smile and hug when I come into his classroom."

While working at home is the perfect solution for Julie, she acknowledges that she's still "learning the ropes." She knows from experience, and from her conversations online in the CompuServe Work-at-Home forum, that maintaining a healthy balance between work and home is *The Big Issue.* "It is so important to take the time to be with your family and make sure your business role doesn't become far more important."

Would she do it again?

*"Yes! I'm the person in control of my time and it's heavenly!"*

## Some Keys to Working Happily Ever After

Experience is a great teacher, and some things about working at home we can't learn until we're actually doing it, within our own walls, with our own families. But every work-at-home parent I interviewed had a few pieces of advice for people who are just starting out. Here are some of the ideas they shared:

1. Get a clear picture of your family priorities.

2. Know what part you want your business to play in your family priorities.

3. Discuss your business with your partner.

4. Use your business resources—first for research; then for support.

5. Enlist the help of your family.

6. Don't be afraid to use daycare.

7. Get—and stay—organized.

8. Be clear about your work schedule and boundaries.

9. Remember why you're working at home. Enjoy your kids.

10. Keep both work and home time in perspective.

11. Learn to leave work at work.

12. Keep talking to your family about the changes and challenges you face together.

13. Do what you love, and love what you do!

Do what you love, and love what you do! (With an extra twist even: You get to do it in a *place* you love, too!) On that note, we'll bring this book to a close. I hope you've enjoyed reading and using it as much as I've enjoyed researching and writing it.

In my own life, working at home is one of the single biggest blessings I've experienced. It's allowed me to raise my children the way my heart

tells me is best. I hope this book helps you get in touch with what you hope and dream for your family; take steps toward raising the family you've always wanted; and achieve the professional goals you've set for yourself.

May you find more smiles than struggles along your path!

—Katherine Murray

# Top Opportunities for Work-at-Home Parents

Not sure what kind of work is for you? According to *Entrepreneur* magazine, the following businesses are hot for potential work-at-home parents[1]:

- Bookkeeping service

- Computer consultant

- Desktop publisher

- Household manager

- Information detective

- Mailing list service

- Party planner

- Word processing service

Remember that many of the routine, in-office jobs done today on a personal computer can now be done from home. Ask yourself what skills you have, what equipment you need, and where you'll find the opportunity.

This list shows jobs from the *Occupational Outlook Handbook* that can be based from home, performed at home, or performed in a home-based shop or office. While many of them obviously require on-site work, these jobs have high numbers of self-employed people, operating businesses (often consulting) from home offices or shops.

- Accountants and auditors

- Actuaries

- Adult education teachers

- Agricultural scientists

- Animal caretakers, except farm

- Apparel workers

- Architects

- Automotive body repairers

- Automotive mechanics

- Barbers and cosmetologists

- Bricklayers and stonemasons

- Carpenters

- Carpet installers

- Chiropractors

- Computer programmers

- Computer scientists and systems analysts

- Concrete masons and terrazzo workers

- Counselors

- Dancers and choreographers

- Dental laboratory technicians

Dentists

 Designers

 Dietitians and nutritionists

 Drywall workers and lathers

 Electricians

 Farm operators and managers

 Fishers, hunters, and trappers

 Gardeners and groundskeepers

 Geologists and geophysicists

 Glaziers

 Heating, air-conditioning, and refrigeration technicians

 Home appliance and power tool repairers

 Homemaker-home health aides

 Insulation workers

 Insurance agents and brokers

 Janitors and cleaners and cleaning supervisors

 Jewelers

 Landscape architects

 Lawyers

 Mail clerks and messengers

 Management analysts and consultants

 Motorcycle, boat, and small engine mechanics

 Musical instrument repairers and tuners

 Musicians

 Occupational therapists

 Optometrists

 Painters and paperhangers

 Paralegals

 Photographers

 Physical therapists

 Physicians

 Plasterers

 Plumbers and pipefitters

 Podiatrists

 Preschool teachers and child-care workers

 Private detectives and investigators

 Private household workers

 Property and real estate managers

 Psychologists

 Public relations specialists

 Real estate agents, brokers, and appraisers

 Roofers

 Shoe and leather workers and repairers

 Speech-language pathologists and audiologists

 Stenographers, court reporters, and medical transcriptionists

 Surveyors

 Taxi drivers and chauffeurs

- Tilesetters
- Travel agents
- Typists, word processors, and data entry keyers
- Underwriters
- Upholsterers
- Veterinarians
- Visual artists
- Woodworking occupations
- Writers and editors

# Note

1. *Complete Guide to Home-Based Businesses,* by the editors of *Entrepreneur* (New York: Bantam Books, 1990).

# Online Addresses for Work-at-Home Parents

If you've got a personal computer and a modem, you're halfway onto the Information Superhighway. With the right software—which may be a hookup to CompuServe, America Online, Prodigy, or the Internet—you can have access to all kinds of discussion groups, information pages, files, games, programs, books, and more, via your PC.

## Electronic Things Happened on the Way to the Forum

Let's define a few things first.

The Internet is a worldwide network of computers, all linked together to trade and send information. You can use the Internet to find information about virtually any subject, play games, contact clients, and much, much more.

The World Wide Web is one component of the Internet that displays information in easy-to-use and easy-to-understand pages. These pages are fun to read and inviting, with pictures, text, and sometimes animation, sound, video, and more. You move from one page to another on the World Wide Web by clicking links that take you to areas you want to explore.

Online services are commercial services that provide you, the user, with links to all kinds of information, discussion groups, chat rooms, and more. You'll find other people with similar interests in groups called forums based on different topics, such as parenting, boating, business, games, and a world of other choices. Some of the more popular online services include CompuServe, America Online, The Microsoft Network, and Prodigy. As of this writing, all the major online services offer Internet access, as well, which means you can search and send mail on the Internet without having a separate account with an Internet service provider.

# Where Should You Look?

 CompuServe

 The Entrepreneur's Forum (Go SMALLBIZ)

 Working from Home Forum (Go WORK)

 Small Business Square (by *Entrepreneur* magazine—Go BIZSQUARE)

 America Online

 Your Business, links you to all kinds of business resources

 Microsoft Network

 Go to Business Know-How Forum

 Go to Small Business

 Go to Marketing

# Must-See Web Sites

Web sites are pages on the World Wide Web you can visit and find links to other pages with helpful information. Here's a smattering of Web sites I've found that have interesting and/or helpful information related to small businesses, parenting, working at home, or a combination of the three:

## Parents and Kids

**Child Secure** http://www.childsecure.com/

**Nap Time Notes** http://ddc.com/napnotes/

**At-Home Dads** http://www.familyinternet.com/dad/dad.htm

**Home Business/Home School** http://iglobal.net/sagecreek/hmbuschl.htm

**KidsHealth** http://kidshealth.org

**KidsSource Online** http://www.kidsource.com

**ParentsPlace** http://www.parentplace.com

**Nashville Parent** http://www.nashville.parent.com

**The Fathers' Forum** http://www.fathersforum.com

**Spencer's Parenting Links** http://www.spencers.com/links.htm

**The National Parenting Center** http://www.tnpc.com

http://yellodyno.safe-t-child.com/html/ratesfty/ratesfty.html

http://parentsplace.com

http://www.happypuppy.com/games/link/index.html

## Home Business

**Home Business Review** http://www.tab.com/
Home.Business/

**Home Business Franchises** http://
home.earthlink.net/ ~jbayhi/

**WorldWide Home Business Mall** http://
www.wwon.com/mall.htm

**National Home Business Association** http://
nhba.com/

**Hard@Work** http://www.hardatwork.com

**Business Opportunities** http://
webmall.clever.net/infohwy.htm

**Home Business Institute** http://
www.hbiweb.com/

**Home Business Solutions** http://netmar.com/
mall/shops/solution/

**Home Business Opportunity Center** http://
www.bizopp.com/

**Home Business Network** http://
www.empnet.com/thbn

http://www.sba.com

http://homebusiness.com

http://www.ai.org

Web sites are notorious for changing
addresses, so if you get an error telling you
that any of these addresses are no longer
available, do a search for the topic you're
looking for and choose the sites you want
from the displayed list.

# Important Addresses for Work-at-Home Parents

American Federation of Small Businesses
407 S. Dearborn Street
Chicago, IL 60605
(312) 427-0207

National Federation of Business and
Professional Women's Clubs, Inc., of the
U.S.A
2012 Massachusetts Avenue, NW
Washington, DC 20036

National Small Business Association
1155 15th Street, NW
Washington, DC 20005

Toastmasters International
P.O. Box 9052
Mission Viejo, CA 92690
(714) 858-8255

Independent Computer Consultants
Association
933 Gardenview Office Parkway
St. Louis, MO 63141
(314) 997-4633

National Association of Desktop Publishers
1260 Boylston Street
Boston, MA 02205
(617) 426-2885

FEMALE (Formerly Employed Mothers at the
Leading Edge)
P.O. Box 31
Elmhurst, IL 60126
(708) 941-3553

Home by Choice
P.O. Box 103
Vienna, VA 22183
(703) 242-2063

The National MOMS Club
814 Moffatt Circle
Simi Valley, CA 93065
(805) 526-2725

Mothers at Home
8310-A Old Courthouse Road
Vienna, CA 22182
(703) 827-5903

Mothers' Home Business Network
P.O. Box 423
East Meadow, NY 11554
(516) 997-7394

Fatherhood Project
c/o Families and Work Institute
330 7th Avenue, 14th Floor
New York, NY 10001
(212) 268-4846

Parent Action, the National Association of Parents
2 N. Charles Street, Ste. 960
Baltimore, MD 21201
(410) 727-3687

Family Research Council
700 13th Street, Ste 500
Washington, DC, 20005
(202) 393-2100

# The Working Parents' Handbook

# We've Got to Start Meeting Like This!

**Revised Edition**

### How to Succeed at Work, Raise Your Kids, Maintain a Home, and Still Have Time for You

*By Katherine Murray*

**The entertaining, fun how-to guide for all working parents!**

*"Terrific insight and advice, anecdotes and tips. I enjoyed reading it and found myself wanting more. Parents everywhere will benefit from it."*
–Pamela Fettig, editor, *Indy's Child* magazine

Today, about 70 million men and women are juggling at least two important jobs: careers outside the home and parenting. Working mom Katherine Murray shows how to keep work, home, family, and personal priorities in balance in this witty, thought-provoking, easy-to-read book.

- A great book for working mothers and fathers, single parents—all working parents
- Special appendices with checklists and lists of family-friendly resources for parents and kids
- Sound advice in an entertaining format, with many illustrations and "information-at-a-glance" graphics
- Tips on balancing priorities, finding child care, handling stress, making personal time, and much more

### A Guide to Successful Meeting Management

*By Roger K. Mosvick & Robert B. Nelson*

*"Valuable insight and techniques for handling the growing problem of excessive and ineffective meetings in business."*
–Ken Blanchard, author of *The One-Minute Manager*

Almost every business person would like to have more productive meetings — and fewer of them! Here's advice based on a five-year research project by two communication professionals that shows business people how to get the most out of meetings. The first edition sold more than 50,000 copies!

- Excellent for meeting and event planners, executives, managers, small business owners, and all business people
- Details the six most common problems contributing to meeting mismanagement and their solutions
- Includes advice on appropriate setting, effective meeting formats, agendas, and more
- Techniques endorsed by Ken Blanchard, author of *The One-Minute Manager*

Business/Parenting
6 x 9, Paper, 275 pp.

1-57112-075-0 - $14.95

Business
6 x 9, Paper, 312 pp.

1-57112-069-6 - $14.95

## Job Search 101: Getting Started on Your Career Path

Authors: Pat Morton & Marcia R. Fox, Ph.D.
ISBN: 1-56370-314-9
Price: $12.95
Pub Date: March 1997

## The Federal Resume Guidebook

Author: Kathryn K. Troutman
ISBN: 1-56370-313-0
Price: $34.95
Pub Date: April 1997

## Beat Stress with Strength
### A Survival Guide for Work and Life

Authors: Stefanie Spera, Ph.D. & Sandra Lanto, Ph.D.
ISBN: 1-57112-078-5
Price: $12.95
Pub Date: March 1997

## Jobscape
### Career Survival in the New Global Economy

Author: Colin Campbell
ISBN: 1-56370-316-5
Price $16.95
Pub Date: June 1997

## America's Top Military Careers, Revised Edition

Author: U.S. Department of Defense
ISBN: 1-56370-310-6
Price: $19.95
Pub Date: March 1997

## Healthy, Wealthy, & Wise
### A guide to Retirement Planning

Compiled by the editors at Drake Beam Morin
ISBN: 1-57112-081-5
Price $12.95
Pub Date: July 1997

## Inside Secrets to Finding a Teaching Job

Authors: Jack Warner and Clyde Bryan with Diane Warner
ISBN: 1-57112-079-3
Price $12.95
Pub Date: April 1997

## Be Your Own Business!
### A Definitive Guide to Entrepreneurial Success

Edited by Marcia R. Fox, Ph.D.
ISBN: 1-57112-082-3
Price: $16.95
Pub Date: August 1997

## Job Savvy, Second Edition
### How to Be a Success at Work

Author: LaVerne L. Ludden, Ed.D.
ISBN: 1-56370-304-1
Price: $10.95
Pub Date: April 1997

# JIST Customer Information

JIST specializes in publishing the very best results-oriented career and self-directed job search methods. For sixteen years we have been a leading publisher in career assessment devices, books, videos, and software. We continue to strive to make our materials the best there are so that people can stay abreast of what's happening in the labor market, and so they can clarify and articulate their skills and experiences for themselves as well as for prospective employers. **Our products are widely available through your local bookstores, wholesalers, and distributors.**

## The World Wide Web

For more occupational or book information, get online and see our Web site at **http://www.jist.com/jist**. Advance information about new products, services, and training events is continually updated.

## Quantity Discounts Available!

Quantity discounts are available for businesses, schools, and other organizations.

## The JIST Guarantee

We want you to be happy with everything you buy from JIST. If you aren't satisfied with a product, return it to us within 30 days of purchase along with the reason for the return. Please include a copy of the packing list or invoice to guarantee quick credit to your order.

## How to Order

For your convenience, the last page of this book contains an order form.

24-Hour Consumer Order Line: Call toll-free 1-800-547-8872

Please have your credit card (VISA, MC or AMEX) information ready!

**Mail:** Mail your order to the address listed on the order form: JIST Works, 720 North Park Avenue, Indianapolis, IN 46202-3490

**Fax:** Toll free 1-800-547-8329

# JIST Order Form

Purchase Order #: _____

**Billing Information**
Organization Name: _____
Accounting Contact: _____
Street Address: _____
_____
_____
City, State, Zip: _____
Phone Number: ( ) _____

**Shipping Information (if different from above)**
Organization Name: _____
Contact: _____
Street Address: (we canNOT ship to P.O. boxes)
_____
_____
_____
City, State, Zip: _____
Phone Number: ( ) _____

**Phone:**
**1-800-547-8872**
**1-800-JIST-USA**
**Fax:**
**1-800-547-8329**

Credit Card Purchases:
    VISA_____   MC_____   AMEX_____
Card Number: _____
Exp. date: _____
Name as on card: _____
Signature: _____

| Quantity | Product Code | Product Title | Unit Price | Tot |
|----------|--------------|---------------|------------|-----|
|  |  |  |  |  |
|  |  |  |  |  |
|  |  |  |  |  |
|  |  |  |  |  |
|  |  |  |  |  |
|  |  |  |  |  |
|  |  |  |  |  |
|  |  |  |  |  |
|  |  |  |  |  |
|  |  |  |  |  |

| | | | | |
|---|---|---|---|---|
| | | Subtotal | | |
| | | **+Sales Tax**<br>*Indiana residents add 5% sales tax.* | | |
| | | **+Shipping / Handling**<br>*Add $3.00 for the first item and an*<br>*additional $.50 for each item thereafter.* | | |
| | | **TOTAL** | | |

**JIST Works, Inc.**
720 North Park Avenue
Indianapolis, IN 46202

**JIST thanks you for your order!**